TRUE TO THE SPIRIT

TRUE TO THE SPIRIT

Film Adaptation and the Question of Fidelity

EDITED BY COLIN MACCABE,
KATHLEEN MURRAY, AND
RICK WARNER

OXFORD
UNIVERSITY PRESS

OXFORD
UNIVERSITY PRESS

Oxford University Press, Inc., publishes works that further
Oxford University's objective of excellence
in research, scholarship, and education.

Oxford   New York
Auckland   Cape Town   Dar es Salaam   Hong Kong   Karachi
Kuala Lumpur   Madrid   Melbourne   Mexico City   Nairobi
New Delhi   Shanghai   Taipei   Toronto

With offices in
Argentina   Austria   Brazil   Chile   Czech Republic   France   Greece
Guatemala   Hungary   Italy   Japan   Poland   Portugal   Singapore
South Korea   Switzerland   Thailand   Turkey   Ukraine   Vietnam

Published by Oxford University Press, Inc.
198 Madison Avenue, New York, New York 10016

www.oup.com

Oxford is a registered trademark of Oxford University Press

Library of Congress Cataloging-in-Publication Data
True to the spirit : film adaptation and the question of fidelity /
edited by Colin MacCabe, Rick Warner, and Kathleen Murray.
     p. cm.
Includes bibliographical references and index.
ISBN 978-0-19-537466-7; 978-0-19-537467-4 (pbk.)
1. Film adaptations—History and criticism.   2. Motion pictures and
literature.   I. MacCabe, Colin.   II. Warner, Rick, 1977–
III. Murray, Kathleen, 1975–
PN1997.85.T78 2010
808.2'3071—dc22   2010013479

Printed in the United States of America
on acid-free paper

To the English Department of the University of Pittsburgh,
where film and literature have been taught and studied together since 1975

PREFACE

Grading papers is, for almost all professors, the most unwelcome of tasks. In most cases it requires strenuous attention to writing that outside the educational context would not warrant such attention, and this effort is accompanied by a constant anxiety about parity, that one is maintaining the same standards for one student as for another. That's the upside. The downside is mangled thought and argument, often your mangled thought and argument, which reveals that what one had thought to be a successful seminar was no more than a lot of nodding heads. It is true that there are always one or two excellent papers where the fluency of the argument and the ease of exposition means that one finishes the paper without realizing it, but most grading involves constant checking on how many pages remain to read while reevaluating your own abilities as a teacher.

In April 2005, I sat down to grade the papers from a class I had taught on adaptation and had a more-than-welcome surprise. Each paper was not simply a delight to read but was clearly publishable. At first I thought of individual publication, but it soon became clear that the most appropriate form was a book. This was not simply a question of the quality and range of the essays but the fact that they shared a perspective that had been elaborated in the course of the seminar—they were interested in examining adaptation from the perspective of fidelity. Once I thought of a book, I also thought of editing it with students from the class and asked Kathleen Murray and Rick Warner to join me in the task. Their hard work, acute insights, and wide-ranging knowledge have been invaluable.

Any teacher runs the risk of overvaluing their students and so the next step was to send the essays to those we most respected in film studies and to ask them if they would come to Pittsburgh to talk with us. The conference held in March 2007 at which Dudley Andrew, Tom Gunning, Laura Mulvey and James Naremore delivered the papers collected here convinced us all that a book was a real possibility. A final addition was to ask Fredric Jameson, our chief of cultural critics, for his thoughts on the subject. His paper was followed up by an informal seminar with the students in Pittsburgh in March 2009.

The final touches were added and the title chosen in response to the extremely thoughtful and detailed comments of the two anonymous reviewers commissioned by Oxford University Press.

Thanks for commissioning those reviews and for her general enthusiastic and informed support go to Shannon McLachlan of OUP and her assistant Brendan O'Neill. Last but not least, Carol Mysliwiec contributed good-humored and unstinting organizational support at all stages of the project.

CONTENTS

TRUE TO THE SPIRIT

The Butcher Boy (Jordan, 1997)

Introduction

Bazinian Adaptation: The Butcher Boy *as Example*

Colin MacCabe

HISTORICAL PERSPECTIVE

Adaptation as a process is so basic that it covers not simply a wide range of human activities but arguably one of the most fundamental of biological processes. Adaptation is the term Darwin uses to stress that the structure of an organism is a function of its environment. In place of a divine design, we have a continuous process. Indeed, much of human history in its production of a built environment and the institutions that grow with it can be described as adaptation.

There is, however, a meaning that is peculiar to the history of the cinema, where an adaptation refers to a film that relies for some of its material on a previous written work and the word differentiates such films from films produced from an original screenplay. This distinction is recognized at every level of the industry up to the categories of the Oscars. But this categorization is the product of a long and complex history. If we cast our eyes back over classical antiquity, medieval Europe, and the Renaissance, we will find that almost all of the canonical texts are adaptations in the sense they involve a reusing of previous material. From Sophocles's *Oedipus the King* to Chaucer's *The Knight's Tale* and to Shakespeare's *Macbeth,* we find that adaptation is the norm rather than the exception. Indeed, if we take Shakespeare's thirty-seven plays, almost all use previous sources. And yet it would be odd to call Shakespeare's or Sophocles's plays adaptations, both because to do so does not distinguish one play from another and because it awards an importance to the source text that would have seemed alien to a culture for which fictions were naturally the retelling of stories. The process that transformed those cultures into our automatic expectation that fictions be original is so complex that a full explanation would be nothing less than a history of capitalist modernity. But we do know that it required not simply the emergence of a genre but a genre that claimed that its fictions were new: for the novel declares the importance that its stories are original in its name.

There was at least one clear reason that the post-Renaissance world needed to both produce and consume novel fictions, and it can be grasped emblematically in one of the two Shakespeare plays for which there is no clear source narrative: *The Tempest*. It is generally accepted that Shakespeare's inspiration came not from a previous romance or history but from a letter written by William Strachey in which he described how the ship on which he was sailing to Virginia as part of a convoy of colonists got separated in a storm and found land on the island of Bermuda, where they spent ten months and built the boats that conveyed them, miraculously saved, to Virginia.[1] Neither the cycles of classical antiquity or medieval Europe, nor the romances of the Renaissance that reworked oral folktales, could possibly offer models for the narrative of these brave new worlds. Indeed, we only have to think of the importance of *Oroonoko*, *Robinson Crusoe*, or *Gulliver's Travels* for any traditional history of the novel to understand that one very important component in the development of original fictions is the simple lack of available models for subject matter dealing with the Americas or the South Seas.

However, if this provides one important element in the development of an expectation of originality in fiction, unknown for the first two thousand years of Western culture, there is no doubt that an ideology of originality is much more dependent on that complicated European movement that we know as Romanticism.[2] However we wish to analyze that cultural moment, there is no doubt that its emphasis on the individual consciousness as the seat of the most important aesthetic creativity is determining. By the first decades of the nineteenth century, developments in technology, distribution, and education have combined to make the novel culturally dominant. This and the hegemony of Romanticism mean that adaptations, despite their continuing importance both in middlebrow culture (Lamb's *Tales of Shakespeare*) and within the poetic tradition (Tennyson's "Ulysses," *Idylls of the King*), are understood as inherently inferior.

A NEW KIND OF ADAPTATION

If high modernism, Joyce's *Ulysses*, Eliot's *The Waste Land*, and Pound's *Cantos* all offer a new model of adaptation from classical sources, this has little effect either on the vast majority of novels or the dominant ideology, which continues to treat adaptation as inherently vulgar. However, that very high modernism is itself in part a reaction to the new medium of film, and this new medium of film produces a new kind of adaptation. It might be tempting to read this new medium's dependence on adaptation as a return to the conditions of premodern Europe. Such a reading is impossible for two reasons. First, despite the fact that roughly a half of Hollywood's production in any year from the 1920s onward is an adaptation, it is also the case that roughly half are original screenplays. If we look to previous eras, we find that every story is a retelling and, further, a retelling of retellings. The dramatists of Athens take much of their material from the Homeric cycles. In Europe, the Grail legend and in England the Arthurian myths occupy analogous if slightly less dominant models. Hollywood, to limit ourselves simply to the United States, is not concerned simply with a general process of retelling but with a very specific retelling, within a new media, of material that usually has exactly that claim to originality that is such a pronounced feature of post-Romantic culture.

Second, the cinema promotes a new form of adaptation in which the relation to the source text is part of the appeal and the attraction of the film. We know that Shakespeare's treatment of his sources is, to put it mildly, cavalier. Even in a play like *Henry V,* where he follows his historical sources closely, he is perfectly willing to invent and to ignore the historical record when it suits his purpose. Thus the first scene with the French princess, in which a series of obscene puns attend the naming of the parts of the body in English, has no warrant of any kind within the sources, and the second scene with the princess, in which Henry is unable to speak French, is simply at odds with every source that Shakespeare could possibly have consulted. It is quite consonant with Shakespeare's aim, which is to produce the ideal figure of an English king who masters both languages and bodies.[3] Of course, this kind of adaptation is perfectly possible in the cinema as well. When Robert Aldrich and his screenwriter A. I. Bezzerides took Mickey Spillane's hero Mike Hammer and turned him into a sadistic thug in *Kiss Me Deadly,* they were quite conscious of taking a figure of postwar paranoia and turning him to purposes which were very far from the original author's intention.[4]

The cinema, however, also produces a completely new kind of adaptation that claims that the source material is being faithfully translated into a new medium. It is important to stress that this relation between source and adaptation is effectively unknown to previous cultural eras, although it has a prehistory in nineteenth century theatre.[5] In a history as old as narration, this form of adaptation constitutes a new chapter. The film theorist who understood this most clearly was André Bazin who, in two particularly luminous articles, sketched out the basis for understanding this new form of adaptation that could not be understood as one medium translating another but as two media making a whole that was not reducible to the sum of its parts. Bazin's first article was published in the July 1948 issue of *Esprit*, and it concluded with the following passage:

> All things considered, it's possible to imagine that we are moving toward a reign of the adaptation in which the notion of the unity of the work of art, if not the very notion of the author himself, will be destroyed. If the film that was made of Steinbeck's *Of Mice and Men* (1940; dir. Lewis Milestone) had been successful (it could have been so, and far more easily than the adaptation of the same author's *Grapes of Wrath*), the (literary?) critic of the year 2050 would find not a novel out of which a play and a film had been "made," but rather a single work reflected through three art forms, an artistic pyramid with three sides, all equal in the eyes of the critic. The "work" would then be only an ideal point at the top of this figure, which itself is an ideal construct. The chronological precedence of one part over another would not be an aesthetic criterion.[6]

Bazin's fundamental insight that a source text and film form an "ideal construct" can be developed independently of the theatrical face of the pyramid.[7] Four years later, Bazin returned to the topic of adaptation in his article "Pour un cinéma impur," and once again he argued that what was at stake was not a copy of one medium by another or a substitution but the production of "a new dimension." It was this theoretical insight that Truffaut used in his famous article "A Certain Tendency in French Cinema," written in 1953 and clearly massively influenced by Bazin's two articles. Truffaut's entire argument turns on the possibility of producing this new form of adaptation in which film develops and expands the source text. This article was of course the manifesto that announced that *Cahiers du cinéma* constituted a corps of young Turks waiting to assault the old guard of French cinema.

FIDELITY AND VALUE

Given the importance of this conception of adaptation in the history of the cinema, it is surprising that it has not given rise to a whole series of critical studies. However, by 1958, Truffaut had abandoned criticism and Bazin was dead. My own interest in adaptation did not come from my period as an editor of *Screen* in the seventies, when questions of adaptation were simply absent from theoretical questions about the cinema. Indeed if, at that time, I knew Truffaut's manifesto as a crucial part of the history of the cinema, I had not even read Bazin's articles on adaptation. It was only as a film producer in the eighties that I became aware of the importance of adaptation to the business of film. It was then that I first pondered a graduate class on the subject and was astonished to find that so little had been written. There was of course Bluestone's pioneering study, still full of information and insight. However, so concerned was Bluestone to dispute notions of fidelity that would reduce film to novel that he certainly did not consider Bazin and Truffaut's fidelity, which made film and novel combine to produce an "ideal construct" greater than the sum of its parts. Indeed, while his footnotes and bibliography make clear Bluestone was familiar with German and Russian criticism, they suggest that he had not read Bazin or *Cahiers du cinéma*.

In fact, it was to be nearly another twenty years before I finally scheduled my graduate class on adaptation. By then I had read and reread Bazin's texts, and I had in *The Butcher Boy* a perfect example of that "ideal construct" which Bazin had theorized. There had also been a veritable explosion of academic work on adaptation. But almost none of that work was devoted to illuminating the particular form of adaptation that is so specific to the cinema. In the terms of Dudley Andrew's contribution to this volume, modern studies of adaptation are primarily interested in the horizontal meanings that adaptations perform in the present rather than the vertical meanings that tie them to the past. The endless attacks on fidelity, common to almost all the new literature on the subject, meant that they were ill equipped and unwilling to sketch that particular form of productivity that preserves identity at the same moments that it multiplies it.

While many of the recent studies add to our knowledge of the performativity of adaptation,[8] they ignore how audiences talk about film adaptations, and, perhaps even more importantly, how the cast and crew of a film talk about making an adaptation. The shorthand this volume adopts to crystallize such discussions is the phrase "true to the spirit." This expression has the advantage that it avoids in its very formulation any notion of a literal fidelity and demonstrates a much greater sophistication in the general culture than adaptation studies allow. It is over fifty years since Jean-Luc Godard wrote, "We won the day in having it acknowledged in principle that a film by Hitchcock for example is as important as a book by Aragon. Film auteurs thanks to us have finally entered the history of art."[9] However, adaptation studies, rather like Don Quixote, continue to fight the day before yesterday's battles. It is conventional wisdom within much adaptation studies that the question of the aesthetic primacy of literature or film is the key debate. This made sense in 1957 when Bluestone wrote his book and when T. S. Eliot and I. A. Richards, among others, had constructed the university discipline of English as a valorization of literature against popular culture in general and film in particular.[10]

However, it always made less sense in the general culture, where from very early in the twentieth century, as Tom Gunning makes clear in his contribution, film and literature were engaged in the most complicated of cultural interactions. Indeed, if we take our perspective from the late twentieth century, writers and filmmakers move between film and literature with an ease that has no place in adaptation studies. At random, and emblematically, one could cite J. G. Ballard's pronouncement that Cronenberg's *Crash* (1996) was superior to his source novel,[11] and Salman Rushdie's claim that the film version of *The Wizard of Oz* (1939) was his "very first literary influence."[12] Even in the university, English departments are now much more influenced by thinkers such as Raymond Williams, for whom film was an art every bit as important as literature, than they are by older notions of literature's primacy.

The essays collected here are unified by the equal importance that they attach both to source text and film adaptation rather than by any attempt to promote one over the other. If all these essays take Bazin's "ideal construct" as a topic worthy of proper investigation, it should be stressed that they provide neither a model nor a manifesto. Thomas Leitch has pointed out that one of the abiding weaknesses of adaptation studies is its drive to taxonomize.[13] Why this drive is doomed to failure is that the number of variables involved in any adaptation from the linguistic form of the novel or short story to a film's matters of expression approach infinity. There are thus no models of how to adapt in this volume. There are, however, a series of case studies that investigate, across a wide variety of material, films where source text and film enjoy that complicated relation peculiar to the cinema and which Bazin was the first to identify. The source texts can be as different as the autobiography *Seven Pillars of Wisdom,* in Ali Patterson's contribution, or the graphic novel *Ghost World,* in Jonathan Loucks's essay. What unifies all the contributions is the way in which comparison of film and source text illuminates both.

This volume goes against the academic grain in that it considers the question of "truth to the spirit" to capture something important but, further, it also implicitly raises questions of value that are routinely dismissed by adaptation studies. There is here no version of the intellectually dull and unproductive question "is the film better than the book?" or its equally dull and unproductive response "the book is better than the film." There is, however, an assumption that the books and films considered are of real value, a value in most cases that has been augmented by the process of adaptation. Much humanist study of the past generation has reacted to the understanding of how far the greatest of Western art is intimately connected with the exploitation of labor, sexual discrimination, and imperialist domination by abandoning any notion of the value of art. But when Benjamin stressed that all monuments of civilization were also monuments of barbarism, he did not suggest for a moment that we abandon the attempt to civilize ourselves. When Williams demonstrated how Jonson's "To Penshurst" was rooted in a vision of a society where economic inequality was naturalized, he did not mean that the poem's vision of a harmonious society was without value. When Woolf pondered what Shakespeare's sister might have achieved, she was not suggesting that her brother was not a great poet. Of course, all three would have stressed that the question of value is always contemporary and always in question, but none of them would have considered that it could simply be foreclosed. Indeed, there are two very important practical reasons why academic abandonment of questions of value is not simply theoretically ignorant but also practically disastrous. The first is "the grammar of value," that is to say those colloquial forms that are used to discuss books and films. These colloquial forms are highly evaluative not least because they are often directed at immediate questions of choice: "Do you recommend that I go and see this movie or that?" "In your opinion is this book worth buying?" For academic discourse to discount completely such discussion is to seal itself hermetically off from the general culture. The second, and perhaps more important, reason is that questions of value are always in play in those allocations of resources that determine questions of access: what shall be preserved in this archive or library, what should be placed on a national curriculum or an individual syllabus. It is of course the case that there are a variety of sociological and formal enquiries, from Moretti's distant readings to Bordwell and Thomson's statistical analysis of classic Hollywood, which must, by their very methodology, ignore questions of value. That should not mean, however, that questions of value should be ignored either in relation to the traditional humanist canon or the more expanded field of cultural studies. This is not, of course, a plea for a return to the ghastly hectoring of an F. R. Leavis obsessed with inflicting his own narrow judgments on generations of students. Evaluation is a complex and collaborative effort, and individual judgments can only enter into a vast and continuous exchange. It is important to stress, however, that all the essays written here are animated by the authors' commitment to the value of both books and films analyzed.

OPTIONING *THE BUTCHER BOY*

A producer who options a critically successful book is engaging in that curious mixture of culture and commerce which makes film so fascinating a medium to study. For in brandishing the source text as part of the marketing of the film, the producer is claiming both a cultural ambition and an existing audience. Neil Jordan's original engagement with the book *The Butcher Boy* was as a producer. So prolific is Jordan as both a writer and director that it is easy to forget his considerable career as a producer.[14] However, when, in 1992, he optioned what was from the moment of its publication recognized as a great Irish novel, perhaps the greatest since *Ulysses,* Jordan was not thinking of directing it himself. Any producer would know that while the book was guaranteed a considerable audience in Ireland, such an audience would in film terms be small.

Any thought of widening the audience globally would first of all have to cope with the problem of the novel's fundamental narrative, in which a young boy causes his mother's suicide by running away from home, finds himself incarcerated in an industrial school where he is blithely unconcerned by the sexual abuse visited on him by a priest, returns home in time for his father's death, whose body he keeps at home, after which episode he is placed in a mental hospital before returning to his town where he butchers an innocent woman and attempts to kill himself. Even when one admits that this summary is as far from the ecstatic and life-affirming tone of the novel as it is possible to get, one does not need to be a marketing genius to recognize that this film was unlikely to enjoy the very widest appeal. There is, however, a much more important reason that would limit the audience for this adaptation, particularly in the vital market of the United States.

James Joyce had brought Dublin, the capital of Ireland, to a global audience in the first decades of the twentieth century. But Joyce himself was all too conscious that he had nothing to say about Ireland outside Dublin. These absences are figured in a variety of ways. His fellow student Davin's encounter with a peasant woman on his way home from a hurling match and Stephen's dream of a struggle all through the night with an old peasant just before he leaves home are two of the most obvious instances in *A Portrait of the Artist as a Young Man.*[15] McCabe's novel spoke from outside Dublin, from the heart of County Monaghan, and it spoke in the tones of that county, neither Belfast rasp nor Dublin drawl. One thing that Jordan and McCabe agreed from the first was that the film would speak the language of Monaghan. From the Hays Code on, Hollywood has demanded a very standard American English for almost all dialogue, and Jordan and McCabe's linguistic ambition meant that the film would have difficulty finding an American distributor.

Jordan himself was at stage in his career where, apart from any other considerations, he was unlikely to want to direct a small film. He had just brought his career back from the dead, and his sights were set on an Irish epic, the story of Michael Collins. Jordan had wanted to make this film about Ireland's national liberation ever since his initial success as a director with the thriller *Angel* in 1982, and draft had followed draft as personnel changed at Warner Brothers, who had first commissioned the project. It is worth noting that Jordan's initial ambitions were all in terms of writing, and it was only after dissatisfaction with the fate of early scripts that he decided to take the helm himself. Indeed, it is doubtful if there is any director in the history of cinema who has been as accomplished a writer as Jordan. Even Pasolini cannot match Jordan's achievements in novel and short story. Jordan's own career offers a very good example of how central adaptation is to cinema. One might expect that a writer as talented as Jordan would work only with his own original scripts, but in fact he has been as happy to adapt as to write original screenplays. His first major success, *The Company of Wolves* (1984), was an adaptation of short stories by Angela Carter. Jordan's initial roll—the widely acclaimed *Mona Lisa* (1986) had followed *The Company of Wolves*— came to an abrupt end with *High Spirits* (1988), an extremely expensive and ill-judged comedy which planted American stars in a stage Irish setting.

Jordan's recovery from this disaster was in three stages. As a start, he worked, for the first time, as a director for hire on *We're No Angels* (1989) with Robert de Niro, Sean Penn, and Demi Moore. Although the film did not make money, it proved that Jordan could handle both Hollywood budgets and stars. He then returned to Ireland and made a small film, adapted from his first collection of short stories, entitled *The Miracle* (1991). This is one of Jordan's finest films as he takes material from his youth and gives it the perspective of maturity. In retrospect, it is cut from the same cloth as *The Butcher Boy*, with a plot that features a weak alcoholic father and a style that moves easily between dream and reality. Also in retrospect, it marks the beginning of a tremendous creative surge that would culminate in *The Butcher Boy*. Most immediately, it allowed him to make a script entitled "A Soldier's Wife" that he had been tinkering with since *Angel*. The theme is an old one in Irish republican history—the relationship between a British soldier and the IRA unit holding him hostage. Its first outing came in the 1931 Frank O'Connor short story "Guest of the Nation," and it was reprised in Brendan Behan's 1958 play *The Hostage*. Jordan added two twists: he made the soldier black and the second half of the play had the IRA volunteer setting out to the London of the seventies, which Jordan had known as a casual laborer, to seek out the dead soldier's wife. Very late in the project Jordan added a third twist—the wife became a transvestite—and he changed the title to *The Crying Game*. In Ireland, the film had a mixed reception, and its unflinching portrayal of IRA violence did not please ardent republicans; in England, it was received with the guilty boredom that is reserved for any reminder of England's history with its most intimate neighbor. But in the States, a tremendous marketing campaign by Miramax and a world in which, to use Derek Jarman's words, "everyone wants a touch of black cock"[16] saw the film gross $68,000,000 and garner six nominations for the Academy Awards, while Jordan received an Oscar for best original screenplay. It was in the midst of this extraordinary success that Jordan optioned *The Butcher Boy* and asked Patrick McCabe to make a first attempt at adapting it for the screen.

MCCABE'S ADAPTATIONS

When McCabe sat down to work at the adaptation, it was the fourth time he was adapting material that he had wrestled with for decades. McCabe was born in Clones in County Monaghan, and the town occupied much the same place in his imagination that Yoknapatawpha County did in the psyche of William Faulkner. Indeed, the comparison with Faulkner goes much further than this, for McCabe's mature style using spoken rhythms in elaborately written prose bears many resemblances to Faulkner. The style did not arrive fully formed, and McCabe's first two novels, *Music on Clinton Street* and *Carn*, are written for the most part in a conventional third person where the divorce between the author's and character's voices, except in very few passages, remains that of a classic realism. When McCabe, now teaching in England, sat down to write his third novel, his focus remained Clones, but he went for a very different form. McCabe himself says that he wanted to "find a style that suited my soul."[17] His starting point was a radio play by Patrick Shay entitled "He Lies in Armagh Jail," which was itself a dramatization of a series of famous trials that followed a murder in Clones in 1902. Two friends, one a slaughterhouse worker and the other a seller of chickens and eggs, met up, and subsequently the chicken seller disappeared. Many months later, a local policeman ordered that the slurry at the back of the slaughterhouse be cleared, and the body of the chicken seller, only half dissolved in quicklime, was discovered. There were three trials in all of the slaughterhouse man before, finally, on the gallows he confessed to the crime, which had apparently been caused by the more prosperous chicken seller calling in a small debt.

McCabe felt that the story captured many of the class conflicts of rural and small-town Ireland, conflicts buried by the myths of national liberation, and he set the story in the present. The murderer, called Francie Brady, is a half-mad, drug-fuelled adolescent living wild in an abandoned railway station. His victim is Joe Pop Purcell, the vet's son from whom Francie has become alienated since Purcell was sent away to private school. Indeed, the murder is explicitly caused by class distinction when Joe comes to the slaughterhouse to try to persuade Francie to come with him to America on a holiday. "Then he smoothed back his hair that way. As long as I'd known him before he went away to the boarding school he had never touched his hair like that." Francie refuses all Joe's entreaties, provoking Joe to lose his temper: "Stay here, then. Stay with the pigs where you belong."[18] Francie's response is to butcher him.

The book's form is very different from McCabe's first two novels. It is episodic, flashing back and forth, as if set in a mind fundamentally disorientated by hallucinogenic drugs. This makes the story very difficult to follow. Indeed, for any reader unfamiliar with *Music on Clinton Street* (from which much of the material is transformed) and *The Butcher Boy* itself, the narrative would be close to incomprehensible. While the episodic narration leads to a great gain in the intensity of the writing, the book also lapses back into third-person description as its fundamental authorial voice. The result is a mess (albeit fantastically interesting and fertile), and it is perhaps not surprising that it was rejected by the publisher Aidan Ellis who had, until then, been one of McCabe's staunchest supporters. The rejection was a terrible blow for McCabe, but he sat down and very quickly adapted the material again, changing the title from "Baby Pig" to *The Butcher Boy*.

The changes in content were dramatic. The material from *Music on Clinton Street,* which featured a wide cast of characters, is gone. It is Mrs. Nugent, not Joe Purcell, who is murdered. Both industrial school and mental asylum are introduced. And Francie, although he becomes the feral nightmare of "Baby Pig" at the end of the book, is for the first three quarters an engaging and charming young boy. More important is the change of form—the book is told as a retrospective continuous narrative. Most important, however, is the production of a voice which fuses character and narrator, unforgettable from the first paragraph:

> When I was a young lad twenty or thirty or forty years ago I lived in a small town where they were all after me on account of what I done on Mrs. Nugent. I was hiding out by the river in a hole under a tangle of briars. It was a hide me and Joe made. Death to all dogs who enter here, we said. Except us, of course.[19]

There is now no divorce between the narration and Francie Brady's voice, and it is that voice that is our sole access to the events of the novel. It was a voice as distinctive and as immediately engaging as Holden Caulfield, and *The Butcher Boy* was an immediate critical and commercial hit. It was also immediately optioned by Neil Jordan, riding the wave of *The Crying Game's* astounding success. McCabe himself produced the first draft adaptation.

It is often said that there is very little difference between plot of film and book.[20] While this may testify to the way in which the film and book have become that one cultural object of which Bazin speaks, it is extraordinarily inaccurate about the number and importance of the changes from novel to film. Even in McCabe's first version, which was overlong and overliteral, McCabe excised two key passages in which Francie imagines himself choking on Mrs. Nugent's breast. In counterpoint, the Virgin Mary, whose appearance to Francie in the novel is simply a ruse to ingratiate himself with the industrial school authorities, appears in this first film script with a speaking part. McCabe's second draft was much more crafted;

both Uncle Alo's arrival and Francie's return from his unauthorized jaunt to Dublin are staged in the central square of Clones—the Diamond—thus cutting out secondary business and emphasizing the centrality of the town. More crucially for the final film, Joe's friendship becomes much more of a reality. The novel's heartbreaking solitary reflection, "As long as I walked the streets under them stars there'd be only one thing anyone could say about me and that was: I hope he's proud of himself now, the pig, after what he did on his poor mother,"[21] is in the film said to Joe, who manages to console Francie. In a similar affective switch, Joe pledges undying loyalty as Francie, en route to the industrial school, is driven from the square incarcerated in a police car.

MICHAEL COLLINS

McCabe delivered this second script as Jordan was editing *Interview with the Vampire*. Amongst the many who had been impressed by *The Crying Game* was David Geffen, the legendary music mogul who was to go on to cofound DreamWorks and who at that time had both a deal with Warner Brothers and an option on Anne Rice's *Interview with the Vampire*, which he asked Jordan to write and direct. For the first time, Jordan was offered the possibility of full access to what Orson Welles called the "biggest electric train set a boy ever had." He had Tom Cruise and Brad Pitt as his leads and a full period piece ranging from antebellum New Orleans to nineteenth-century Paris.

Jordan now sat down and rapidly wrote a third draft of the script. He pruned radically. Out went the over-tedious description of the failure of Joe and Francie's friendship. Out too went a subplot that McCabe had introduced, which had Sergeant Sausage and Leddy the pig slaughterer keeping a weather eye on Francie as pledges of their youthful ardor for his mother (there is the faintest trace of this subplot in the very opening scene of the final film). Jordan, however, kept many of McCabe's changes. The most significant aspect of this third draft is that Jordan now felt himself possessed by Francie's voice and decided that he would direct the film himself.

The making of *Interview with the Vampire* had been fraught with public difficulties. Anne Rice had taken out a page-long ad in *Variety* to denounce the casting of Tom Cruise as the vampire Lestat. Jordan, however, had directed Cruise against type as a mincing little leather boy in a blond wig, and once Anne Rice had seen the final film, she took out another page ad in *Variety* to say that she had been wrong. The film took over $100,000,000 at the box office. Jordan had now had two cultural and commercial hits in a row. Warner Brothers offered him carte blanche for his next movie. Jordan explained that the film that he had wanted to make for over ten years was *Michael Collins,* a film that the studio had probably forgotten they owned.

Michael Collins is one of the most memorable figures in all of Irish history. In the aftermath of the Easter Rising and the elections of 1918, he organized the embryo state's finances while at the same time forging the Irish Republican Army into a formidable weapon. Indeed, the terror campaign he waged was so successful that it forced the British government, then at the height of its global power, to the negotiating table. De Valera, who was to become the dominating figure in the first four decades of Irish independence, declined to attend these negotiations, and it was Collins who was probably the dominant voice in the decision to accept the twenty-six-county Ireland that Lloyd George offered as an alternative to unleashing the full military power of the British state. Much ink has been spilled and many lives have been lost over this decision, and as a small child in London, my blood was both thrilled and chilled by the story of these negotiations. In particular, my father was obsessed by the final hours of the five-month negotiation when the five-man delegation walked the nighttime streets of London, having agreed to final terms but not yet having signed the final documents. When they returned to Downing Street, Churchill, who was negotiating beside Lloyd George, recorded of Collins that he had never seen a man in the grip of such powerful emotions. As he signed the treaty, Collins remarked that he was signing his death warrant.

This comment proved uncannily prescient. Not a year later, and in the uniform of the commander in chief of the army of the newly formed Irish state, he met his death on 22 August 1922 at the hands of an IRA flying column in the civil war that had been provoked by the treaty. The date has been burned into my own memory since my very earliest years, for it was on that day that my father was born, and my grandparents' reaction to the death was to change the name they had decided for a boy from Michael to the more safely Gaelic Myles. In the sixties, all this was ancient Irish history, but in the seventies as a new civil war broke out in Northern Ireland and as the Provisional IRA started bombing campaigns on what some called the Mainland, the debates over the treaty became current once again. Indeed, when I was head of production at the British Film Institute in the late eighties, I commissioned the poet and critic Tom Paulin and the director Thaddeus O'Sullivan to write a script on the period. They had carte blanche, but I advised them to concentrate on the five months that Collins was negotiating in London, perhaps even to set the whole film on that final fateful night. The film never got out of development, but it meant that when Jordan told me at a very early screening of *The Crying Game* that he had written a script on Collins I couldn't wait to read it. If I have never sat down to read a script with greater expectations I certainly have never been more disappointed.

The five months and the fateful night did not appear in a version of Collins's life that was a traditional epic in which a nation takes shape around a great man. Virgil had trademarked this form early, and Attenborough's *Gandhi* (1982) and Lean's *Lawrence of Arabia* (1962) were recent examples in Anglophone cinema. It seemed to me untrue to the history and to ignore the most important lessons about a man of war abandoning violence.

What became clear on the release of the film was that Jordan had a much more acute understanding of what was at stake in his native country. *Michael Collins* broke every box-office record ever set in Ireland and allowed huge numbers of Irishmen and women fresh access to their own history. By ignoring the endlessly repeated debates about the treaty, Jordan had produced a cultural legitimation of the twenty-six-county state. And he produced it at the moment when the people of that state were to be asked a question practically without historical parallel. For the film was released in Ireland in November 1996, in the period leading up to the referendum when the Irish would vote, by a huge majority, to renounce any absolute claim to the six counties of the North. Yeats famously asked if "that play of mine sent out certain men the English shot." Jordan can ask himself the less agonizing question of what role *Michael Collins* played in the peace process. If one wanted to take one example of how the film constructs a unified image of the nation, the truly epic scene that ends the film with Collins's death has on the soundtrack Sinead O'Connor, a noted IRA supporter, singing "She Moved Through the Fair," one of the most popular of the traditional songs popularized by the Gaelic revival. Film's ability to add music to text and image remains an area worthy of much further exploration, and Stephanie McKnight's brilliant essay on the use of nondiegetic sound in *The Virgin Suicides* (1999) shows how crucial it can be in adaptation.

However, if the political role of the film is simple to defend, its easy glamorizing of violence, particularly in the central sequences, which are shot as a gangster movie, pose much more difficult questions. Jordan's diary of the production shows that he fully understood how complex was the nationalist legacy of violence, but his film could be accused of contributing to the myths that underlie that legacy. Fancifully, one might construct a narrative in which Jordan's determination to make *The Butcher Boy* his next film was his determination to investigate the myths of Irish nationalism. More certain is that Jordan was in the position after the critical success of *Michael Collins* to ask Warner Brothers to fund to the tune of $11,000,000 a small Irish film about child abuse and matricide. It is difficult to stress how unusual a moment this was in film history—a low-budget Irish film was being made with a Hollywood studio as U.S. distributor. This allowed both a generous eleven-week shoot and the ability to dress sets so that Jordan could shoot wide. Even more important, he could afford the special effects so crucial to the final film. Best of all, the budget was so low that Jordan was left to his own devices. Perfection.

A DIRECTOR'S ADAPTATIONS

Long before the film was greenlit and just having shot *Michael Collins*, Jordan sat down to write a further draft of *The Butcher Boy*. This time he made a momentous decision, arguably more a director's than a writer's decision. In the final quarter of the book when Francie has been released from mental hospital, he is no longer a child but the terrifying adolescent that had been created in the pages of "Baby Pig." It had been understood from the first that if the film were to faithfully represent the book there would need to be a change of actor at this point. Jordan now decided that he could only make the film with one actor: Francie would remain a schoolboy throughout. Although the script was to go through another draft and many final tweaks of the voice-over, this fourth draft is very much the script of the film that we know. It should be stressed that the complex textual history of *The Butcher Boy*—with two versions lying behind the published book and five drafts between book and film—is not, in my view, unusual. James Naremore, in his essay on Welles's attempts to make *Heart of Darkness,* gives another example of how fluid is the process of writing an adaptation.

Jordan's decision to use only one actor and to keep Francie a child also saw the deletion of much of the extreme violence at the end of the book, when in a state of hypomania and fuelled by alcohol, Francie delights in his newfound physical strength to terrorize. Gone are the scenes where he frightens Mrs. Connolly when she tries to help him after he has been released from the mental hospital. Gone too is Francie's pleasure in making Mrs. Nugent beg for her life and beating her up before he kills her.

Jordan is a master of screen violence, and the occasions when Francie (played by Eamonn Owens) erupts into murderous rage are very powerful, but they are very brief. It would have been impossible to show the repeated brutality of the final stages of the book on screen. As readers, we almost fail to notice the details, carried along as we are by the torrent of Francie's words and transfixed as we are by the burden of rejection that Francie is accumulating. On screen, such violence would have alienated us from Francie. Bazin claimed that the mark of a true adaptation was the ability was to find in other matters of expression material that could not be transposed directly. The violence that Jordan drops from the end of the book now emerges much earlier in the film as a threat to the very existence of the species. In the book, the fear of human extinction unleashed by the Cuban missile crisis and the impact of television on the culturally isolated state of de Valeran Ireland are two separate themes. The film brings them powerfully together in the image of the mushroom cloud exploding on the television screen as Francie's mother reaches for Dr. Roche's useless tablets. Similarly, when Francie breaks into the Nugents to dump on their living room floor, the television is screening footage from an imaginary atomic attack rather than *Voyage to the Bottom of the Sea* as in the novel.

The movie's most striking image, the atomic mushroom cloud, identifies Francie's inability to find himself a symbolic space in the town, and his consequent violence, with the death drive that threatens the future of the planet. Francie's psychotic collapse as he refuses to accept his father's death takes form as a nuclear explosion that devastates the town. Francie's inability to symbolize his father's death, his inability to come to terms with the inevitable mortality of the father, makes Francie not simply a native of Clones but a representative of the human race. Lacan argued that it was just this inability to accept that the father is no more than a name, a further term in a symbolic progression, which is at the root of all psychosis. One could argue, however, that Francie's condition is peculiarly Irish. After Catholic Emancipation in 1829, Catholic men in Ireland, while enjoying freedom to practice their own religion, were still discriminated against as citizens. The effort to claim a full Irish citizenship is guyed in the Cyclops chapter of Joyce's *Ulysses* where "The Citizen" stands for a crippled masculinity constitutionally wedded to violence as a defense and a disavowal. The problem for Ireland, and this is the failure of national liberation, is that the form of subjectivity that is aspired to is exactly that of the imperialist oppressor, albeit with a different Gaelic content. The real liberation from colonialism would be to accept the weakness of the father and to move beyond attempts to identify with an all-powerful individual. It would be to accept that we are all brother pigs.

What stands in the way of this liberation in both Joyce's work and *The Butcher Boy* are overcompensatory mothers who continue to hold out the promise of power to the son when it has visibly failed in the father. This remains the deepest symbolic center of McCabe's novel, and it is emphasized in Jordan's film. The fundamental change from Baby Pig to *The Butcher Boy* is the change from butchering the blood brother, Joe Purcell, to murdering the mother, Mrs. Nugent. In fact, Mrs. Nugent is the second mother that Francie has killed, and the film stresses this equivalence. In the novel, Francie is released from the mental hospital in order to engage in his spree of violence. In the film, he is too young for such a release to be remotely plausible, and instead he escapes through a window—his actions "rhyming" back to his earlier flight from domestic violence and stressing the symbolic equivalence between the death of Annie Brady and Mrs. Nugent, the real mother unable to nourish Francie and the imaginary mother on whose too-ample breast he chokes.

THE POLITICS OF MATRICIDE

That the mother whom Francie is engaged in slaughtering should be understood politically is marked in the book by Mrs. Nugent's name, for Grace Nugent is the heroine of Maria Edgeworth's 1812 novel *The Absentee,* where she functions as the representative of the Irish and Gaelic traditions, and she is also the subject of both poem and song as "Gracey Nugent."[22] Nugent's name reminds us that the Gaelic revival was originally an Anglo-Irish project and that to accept this identification of Ireland is to accept the identification of the imperialist oppressor.[23] In the film, Jordan accepted the designer's suggestion that Mrs. Nugent be clothed in brilliant greens, thus identifying cinematically with the Wicked Witch of the West and politically with Mother Ireland. When Francie murders her, he is disemboweling a whole tradition that has attempted to deny the weakness of the father by producing maternal figures that will empower the son.

In the book, the maternal function is replaced by the music of the language of Monaghan that sustains Francie's speech and by the forms of popular culture both English and American that sustain his imagination. The end of the book is one of ecstatic happiness as Francie, reverting to his first meeting with Joe Purcell, starts hacking at an ice puddle with one of the bogmen who is incarcerated with him. The endless problem of class division that has so perplexed and wounded Francie, the problem that he comes from a family of pigs, is abandoned for the most elementary relation of brotherhood. The film goes much further. It produces an alternative maternal image, unthinkable in the book, in the person of Sinead O'Connor. Jordan claims that he cast O'Connor in the dual role of the Blessed Virgin Mary and Irish colleen because her face so resembled those statues of Mary that decorate the many nineteenth-century churches of Ireland. While this visual resemblance is striking, it is also the case that O'Connor is one of the most visible faces of the abuse that the Catholic Church was revealed to have visited on the thousands of children that the Irish state had entrusted to its care for decades. Indeed, much of the success of *The Butcher Boy* was that it tapped into the anger and fury at a church that had embodied all the hopes and aspirations of the nation for so long and had betrayed its citizens so heartlessly.

Both Jordan and McCabe were determined that the film would not lapse, as it could so easily have done, into a dismal realist account of abuse, but the film does succeed in producing an alternative reality to that embodied by the Catholic traditions of Ireland. Francie Brady and Neil Jordan were both born in 1950, which is the date of the only infallible papal pronouncement ever made. In that year, Pope Pius XII announced after prolonged pressure that Mary, the Mother of God, did not die but was assumed directly into heaven. This belief finds no sanction in the New Testament, and it is plausible to think that its contemporary power is the promise of a maternal function that can overcome the ever-more-terrible forms of species death threatened by industrial civilization. Indeed, the frequency of the references to the book of Revelation in the service proscribed for this new holiday of obligation suggest that the elaboration of the doctrine of the assumption was a direct answer to the fears posed by the bombs that had destroyed Hiroshima and Nagasaki.

In Irish terms, the significance of Mary has to be linked to her image as a maternal figure who escapes the ravages of sexual desire, and this refusal of female sexual desire also runs through the narratives and images of nationalism. However, it is this renunciation of sexuality and the body that produces both the aristocracy of an abusing priesthood and the class divisions which differentiate the middle-class "English" Nugents from the impoverished Brady pigs. The film offers us, instead, a sexually explicit mother in the figure of Sinead O'Connor, and it is this acceptance of sexuality and the body which produces the promise of an ideal fraternity, "blood brothers till the end of time."[24] It also allows that crucial identification with the failed father that the history of Ireland makes so difficult. For perhaps the most crucial difference between book and film is that while Francie Brady tells his story from the future, the voice is the voice of a child. From the first moment of the voice-over in the film we know that Francie is going to achieve adulthood.

That Jordan should have cast Stephen Rea in this crucial part, complete at the end with ridiculous ginger wig, gives further weight to this change. For since *Angel*, Rea has been Jordan's actor of choice, that crucial figure against whom he has played his own identifications like Truffaut with Léaud, Ford with Wayne, or Almodóvar with Cruz. There could be no clearer statement of Jordan's identification with Francie as representative of his own generation. It is also significant that Rea accepted such a relatively small part. But Rea, like many, perhaps all, of the cast realized quite what a significant moment *The Butcher Boy* was in Irish history, and he was determined to add his contribution to render it on screen, not as a "dismal little Irish film"[25] but as ecstatic affirmation. Benny Brady, like many of the characters in *The Butcher Boy*, verges on the stereotype of the Irish drunken father. It took an actor of Rea's ability, and all Jordan's skill as a director, to produce an individualized tragedy rather than generalized farce from the part. Indeed, this was the problem for all of the cast, perhaps the most stellar Irish ensemble ever gathered together. Jordan realized that stereotype was the constant risk in the performances and was ruthless not only in reshooting, but also in recasting, to ensure that his magnificent actors found the individual in the stereotype: in this most Irish of films there could be no room for the stage Irish.

ADAPTATION AND AUTHORSHIP

In reading novel and film as illuminating each other, I have been guided by Bazin's notion of an ideal construct, and *The Butcher Boy* seems the perfect example of such a construct. However, one could add rapidly, and in no way exhaustively, to Bazin's original list of *The Grapes of Wrath* (1940), *A Day in the Country* (1936), and *Man's Hope* (1945) with *Blade Runner* (1982), *Crash,* and *Lord of the Rings* (2001–3) to indicate that *The Butcher Boy* is not an isolated phenomenon. In the final paragraph of his 1948 essay on adaptation, Bazin spoke of how adaptation would alter our very notion of authorship, and it seems to me that here too *The Butcher Boy* can offer useful lessons. It is nearly a century since T. S. Eliot wrote "Tradition and the Individual Talent" and launched a coruscating attack on the Romantic ideal of the conscious artist controlling the meanings in his or her work. Barthes's and Foucault's closely linked essays of the late sixties bought considerable gains to Eliot's position with their emphases on the transindividual genres and codes (Barthes) and on the institutional definitions of authorship (Foucault). However, these later essays have given rise to a debilitating academic orthodoxy that blithely assumes, against every common sense, commercial and biological consideration, that authors have no reality whatsoever. Film, completely ignored by Eliot (unsurprisingly) as well as by Barthes and Foucault (much more surprisingly), offers a very good example of how we need to retain some notion of the individual author without relapsing into the Romantic concept of a unified creative source. There are two reasons why film is a particularly good place to reevaluate authorship. One of Barthes's major objections to the concept of the author was that it obscured the genres and codes from which each work is composed. However, the concept of a film "auteur" was elaborated in terms of those genres and codes from—and this is the historical originality of *Cahiers*—the point of view of the audience. If we reverse the perspective and look at it from the point of view of the producer, then it is quite clear that there must be an author on the set. For when each take finishes, actors, wardrobe, cinematographer, hair and makeup, continuity and more all look to the director to decide whether another take is needed. The director will consult and the crew will contribute, but only one person on the set is actually able to see the full picture.[26] If then every film must have, at least during shooting, an authority, and if a director like Jordan also has the final say during script and prepro-duction as well as during editing and release, then it is clear that it is his authority that creates the film. However, even this brief a description makes clear how that creation is as much an editing as an originating function, that the codes that the young *Cahiers* critics delighted in are the result of relationships between the director and his cast and crew, that the author finds himself in the audience with whom he is trying to make the film. Indeed when the script is produced from a novel, and when the final film preserves at its center the same main character, then Romantic notions of authorship are impossible to maintain, for who can claim to be the author of Francie Brady? Eamonn Owens, Stephen Rea, Neil Jordan, and Patrick McCabe all have valid claims. Indeed, if we now turn to Patrick McCabe in 1990, writing in England, amongst a cacophony of unfamiliar accents and idioms, and if we keep in mind the image of the anthropology of a film set, then it should become clear that McCabe's function is as much editor as originator as he attempts to listen to his town and as the dead and the living throng about him from as far back as 1902 and beyond, their voices mingling and fusing to become the novel that we love, in a process so com-pellingly described in Eliot's essay. To forget that a text is based in an indi-vidual body or bodies with their specific historical trajectories is to engage in the worst kind of academic idealism. However, those individual bodies need to be understood as dividual, divided by the multitude of dialogues, both past and present, which constitute them.

It might be tempting at this point to think that the new kind of author-ship of which Bazin was talking would be some way of adding Jordan and McCabe together into some "super-author," but the move is not of addition, but of division and multiplication as the effort to communicate experience involves the constant testing of form and content across a range of inter-locutors. Crucial here is some notion of shared social experience. Perhaps the most useful formulation remains that of Raymond Williams's *The Long Revolution:* a "structure of feeling."[27] Williams's term was an attempt to grasp something socially and historically precise in the word structure while cap-turing the most evanescent depths of personal emotion. The term, which Williams attempted to apply generationally, had a certain currency in the sixties, but it disappeared both because of academic fashion and also because there seemed no way to specify what was at stake, no procedures by which one could detail or even fix chronologically what was being described. Since Williams, however, we have paid much more attention to the audience in our understanding of meaning, and if we wish to speak of a structure of feeling which Jordan and McCabe, cast and crew of *The Butcher Boy* shared, then we do not go back into the history of Ireland to find this structure. Rather, we find it in the film itself, and it is the film which then reveals the structure in the history. This at least was what I felt when I first saw *The Butcher Boy*—that the Ireland of the sixties was dramatizing itself before my eyes.[28]

If *The Butcher Boy* perhaps furnishes the perfect example of the new kind of adaptation peculiar to film, then Kathleen Murray offers us perhaps a limit case in her analysis of *To Have and Have Not*, where she argues persuasively that despite the radical departures which mark novel and film, there is an "ideal construct" of the kind Bazin describes. It should not be thought either that this collection is arguing for a necessary superiority of the "ideal construct," or that all of the contributions are concerned with the kind of adaptation Bazin described. Laura Mulvey, for example, offers a penetrating example of three Max Ophuls adaptations where the interest in the alterations of the considerable source texts is not the way in which they develop elements in those texts but how they reveal the repetitive concerns of the film auteur. Finally, this collection perhaps reveals a new category altogether when the film is produced from a close engagement with the original novel but where the aim of the adaptation is not to develop and enhance but to discard and contradict so as to produce a vision which has little to do with the source text. J. D. Wright's analysis of Kubrick's version of King's *The Shining*, Rick Warner's acute examination of Godard's adaptation of Moravia's *Contempt*, and Fredric Jameson's magisterial dissection of Tarkovsky's treatment of Lem's *Solaris* all reveal a form of adaptation which is neither true to the spirit nor casually appropriative of the underlying source. Jameson goes so far as to suggest, in his provocative and fertile conclusion, that this form of adaptation is the most faithful—faithful to each medium's desire to vaunt its superiority. It would be foolish to dismiss this thesis, in which each adaptation allegorizes a conflict between film and novel as form, strongly anchored as it is in Bakhtin's theory of the novel, and responding as it does to something which is in the current intermedial air.

However, this allegory of conflict can only be a part of a dialectic that has also to include the realities of intermedial cooperation. Indeed if we were to descend from the sublime of Jameson's intermedial *agon* to the ridiculous of personality, it might perhaps be worth noting that Kubrick, Godard, and Tarkovsky are all famously uncooperative, all determined to claim total priority for their own efforts, even when, as in Godard, committed to ideologies of cooperation. If we take the analysis to this level, then it is worth stressing again that Jordan is a major Irish writer, that his first collection of short stories was immediately hailed as announcing a major new talent, and that even as recently as 2003 he took a year off from filmmaking to write a major novel, *Shade*. Jordan quite evidently has nothing to fear from a rivalry with literature in general or individual writers such as Angela Carter or Patrick McCabe in particular. It may, however, be possible to raise the argument to a more interesting plane than that of personal psychology if we consider the different roles that film plays from a national perspective. If the novel assumed dominance as the major fictional form at the end of the eighteenth/beginning of the nineteenth century, then it was film that displaced it from the end of the First World War onward. This process is clearest in the United States, but the lag is very little in any of the major industrial countries. The situation in countries too small to sustain their own film industry is very different, and if Francie Brady's visual imagination is full of films, those films are American. Indeed, the first Irish film to achieve any kind of commercial success was Neil Jordan's own *Angel,* and so in Ireland, it could persuasively be argued, the novel maintained its cultural dominance until very recently. It may be that it is this very particular national history that allowed a country's finest fiction writer and finest film director to join forces. Together they harnessed the full resources of both media to perform the reality of the Ireland that made them.

NOTES

1. William Shakespeare, *The Tempest*, ed. Virginia Mason Vaughan and Alden T. Vaughan (Surrey: Thomas Nelson and Son, 1999), 287–302.
2. Elisabeth Decultot, "Les pérégrinations européennes du mot romantique," *Critique* 65, no. 745–46 (juin–juillet 2009): 456–66.
3. There is a scene between Henry V and the French princess in the anonymous source play *The Famous Victories of Henry the Fifth*, but it contains no linguistic element.
4. Stephen Prince, *Visions of Empire: Political Imagery in Contemporary American Film* (New York: Praeger, 1992), 54. Ronald Bergan, obituary for A. I. Bezzerides, *The Guardian*, 6 February 2007.
5. Martin Meisel, *Realizations: Narrative, Pictorial, and Theatrical Arts in Nineteenth-Century England* (Princeton: Princeton University Press, 1983).
6. André Bazin, "Adaptation, or the Cinema as Digest," in *Bazin at Work: Major Essays & Reviews from the Forties & Fifties*, ed. Bert Cadullo (New York: Routledge, 1997), 49–50.
7. Patrick McCabe did write a theatrical version of *The Butcher Boy* called *Frank Pig Says Hello* (1992), but it was written contemporaneously with the novel and did not play an active part in the transformation of novel to film. Historically, many Hollywood adaptations of novels were based on previous dramatizations, including most famously *Birth of a Nation*. More recently, stage adaptations of films—*Spamalot, Billy Elliot*—show the continuing validity of the Bazinian pyramid.
8. See, for example, Christine Geraghty, *Now a Major Motion Picture: Film Adaptations of Literature and Drama* (Lanham: Rowman and Littlefield, 2008).
9. Jean-Luc Godard, *Godard on Godard*, ed. Jean Narboni and Tom Milne, trans. Tom Milne (New York: Da Capo, 1972), 147.

10. See my introduction to David Trotter, *Cinema and Modernism* (Oxford: Blackwell, 2007).

11. In conversation, September 1994.

12. Salman Rushdie, *The Wizard of Oz* (London: British Film Institute, 1992), 1.

13. Thomas Leitch, "Adaptation Studies at a Crossroads," *Adaptation* 1, no. 1 (2008): 64.

14. Among Jordan's more than ten producing credits is the magnificent *Intermission* (2003), from a script by the Irish playwright Mark O'Rowe.

15. For further analyses of Joyce's relation to the Irish peasantry and the ideology of the Gaelic revival, see my *James Joyce and the Revolution of the Word*, 2nd ed. (London: Palgrave, 2003).

16. In conversation, November 1992.

17. Interview with Patrick McCabe, March 2005.

18. Patrick McCabe, "Baby Pig," unpublished typescript, 94–96.

19. Patrick McCabe, *The Butcher Boy* (New York: Fromm International Publishing, 1993), 1.

20. For example, Jessica Scarlata describes the film's ending as "one of its few departures from the plot of the novel" in "Carnivals and Goldfish: History and Crisis in The Butcher Boy," in *Literature and Film: A Guide to the Theory and Practice of Film Adaptation*, ed. Robert Stam and Alessandra Raengo (Oxford: Blackwell, 2005), 235.

21. McCabe, *Butcher Boy*, 44.

22. For more details, see Dana Och, "Straying from the Path: The Body and Movement in the Films of Neil Jordan," in "The World Goes One Way and We Go Another: Movement, Migration and Myth in Irish Cinema," (PhD diss., University of Pittsburgh, 2006), 162–216. See also Thomas J. Tracy, *Irishness and Womanhood in Nineteenth Century British Writing* (London: Ashgate, 2009), 27–29.

23. This is, of course, the analysis of James Joyce's *Ulysses*. See particularly chapter 1 and the character of Haines.

24. The themes of fraternity and sisterhood are investigated further in Jordan's 2005 adaptation of McCabe's *Breakfast on Pluto*, which enlarges the "ideal construct" of *The Butcher Boy*.

25. In conversation, Dublin, 16 June 2004.

26. See my article "The Revenge of the Author," in *The Eloquence of the Vulgar* (London: British Film Institute, 1999), 33–41.

27. Raymond Williams, *The Long Revolution* (New York: Columbia University Press, 1961), 41–71.

28. The analysis of *The Butcher Boy* here condenses many of the themes and emphases of my monograph *The Butcher Boy* (Cork: Cork University Press/Irish Film Institute, 2007).

Sanshô Dayû (Mizoguchi, 1954)

1

The Economies of Adaptation

Dudley Andrew

The sign of the problematic of adaptation is the signature of the author, sometimes reproduced in facsimile on screen. More often, adaptations open with a fade-in on a stately volume on whose cover the title and author are elegantly inscribed. There follows the rest of the credits as pages turn. Even without picturing the book, a film based on a prominent novel will do more than cite the author; it will graphically feature that famous name so as to let its aura spread to envelop the other names listed, underwriting the production by association. The author's name, a variant of a signature, may be a mere surface mark, but it embeds a fourth dimension, the temporal process that, in the case of adaptation, brought an entire film out of the textual body of a novel. Anchored to a submerged reef of values, all films, but adaptations most notably, float to their audiences secured by that slender line of credits that allows us to trace their genesis.

In the case of adaptation, genesis—and credits are called *générique* in French—goes back to a single treasured source, the book that is the origin and perhaps the final measure of the film. Even in our skeptical age, this lifeline—call it fidelity—just won't be easily cut.[1] Fidelity is the umbilical cord that nourishes the judgments of ordinary viewers as they comment on what are effectively aesthetic and moral values after they emerge from *Romeo + Juliet* (Luhrmann, 1996), *The Color Purple* (Spielberg, 1985), or even *Passion of the Christ* (Gibson, 2004). If we tuned in on these discussions, we might find ourselves listening to a vernacular version of comparative media semiotics.

For some time, the leading academic trend has ignored or disparaged this concern with fidelity, finding the *vertical* line that anchors a film to its literary substrate exasperating and constraining. Scholars today dare to detach the anchor and let the films they write about float free. Why not? In postmodernism every text, including every adaptation, is valued for the way it vibrates the *horizontal* network of neighboring texts, none of them to be taken as "superior," not even the novel that may lend its name, plot and characters to a film. If anything, adaptation feeds cultural studies, a discipline born for this era of proliferation, where textual contagion counts more than does interpretation. Cultural studies takes its cue from producers in their ambition to multiply a text's impact through advertising, spin-offs, translations, and "versions" of all sorts.

I. THE HORIZONTAL

In fact, the industry of adaptation was born with the industrial age itself. *Les Misérables* might be considered its Bible, not just as a moral encyclopedia of the early nineteenth century (a drama of class struggle, crime, and social alienation) but as a bestseller, indeed the blockbuster of the century. Victor Hugo wanted to touch all the major ideas of the day, to give contemporary history a moral significance, and to do so for all humanity. He not only wrote of the masses; he expected to be read by everyone. And so it happened. Everyone did read this book. Frantic crowds lined up in front of French booksellers for each of the three installments, April, May, and June of 1862. Translations came out in many languages within the very year of publication. Hugo profited to the tune of nearly $2,000,000 in today's currency, just from the initial rights. The publishing industry had seen nothing like this, and they made the most of it. Sales responded to advertising campaigns associated with reprints and spin-offs. Five million copies of the first Chinese edition were sold. Coming to America during our civil war, it was perfectly timed to support Lincoln's "emancipation proclamation." It has been a bestseller here ever since, with sales jumping every twenty years or so on the backs of adaptations for stage and then screen.

Les Misérables offered itself up to adaptation. Having launched his career with *Cromwell* and *Hernani,* Hugo undoubtedly thought about the stage in laying out his plot, characters, and settings. Indeed, *Les Misérables* became a play only a month after the novel's publication, adapted by Hugo's brother Charles. Although banned by the Parisian authorities, it opened in Brussels and in London before a year was out. Paris wouldn't see it until 1878, the year of a massive republication of the novel featuring five hundred engravings, many by the acclaimed artist Gustave Brion.

On the eve of the century—during the dark years of the Dreyfus affair—a fabulous production of the Charles Hugo play was staged in Paris consisting of seventeen tableaux. Since then, impresarios have been ready to revive *Les Misérables* to exploit the talents of a star actor or the fever of a troubled political moment. Of course, it was also revived to make money…something it always has done, as the musical *Les Miz* reminds us tour after tour.

It has been even more tempting to film a novel whose outsized sentiments can echo within heroic and picturesque locations, as they do in the opening scene in the town of Digne ringed by mountains. Hugo seems to have thought like a producer/director and surely would have been one if born a century later. Of the nearly forty filmed versions, several originate from Japan and the Soviet Union, seven from the United States, plus one each from Egypt, India, and Turkey. The five major French film versions carry an overt supplement of national history in the making, for Hugo meant *Les Misérables* to be a modern epic, depicting France in the wake of 1789 and pointing toward the future that France would become and, in its later film versions, has become. The one I prefer came out in February 1934, directed by Raymond Bernard. Photographed by Kruger who had shot *Napoleon* (1927), it aims at the sublimity and humanity of Gance's masterpiece. The script was cleverly whittled down to what seems both essential and distinctive about the novel, but its fame comes mainly through its incredible cast, the Who's Who of France at the time: Harry Baur as Jean Valjean, music-hall star Florelle as Fantine, Charles Vanel as Javert, a young Jean Servais as Marius, Marguerite Moreno and Charles Dullin as the Thénardiers, and Pagnol's favorite actress Orane Demazis as Eponine. Arthur Honegger wrote a large and somber score for a film that was four and a half hours long, shown in three parts, each occupying a different first-run theater for a month. A year later, Hollywood tried to follow on the success of this French version with Fredric March incarnating Jean Valjean against Charles Laughton's Javert, shrinking the length to well under two hours.

Bernard's version seems, and remains, far more vital than its Hollywood competitor because of the thickness of cultural references that naturally surround it. Hugo's magnificent plot and unforgettable characters were never the whole story, so to speak. His novel swims in geography, clothes, food, and other indexes of everyday life. Bernard's film manages to situate the tale and give it resonance so that the moral intrigue that forms such a satisfying abstract geometry takes on palpable social and even political consequences in the specifically French context and, more to the point, in the context of the turbulent years of 1933–34. No film has had a more remarkable premiere, a gala affair at the Marignan theater on February 4, 1934, just two days before the Stavisky riots, the bloodiest of the century in France. The Stavisky scandal and his suicide (or assassination) had been all the Press could talk about for nearly a month. As high-level minister after minister became implicated, a call to arms was sounded on both left and right. With Hitler cockily flaunting Germany's progress in his first year in office, ordinary French citizens were demoralized and angry enough for a street fight. This explains the spontaneous and extended applause that went up when Emile Fabré entered the Marignan. Fabré had earlier in the week been deposed as head of the Comédie-Française for daring to stage Shakespeare's *Coriolanus* during such a politically unstable time, and he had been summarily replaced by a right-wing functionary. Fabré's presence primed the audience of intellectuals and dignitaries to watch *Les Misérables* as an allegory about current life in France. And sure enough, there were cheers and catcalls throughout the screening, the theater nearly erupting once the students and workers took to the barricades, which is unquestionably the film's finest sequence. The audience was transported by a film (and novel) that seemed to mix revolution and compassion. Pouring out of the theater that night were the cream of Paris who would need to react, less than forty hours later, to the riots at the Place de la Concorde and throughout the city. In its February 17 issue, *L'Illustration,* the *Life Magazine* of France, ran six pages of gruesome pictures of the carnage; but then there followed four pages of stills from the movie. The account of the riot and the lengthy review praising *Les Misérables* came from the same pen, that of the magazine's senior editor.

While art and politics seldom conjoin in so obvious a fashion as this, the cultural studies approach has taught us that film art and the cultural economy are invariably tied up with one another, especially when well-known literary texts are involved. This is so much the case today that some historians believe the cine-literary blockbuster best defines Global Hollywood's self-image. Building on the so-called heritage genre of the 1980s, including the hothouse hybrids of Merchant/Ivory, Miramax led a surge of popular adaptations beginning in the mid-1990s that have grown into the industry's proudest, safest genre. Jim Collins has traced the plethora of intertexts that complicate the way canonical novels like *Sense and Sensibility* or *The Age of Innocence* became landmark films. In a virtuosic discussion of *The English Patient* (1996), he demonstrates the feedback loops created when Michael Ondaatje collaborated on Anthony Minghella's film. Those loops spiraled into a storm of advertising, interviews, and talk-show appearances (by both men), not to mention reviews of novel and film in high and low media, and candid photographs. Academic textual analysis played a role as well, for it encouraged the use of both the novel and the film in college courses, while it lifted the prestige of both works. Thus the traditional form of adaptation study (comparing novel to film) now serves as evidence used by the cultural critic who cares not about the meaning of the texts but about their prominence on the landscape of the mid-1990s. How did a text like Ondaatje's grow, split into two, then proliferate so wildly and at so many levels? Thus, differences between texts no longer serve as a focal issue as they did in the eras first of bellelettristic or formal analysis and later of semiotics; now differences are shown to be part of the logic of capitalism, as *The English Patient* in one guise or another appeals to multiple audiences. Cultural studies goes so far as to suspend literature's priority as an institution and a practice in today's media environment. Writing and reading do not transcend the enticements of image and advertising but lead directly to these and are in turn affected by them. Just look at the cover of the mass-market paperback put out after 1996. The English patient looks very much like Ralph Fiennes; meanwhile, Global Hollywood profits from its association with, its dissemination of, a Booker Prize-winning novel. Oprah profited from readers and viewers alike when she hosted the author and the auteur. *People Magazine* sold stories. *The English Patient* grew in all media, and the media grew with it.[2]

Such a compelling argument, and the approach of which it is so fine an example, risks becoming part of the problem it investigates and exploits. For Collins's essay participates in the circulation and expansion of literary and cinephilic culture, gaining readership in the process and confirming the practice it brings to light. While the practice is not new, late capitalism has certainly accelerated what was incipient in the industrial production that was in place in Hugo's day. After the huge success of Baz Luhrmann's *Romeo + Juliet* in 1996, followed two years later by the blockbuster *Shakespeare in Love* (Madden, 1998), the producers of *Pride & Prejudice* (Wright, 2005) could rightly expect the phenomenal return on their relatively inexpensive production. No wonder that in the past decade especially, cherished authors and the literature they produced have been frantically tossed onto the roulette table of speculative business. Since this enterprise sends many viewers back to read the books, André Bazin noted years ago, what's the harm even of mediocre adaptations?

Yet many critics and a great many spectators do call "foul." Something has gone awry when producers buy up literary properties only to convert them into poker chips. Strident conservatives would rather see literature atrophy than be travestied by the entertainment industry; equally strident radicals denounce the blunting of art's critical edge by those pandering first to the tastes of a mass audience. And they are right to be concerned, for while not all adaptations are "tasteful"—sugared with delectable faces and ornate cinematography—most do cater to contemporary fashion, even in the decision to go forward with a given project in the first place. Critics of Global Hollywood, both left and right, can only decry the limitless expansion of a casino mentality that seems to have left but one game in town.

II. THE VERTICAL

Adaptation may be the humming motor of uncontrollable textual proliferation—the *horizontal* spread of a title, an author, an idea from medium to medium, language to language—but it can also function as an antidote or alternative. For if the *vertical* line that anchors it to the bedrock of its source remains intact, a contemporary film can draw away from the system, submerging its audience in a different sensibility and set of values. That chain bears the troubled name "fidelity."

Because the practice of adaptation chiefly involves literary sources, we can't avoid looking into the moral claims of fidelity in the theory and practice of translation. To question if the Swedish or Japanese renditions of *Great Expectations* are faithful to what Charles Dickens took care to write in English has its counterpart in the way spectators question the propriety of David Lean's 1948 film version of that beloved novel. A prominent theorist of translation, Lawrence Venuti, addresses film adaptation by dismissing at the outset the notion that different languages (verbal or audiovisual) can communicate a self-same content (plot, character, theme, value). What occurs, he believes, is that the original is mediated by an "interpretant" (or ideological grid) while it is on the way to becoming a new or adapted text.[3] The intepretant governs the choices made in adaptation. Rather than a mechanical transfer from one semiotic system to another, the filmmaker interprets the source via an audiovisual form that also includes attitudes and concerns brought to the project. Venuti argues that we should isolate the different "interpretants" operating in the two moments of creation, both to appreciate their respective achievements and also to assess the propriety of the filmmaker's choices. But that assessment should be sensitive to cultural, not just semiotic, values and so would indeed involve a horizontal as well as vertical dimension, since every adaptation takes place within a "horizon" of contemporaneous values, including other texts within the purview of the filmmaker and the projected audience. In his main example, the celebrated but controversial 1968 *Romeo and Juliet,* Shakespeare can be said to have played into the culture's growing concern over bisexuality, while Franco Zefferelli registered certain connotations in the original for the first time. Shakespeare's play grew through a cinematic interpretation that may owe something to other psychologically and stylistically edgy films of the period (Arthur Penn's *Bonnie and Clyde* [1967], Marco Bellochio's *Fist in his Pocket* [1965]), even if scholars were appalled at liberties taken with the text. Certainly cinema grew in stylistic versatility, not to mention prestige, thanks to this encounter with Shakespeare.

Venuti might well have asked about the staging of Shakespeare through the centuries, since theater in its living form always involves directors and dramaturges who embody the role of "interpretant." And he should have asked about *Romeo and Juliet* performed in German or Russian, that is, about the legitimacy of any translation of the Bard. He asks instead of Shakespeare himself what interpretants were at work in fashioning his "version" of a tale of two characters named Romeo and Juliet? What sources did he use? What other plays (by rival playwrights) did he look to? What was in his library? Venuti's hermeneutic approach risks spreading out both horizontally and vertically to infinity. Still, Shakespeare's text makes us stop. Similarly, to take the most canonical example, the Bible makes a billion readers stop. Its interpretations—including translations, adaptations, and illustrations—have been as necessary to the spread of religion and of culture as they have been fraught with discord. Walter Benjamin used the Bible as such in his great essay, "The Task of the Translator."[4]

Is the canonical lineage of the Bible unique? Let's explore fidelity outside the Western tradition and in a medium other than language. Does adaptation involve fidelity elsewhere and otherwise? I choose the opening sequence of Kenji Mizoguchi's 1946 *Utamaro and His Five Women*, where the artist-hero is challenged to a duel by a cocky exponent of the aristocratic Kano school of painting. How could someone from the popular class who draws for money stand up to a Kano-school painter for whom art is a religious calling? Soon he finds himself fighting (and losing) with paintbrushes, not swords, when Utamaro "improves" the painter's rendition of the goddess of mercy with a few swift strokes. "There, that's better. Wouldn't you agree?" says Utamaro triumphantly. "I've put life into the figure." Economy, spontaneity, and the lively representation of an iconic figure are all on the side of the artist who eats, drinks, and sleeps with the people. He even designs tattoos. "Utamaro draws on flesh," cries out the chagrined Kano artist, who has been required meticulously to imitate time-honored forms and colors.

Yet Utamaro has not drawn just anything. He has brought to life "White-Robed Guanyin," a powerful Buddhist icon. Her image was given canonical form in the late thirteenth century by Muqi; Utamaro knows how to animate her on paper not through slavish imitation but by capturing the spirit of movement and life that Muqi invested in his masterpiece. Just like Utamaro, Mizoguchi felt himself and his artform to be at once on the side of the people and yet connected to the sacred mission by which art ties humanity to the domain of the sacred. He would soon resurrect several near-sacred texts from the Japanese patrimony, introducing them to the West. The film that first grabbed Bazin was the 1951 *The Life of Oharu,* whose Japanese title carries the name of the renowned seventeenth century author this film adapts: *Saikaku ichidai onna.* A few years later Mizoguchi faithfully transformed a beloved puppet play by Japan's Shakespeare, again retaining the author's name in his title, *Chikamatsu Monogatari.* In between, he rendered one of Japan's most well-known tales, *Sanshô Dayû,* relying on Mori Ogai's canonical 1917 version, but improving it, perfecting it, finalizing it so that ever after the tale would be known through Mizoguchi.[5]

Borrowing the Sanshô legend from Mori Ogai (who himself had borrowed it from earlier versions) Mizoguchi thematized fidelity in the largest sense.[6] In the tale, two kidnapped children, Anju and Zushiô, are forced to adapt to horrendous conditions in a slave camp far from their parents, who have been scattered to distant parts of Japan. Throughout their long ordeal, Anju prays to an icon of a bodhisattva given to Zushiô by their father, just as he was led into exile. He had made his son touch the icon while faithfully repeating this maxim: "Be merciful to all men." Ultimately, Zushiô holds firm both to the spirit of the statue and to the letter of the maxim, just as Mizoguchi holds firm to the legend he adapted in the grim moral situation of post-occupation Japan. Thus Mizoguchi made of *Sanshô Dayû* an icon that honors another icon, the goddess of mercy lodged in the reliquary of the story. He was seen praying to a Buddhist icon in his Venice hotel room the night before being awarded the Silver Lion.

When Terrence Malick staged *Sanshô Dayû* at the Brooklyn Academy of Music in 1991, did he touch a sacred icon reverentially, faithfully repeating the moral that has accompanied it for a millennium? Today, in a remote site in Western Japan stand statues of Anju and Zushiô awaiting tourists who take their literature or cinema very seriously. Traditional *onsen* (hotels) advertise their proximity to this pilgrimage site. Such a commercial spin-off spreads away from the original icon of the medieval legend, but only after it establishes and maintains a vertical link to that powerful story.

Perhaps better than other uses of the medium (documentary, experimental), adaptations show cinema dead center in a vast two-dimensional cultural economy. The vertical economy is ruled by past and future, measured by the ancestors and the gods from whom literary, religious, and moral

values derive. The horizontal economy creates value in spreading this patrimony out as widely as possible. Bazin challenged his readers to conceive
of cinema as participating in such a vast cultural economy. And with this in
mind, Jean-Michel Frodon has introduced to today's readers of *Cahiers du
cinéma* the work of Marie-José Mondzain, whose central book bears the title
Image, Icon, Economy: the Byzantine Origins of the Contemporary Imaginary.[7]
In her more recent writings, Mondzain has developed the consequences of
Byzantine iconophilia for the cinema.

Economy is the term used by the Fathers of the early church. While ultimately related to an ecclesiastical financial system involving icons, among
other things, the first of three major economies comes in the form of the
doctrine of the Trinity. The first involves the Trinity wherein a unitary God
is split between the Father and the Son, his natural image, related by the Holy
Spirit. This "mystery" of the Trinity amounts to a division within unity, difference within the same that makes creativity possible.

A second economy describes the circuit of exchange between heaven
and earth when Christ became man. Old Testament prophecies, angelic
appearances, and prefigurations led to the New Testament account of the
words and deeds of Jesus right here on earth, in Judea. A special moment,
the transfiguration, visibly joined heaven and earth in their vertical relation
when Christ on Mount Tabor radiated an uncreated light. The transfiguration guarantees the value (that is, the economy) of icons which are themselves auratic images bathed in and radiating light to those who venerate
them.

Icons are special tokens in the currency of a third theological economy, wherein the faithful buy into transcendence through a commerce
of grace regulated by the church. Icons are based on similitude, could be
copied, and their multiplication alarmed the church, which lost the ability to police their use and feared a dispersal of authority. Man-made, they
nonetheless share in the power of the "natural image" when faithfully produced by an artisan of faith. Fidelity guarantees that the supernatural value
invested in the prototype passes into the calque. Even copies of copies par-
take of such power.

Film adaptations are icons of canonical literary creations. With Literature replacing Religion as a source of transcendence, scholars are today's
priests of inherited spiritual wealth. The fight between horizontal proliferation of, say, Shakespeare and academic or artistic vertical authority plays
out today in arguments over cultural studies. Bazin was interested in both
kinds of economy. His 1948 essay "Adaptation, or the Cinema as Digest"
celebrates the way the people use and enjoy classics through popular versions, illustrations, and filmed adaptations.[8] But the rest of his work shows

how cinema can use the "value" of originals to enrich itself only through a kind of fidelity.

Bazin and Mondzain come directly together around a single image. In the appendix to her book, Mondzain shows that we still live with the power of icons. Her illustration is the photograph of the Shroud of Turin. On May 29, 1898, an amateur photographer named Secondo Pia was authorized to remove a protective pane of glass and take a twenty-minute exposure of the shroud. As the paper reported it: "He dipped his glass plates in the developing bath; suddenly the negative in front of the red lamp caused the face of Christ, which no one had contemplated for eighteen centuries, to loom before his eyes." Here we have science and faith, negativity and appearance, icon and index, making the photograph of the shroud as important as the relic itself.

The faithful could now keep personal copies of the official photograph so as to be in touch with Christ, literally in touch with him through a series of physical relays. From pocket photo to the negative that produced it, to the 1898 photo that came from the glass plates, which had been affected in negative by light reflecting or emanating from the cloth, to the resurrected body that for three days more than eighteen centuries ago was in contact with this cloth for a sufficient time to leave a blurred and bloody but indelible impression. So goes the vertical economy of fidelity, where a miserable-looking photo showing scarcely decipherable blotches can "bear away our faith." But outside this economy, whether for the nonbeliever, or for the believer once carbon dating had proven it bogus, the shroud is nothing but an old rag.

Let us turn now to another sort of modern believer and fetishist, the cinephile. This very picture appears as the first illustration in *Qu'est-ce que le cinéma,* accompanying a footnote Bazin composed: "Here one should really examine the psychology of relics and souvenirs which enjoy the advantages of a transfer of reality stemming from the 'mummy-complex.' Let us merely note in passing that the Holy Shroud of Turin combines the features alike of relic and photograph." A fetish (the photograph) of a literal fetish (the shroud), it is an imprimatur or blessing for Bazin's four volumes to follow. But it's a mixed blessing, so to speak, for by 1958 everyone knew the shroud to be fake and the photo only a document of a hoax or at least of a wild superstition. What could Bazin have had in mind in suggesting or permitting such an image to color our reading of "The Ontology of the Photographic Image"?

A paragraph midway through that essay suggests one motivation through a play on the word that is our topic: "A very faithful drawing may actually tell us more about the model but despite the promptings of our critical intelligence it will never have the irrational power of the photograph to bear away our faith."[9] Why wouldn't a "faithful" drawing of the dead Christ not match this impoverished photograph in its psychological power? By now we know the answer: Bazin argues that the iconic properties by which a photograph imitates the visual layout of its referent are far less compelling than the photograph's physical relation to the referent, its status as decal. In this case, the photograph is a decal of a putative decal of Christ, for the shroud served as a contact print of Christ's body. The photo of the shroud is revered for being just two contact prints away from the god-man, the source of salvation. "Faith" in Christ motivates faith in this photographic image despite its evident inferiority to "faithful" drawings or paintings that deliver an illusion of presence. The impurity of the texture of this photographic image, on the other hand, ratifies the eerie presence of the absence of the object to which it is connected, however weakly. All photographs gain from the genuineness signaled by the impurities on their surface. For these indicate that the true subject has withdrawn from the sign. Bazin may lead to Derrida and Deleuze, with their proliferation of difference, but here he leads to Mondzain and to Jean-Luc Nancy, who write not of difference but of "similitude" and of the withdrawal of the image, which leaves us alone in search of its value. Nancy's book *The Ground of the Image,* like Mondzain's *L'Image Naturel,* are both about a kind of fidelity that goes beyond appearance to a truth that is present in its absence from the image.[10] We should use adaptations, just as we use images, Bazin says, to get at the truths to which they point. Cinema brings us closer to a fidelity to truth. This is worth celebrating on Bazin's ninetieth year.

Let me close with a final image, indeed, the final shot of *Diary of a Country Priest* (Bresson, 1951). Bazin reminds us that this is a mere shadow of a cross ("as awkwardly drawn as on an average holy card") cast upon the wall above the priest's corpse by two mullions. This ultimate "assumption" of the image, this spiritual abstraction, has been prepared over the course of two hours through the overlaying of the priest's voice, the inscriptions in his diary, and the black-and-white traces of people and objects, until at last we reach "a sublime achievement of pure cinema. Just as the blank page of Mallarmé and the silence of Rimbaud is language at the highest state, the screen, free of images and handed back to literature, is the triumph of cinematographic realism."[11] Bresson's great film taught Bazin that filmmakers could challenge themselves with uncinematic literary material and produce "impure cinema" of the highest cultural order. Dispensing with the "illusory fidelity" of the replica, they had learned through script construction and mise-en-scène to encounter a novel or a play and thereby produce something close to the equilibrium of form and ideas that operates in the original. Subservient to their source, but not slavishly mechanical in rendering it, they achieved a deeper fidelity. Genuine fidelity, then, is like the "true realism" of the "Ontology" essay, with which Bazin had challenged the surface realism of appearance. Just as true realism gets to the essence of its subject through the negative operations of allusion and ellipsis, so genuine fidelity abandons vain and simple-minded matching for creative transformation. As Benjamin argued in "The Task of the Translator," the result of such a confrontation of languages around the case of a treasured text can reveal something new about the original while always expanding the two languages involved. And so, we can say that its necessary impurity can only alter cinema's identity—and perhaps its ontology—as it becomes itself in and through history.

NOTES

1. J. D. Connor, "The Persistence of Fidelity: Adaptation Theory Today," *M/C Journal* 10, no. 2 (May 2007): http://journal.media-culture.org.au/0705/15-connor.php.
2. Jim Collins, *Bring on the Books for Everybody: How Literary Culture Became Popular Culture* (Durham, N.C.: Duke University Press, 2010).
3. Lawrence Venuti, "Adaptation, Translation, Critique," *Journal of Visual Culture* 6, no. 1 (2007): 25-43.
4. Walter Benjamin, "The Task of the Translator," trans. Harry Zohn, in *Selected Writings*, vol. 1, ed. Marcus Bullock and Michael W. Jennings (Cambridge: Harvard University Press, 2004), 253–63.
5. I elaborate this point in Dudley Andrew and Carole Cavanaugh, *Sanshô Dayû* (London: BFI Publishing, 2000).
6. Dudley Andrew, "The Well-Worn Muse: Adaptation in Film History and Theory," in *Narrative Strategies: Original Essays in Film and Prose Fiction*, ed. Syndy M. Conger and Janice R. Welsch (Macomb: Western Illinois University Press, 1980), 9–17; reprinted in Dudley Andrew, *Concepts in Film Theory* (Oxford: Oxford University Press, 1984), 96–106; and in *Film Adaptation*, ed. James Naremore (New Brunswick: Rutgers University Press, 2000), 28–37.
7. Marie-José Mondzain, *Image, Icon, and Economy: The Byzantine Origins of the Contemporary Imaginary* (Stanford: Stanford University Press, 2005).
8. André Bazin, "Adaptation, or the Cinema as Digest," trans. Alain Piette and Bert Cardullo, in *Film Adaptation*, ed. Naremore, 19–27.
9. André Bazin, "Ontology of the Photographic Image," in *What Is Cinema?* vol. 1, ed. and trans. Hugh Gray (Berkeley and Los Angeles: University of California Press, 1967), 14.

10. Jean-Luc Nancy, *The Ground of the Image*, trans. Jeff Fort (New York: Fordham University Press, 2005); Marie-José Mondzain, *L'Image Naturel* (Paris: Le Nouveau Commerce, 1995).

11. André Bazin, "*Journal d'un curé de campagne* and the Stylistics of Robert Bresson," in *What Is Cinema?* vol. 1, ed. and trans. Gray, 141.

Atlantis (Blom, 1913)

2

LITERARY APPROPRIATION AND TRANSLATION IN EARLY CINEMA

Adapting Gerhardt Hauptmann's Atlantis *in 1913*

Tom Gunning

Like many film scholars, I have often felt uncomfortable with the issue of adaptation. Reviewing the literature on this topic, I find I am not alone.[1] For years, essays on filmic adaptations began by indicating that previous writers have got it all wrong. The discussion of filmic adaptations makes up a history of errors, it would seem. At the risk of oversimplification, I could list the principle errors complained of as:

> First error: Critics claim films have a duty to be faithful to a literary source.
>
> Second error: Critics ignore the unique language of cinema and thus do not acknowledge a filmic adaptation to be an independent cinematic work.
>
> Third error (most recent): Critics restrict adaptation to serious canonical literary works, discussing adaptations of Dickens, Dostoyevsky, or Shakespeare, rather than popular novelists like Vera Caspary, W. R. Burnett or Karl May.

A number of assumptions underlie these complaints. These objections maintain the value of film adaptations as independent works rather than simply re-editions of a classic text. This independence demands that critics acknowledge film adaptations as specifically cinematic, rather than viewing them simply as translations into another medium of the essence of the source work (although definitions of the "cinematic" undergo a fairly constant modification—and are more often assumed than specified). The most recent complaint broadens the range of sources that should be considered

adaptations, reacting against an elitism initially endemic to adaptation studies, as critics distance themselves from the original reformist demand that
filmic adaptations should bring the cultural values of great works of literature to cinema and to their mass audiences.

Although I would basically endorse these objections and principles,
and therefore accept the errors listed above as being in need of correction,
my unease with adaptation studies nonetheless stands. Discussion of filmic
adaptations seems to me to remain stuck in a defensive posture set by earlier
generations of film critics anxious to maintain the value of cinema against
the cultural hegemony of literary studies. Make no mistake about it, cinema
still lacks academic and cultural respectability in many ways, a fact I bewail
publicly (and occasionally celebrate privately as I cling to the last shreds of
outsider status that an undue interest in film still accrues) as the academic
establishment continues to condescend to film studies. But such a defensive posture limits a full historical and aesthetic exploration of the filmic
adaptations of literature. Defensive postures all too often reinforce lingering senses of inferiority, as if film has something to fear from the literary
text, rather than something to gain. I believe our understanding of literary
adaptation can be limited by a premature assertion of cinema's autonomy.
I take for granted the value, the uniqueness, and the power of cinema, but
adaptation might best be approached as an area in which cinema foregoes
this preoccupation with its autonomy (without actually losing its identity)
and becomes sincerely interested in how it can interact with literature. This
investigation must be based in a confidence that such interaction is not
doomed to absolute submission to academic and cultural hierarchies, but,
like a good marriage, should lead to conversation, commingling, frequent
intercourse, and possibly new offspring.[2] Adaptation forges a relation to literature, rather than proclaiming independence from it. Adaptation poses
a central means for cinema to test itself against literature. The question for
a film scholar must be: when, why, and how have films adapted literary
sources, and why has this relation been sought out when it could have been
avoided?

To explore the relation cinema forges with literature through adaptation, I want to introduce a distinction, breaking adaptation into two closely
related, but theoretically distinct, practices. The first practice is familiar from
most studies of adaptation: the transformation that takes place between the
source text and the final film. This includes changes made in the story as
well as the more subtle transformations involved in the transfer to another
medium (although these two aspects may at points be nearly indistinguish-
able). I will call this practice "textual transformation." While detailing and
analyzing this process takes center stage in most adaptation studies, I would
stress that textual transformation is not restricted to literary adaptation but

forms part of the process of narrative film production due to the complexity of the stages of its production and its diverse semiotic levels. Nearly every narrative film undergoes textual transformation as it moves from whatever verbal form its story takes originally: a treatment, a full script, a scenario, or even random notes. In other words, films that we do not think of as literary adaptations, those based on original stories or screenplays, nonetheless undergo a frequently protracted process of textual transformation as they reach their final filmic form. Although there may be a few exceptions, nearly every narrative film moves from a verbal text to the final filmic text, and usually there are many stages in between, including the stage known as preproduction (e.g., the preparation of a shooting script), but also the adjustments that take place during shooting, and quite crucially during postproduction (most obviously editing, but also the addition of special effects, color adjustment, etc.). A production history of specific films can detail these processes, including the transformations the various filmic versions go through before becoming the released film (e.g., new cuts resulting from censorship), and revisions may even continue after the initial release, with the film appearing in various versions (television, foreign release, so-called "director's cuts").

Thus, nearly every narrative film goes through a process of textual transformation as it moves toward its final form. But not every film claims a literary source. Therefore, the second practice that I want to distinguish within the process of literary adaptation consists precisely of claiming a relation to a preexisting text, staking a claim or filiation to a specific work (or sometimes even works). Although I am still looking for a concise phrase for this, I will provisionally call it "literary appropriation." Defining this practice can become thorny, since the ways of making this claim (and the degree of importance accorded to it) may take many forms. But I will maintain that literary adaptation strictly conceived only occurs when a relation between the preexisting literary source and the film itself is made an issue for (at least some) viewers. The minimum degree of this process would be a credit line such as "based on the work by...." But literary appropriation can involve more than this credit line. Publicity for the film or discussions in the form of reviews or critical essays, for instance, can assert the importance of the film's relation to a literary text, appropriating the text as part of the reception of the film (and this can sometimes occur even without the credit line, when a critic spots a relation not acknowledged in the credits, as when critics noted the relation between the Coen brothers' *Miller's Crossing* [1990] to the novels of Dashiell Hammett, *The Glass Key* and *Red Harvest*). One can conceive of appropriation occurring even without transformation of the original text, as in Michael Snow's film *Rameau's Nephew by Diderot (Thanx to Dennis Young) by Wilma Schoen* (1974), which does not in the conventional sense "adapt" the text of Diderot's novel, but whose title asserts an important relation between Snow's film and Diderot's text (an importance traced then by a number of critics in terms of shared themes of language and performance). As a filmic practice with its own discourses and processes, adaptation involves more than the simple fact that a literary text was made into a film. Literary appropriation claims that an interrelation between the text and the film plays an important role in experiencing the film. This drags us into murky waters, because there are so many ways this appropriation of a literary text might be made. It could be made at any time in a film's history, from its preproduction to years after the film was released. But I think factoring in this appropriation moves us away from exclusive focus on the process of textual transformation and opens up a number of other issues. The primary question then becomes what does this film's appropriation of a literary text do: for the viewer, for the scholar, and perhaps most intriguingly, for filmmakers?

I am primarily interested in this question as a film historian, and I will explore it in relation to the history of early cinema, before World War I. In what ways did the appropriation of literary texts shape and transform the nature of narrative film during the first decades of film history? In cinema's first decades, as I have claimed elsewhere, a number of early films "refer" to a literary work without actually adapting its story, characters, or situations.[3] The very brief running time of many early films, often less than two minutes, did not allow the adaptation of substantial narrative action or development. However, a number of early films, especially from the first five years of cinema history, staged famous "peak moments" from the plays of Shakespeare or other canonical works. These appropriations are often iconic, summoning up famous images from plays (*The Duel Scene from Macbeth* [1905], Herbert Beerbohm Tree as *King John* [1899]) more than narrative development, and often refer to preexisting visual appropriations of these moments in paintings or illustrations that had been widely circulated as prints, photographs, or even commercial ephemera.[4] These films appropriate a literary work, often without retelling a story, and therefore without performing the sorts of textual transformation that we usually associate with adaptation. Keeping this in mind not only clarifies that appropriation can be separate from textual transformation (as Snow's film of Diderot's text shows), but that it may form the primordial gesture of adaptation.

As films expanded in length in the first years of the twentieth century, the possibility that a story might provide the principle structure of a film emerged. But even with longer films, the model of "peak moments" often overwhelms a coherent narrative. A number of early literary adaptations remain incomprehensible if a viewer does not know the original source. Thus the publicity *Bulletin* for Biograph's 1903 production of *Rip Van*

Winkle announced, "We have not attempted to show the play in its complete form, but have chosen instead the various dramatic events...."[5] These early adaptations most frequently refer to literary works at one remove by citing theatrical performances first and foremost. Biograph's *Rip Van Winkle* references Joseph Jefferson's famous production (and performance) more than Washington Irving's short story. Charles Musser points out that early adaptations of literary works (such as Porter's *Uncle Tom's Cabin* [1903] or Méliès's *Baron Munchausen's Dream* [1911]) often depend on audience foreknowledge of the source more than on narrative information conveyed exclusively by the film.[6] Invoking audience foreknowledge obviously depends on what I am calling literary appropriation and demonstrates the way appropriation and textual transformation, so carefully superimposed in later cinema, appear slightly askew in early cinema. Literary appropriation can use audience foreknowledge to fill in gaps left in the film text in the process of textual transformation.

In the second decade of cinema history, the rise of narrative integration, in which films increasingly organized themselves around telling a coherent story, rather than simply invoking one (or ignoring story in favor of visually striking cinematic attractions), increased the possibilities of adaptations from literary sources.[7] Appropriation of literary texts played a vital role in this process of focusing filmic discourse on the process of narration. Traditional accounts of the early development of film language often scorned the role literary adaptation played in such unfairly maligned practices as the French *films d'art,* as if works based on theater or novels betrayed an essential cinematic essence. One should not deny the important role of the basically nonliterary genres of action films and comedies in the early evolution of film style, especially editing. The evolution of film editing may well owe more to farce and adventure films with their dynamic chase and rescue sequences than to films that highlight literary appropriation. But fortunately, film historians no longer believe that editing constitutes the only important aspect of early film style. Innovative staging and composition, lighting, décor and styles of acting, and most importantly, a variety of means of conveying characters' motivations or reactions, frequently occur in films that involve literary appropriation, such as D. W. Griffith's adaptations of Browning's *Pippa Passes* (1909), Dickens's *Cricket on the Hearth* (1909), or Pathé's adaptations of Shakespeare's plays.[8] The brevity of the one-reel film that dominated production before 1913, as much as the often-cited lack of spoken dialogue, restricted the textual transformation of these films to what we might call, following André Bazin, "digests" of famous texts.[9] Thus, in this period literary appropriation exerted creative pressure on film style, even when the process of textual transformation remained limited due to film length and lack of dialogue. Appropriation of literary texts not only gained cinema social prestige and cultural capital in the single-reel era, but expanded the range of film genres and placed a new emphasis on character psychology.

A crucial point in the relation between literature and film (including both appropriation and textual transformation) occurs with emergence of the multi-reel feature film around 1912–14. The emphasis given in several contexts to the author in this period (most clearly in the German *Autorenfilm* movement from around 1913) promoted films as equivalent to literary works.[10] Interestingly, a number of these films, while scripted by famous literary authors, were original works rather than adaptations of previous works, such as Hanns Heinz Ewers's *The Student of Prague* (1913). Although Ewers was a well-known author, this film was based on an original script he authored rather than a previously published work. Thus a new era of literary adaptation occurred around 1913, marked especially by an interest in contemporary works and authors. The adaptation of classic works, the dominant source for the literary digests of the one-reel era with versions of Shakespeare and Dante, certainly continued in this period, but a new desire to draw on contemporary literature helped transform the nature of film adaptation.

I want to consider an exemplary adaptation from this era of intensive literary appropriation that lasted from about 1912 to 1915, *Atlantis,* made in 1913 by the famous Danish film production company Nordisk and directed by August Blom. *Atlantis* adapted a novel published in 1912 by a contemporary author who had won the Nobel Prize in that same year, Gerhardt Hauptmann. In this era, Danish cinema not only produced internationally popular films, but also drew on contemporary movements in theater and literature, specializing in films that targeted sophisticated urban audiences around the world.[11] One of the super-productions of this era of early feature films (with a budget that publicity indicated was twice that spent on any previous film) and intended for worldwide exhibition, *Atlantis* was conceived as a film that would not only make a profit on its very large investment, but demonstrate the cultural value of film as a medium.[12] As David Bordwell and others have shown, Danish filmmakers like August Blom, the director of *Atlantis,* not only developed naturalistic acting styles, but pioneered a sophisticated mise-en-scène that depended more on depth in staging than on editing.[13] The influence of these films on the most creative and innovative European directors of the 1910s, in Russia (especially the films of director Evgeni Bauer), Germany (director Franz Hofer) and Sweden (the early films of directors Maurice Stiller and Vilgot Sjöström) demands more recognition. *Atlantis* was widely publicized as initiating a new era in the relation between literature and film, adapting not only a serious work of a celebrated author, but tackling a work that, while far from being avant-garde, raised psychological and metaphysical issues that marked the most modern concerns in literature.[14]

Let me engage in my own act of textual transformation and offer a synopsis of Hauptmann's novel. The novel follows its protagonist Frederick von Kammacher as he departs on a modern ocean liner, the *Roland,* on a trip across the Atlantic to America. He takes the trip somewhat on impulse in the midst of an extended bout of melancholia, fleeing a recent humiliation in his profession as a bacteriologist and marital trouble with his wife, who has gone insane and often been violent. Kammacher is pursuing a young dancer, Ingigerd Halstrom, whom he saw perform a decadent modernist dance, "The Spider's Victim," in Berlin. Ingigerd is traveling to America, where she has a booking at a New York theater. During the long voyage, Kammacher becomes fascinated by the titanic modernity of the *Roland,* even though the stormy condition of the passage makes most of the passengers constantly seasick. He finds Ingigerd both fascinating and infantile in her coquettish behavior and forms friendships with the ship's captain and Arthur Stoss, a man without arms who makes his living as a variety performer, using his legs and feet to do such things as uncork a bottle of wine or fire a rifle. Kammacher also has a sexual affair with a Russian Jewish woman in the steerage. Kammacher engages in long conversations on the nature of the modern world, reviews the apparent failures of his life and contemplates the erotic possibilities that surround him. His dreams are also central to the novel and create a counterpoint to his waking life. In a series of dreams, a realm beyond life inhabited by a mystical brotherhood, the Toilers of Light, makes him aware of another dimension of existence.

One night, Kammacher awakes to find the *Roland* sinking after a collision with a derelict ship. With Ingigerd, Stoss, and a few others, he manages to get into a lifeboat as the ship descends into chaos and then sinks. Another ship picks up Kammacher's lifeboat, which contains the sole survivors of the shipwreck. They are taken to New York, where they become celebrities, with the stage appearances of both Stoss and Ingigerd gaining journalistic attention and commercial success from the publicity generated by the shipwreck. Kammacher, however, is repelled by the superficiality of Ingigerd and by American commercial culture. He spends his time with a group of German artists in New York, discovers a new fascination with sculpture, and new erotic possibility with a young woman artist, Eva Brown. Leaving the metropolis, Kammacher withdraws to the wilds of Connecticut. In this rural area he finds himself more and more subsumed by his reveries. In dreams he relives the shipwreck and eventually dwells in a nearly constant hallucination. Learning that his wife has committed suicide in the asylum, Kammacher succumbs to a life-threatening illness. Eva Brown arrives to care for him and nurses him back to mental and physical health. Becoming engaged, they return to Europe, recrossing the ocean.[15]

A highly psychological novel of ideas, *Atlantis* has little in common with the action-based filmic genres of the early 1910s, whether westerns or slapstick comedies, but it also doesn't correspond to the clichéd image of a stage-bound literary adaptation associated with the *films d'art*. Its focus on intellectual issues of modernity and technology, the new realms of spirituality and the unconscious conveyed by dreams, mark it less as an example of the naturalism that Hauptmann's early plays than as a harbinger of a new modernism, even an anticipation of expressionist issues (although avoiding expressionist syntax or distortion). As material for film, it challenged existing practices and stylistics.

Nonetheless, one can imagine what might have attracted the Nordisk Company and director August Blom to this novel, beyond the cultural capital of a literary adaptation by the recent winner of the most prestigious literary prize. The year of the novel's publication, as well as Hauptmann's Nobel Prize, 1912, also witnessed the *Titanic* disaster. Although Hauptmann's novel was finished before the greatest shipwreck of the modern era (and was set in 1892, the centennial of Columbus's discovery of the new continent), the coincidence heightened interest in the novel and, inevitably, its film adaptation. Along with its cultural prestige, the novel offered sensational attractions: not only the spectacular shipwreck, but the theatrical spectacles of Ingigerd's spider dance and Stoss's armless performance. Hauptmann drew on autobiographical experiences in *Atlantis,* and the film managed to hire as actors the actual dancer, Ida Orlov, and the armless performer, Charles Unthan, who had inspired Hauptmann's fictional characters. Before reading the novel, I had assumed that the armless performer had been added to the film by the producer, a bit of the cinema of attractions grafted onto a literary adaptation to guarantee commercial appeal (Danish film historian Casper Tybjerg notes that "during this scene the narrative stops dead in its tracks"[16]). My mistake shows how foolish it is to essentialize the nature of either literature or film, when in fact each medium aspires to transcend whatever identity it may be seen to have, sometimes resulting in extraordinary innovations, sometimes in apparent disasters and failures. However, some contemporary German critics associated with the reform movement did denounce this variety attraction as "revolting."[17]

Blom's film certainly made full use of the spectacular opportunities Hauptmann's novel offered. It also trimmed, if not eliminated, the long conversations on the nature of modern life, Europe versus America, reality versus dreams, and the erotic lures of life that makes the novel often read like a floating *Magic Mountain*. But most uniquely, *Atlantis* strives to appropriate and adapt a modern psychological novel that chronicles the mental deterioration of an intellectual's sense of reality and the barrier between dreams and life. As Tybjerg succinctly puts it, "*Atlantis* based itself on a modern novel, a novel that seeks to explore the predicament of modern man."[18] I would like to suspend judgment on the film's success, while drawing attention to its extraordinary ambition: an interior psychological narrative in a specifically modern vein that deals with a modern understanding of mental depression and ennui. I must in all honesty add that I think Blom's achievement of this ambition remains limited, but there is no question in my mind that *Atlantis* stands as the predecessor, perhaps premature, of the interior journeys of Michelangelo Antonioni and the art cinema of the 1960s and '70s.

Analyzing the textual transformation from novel to film helps us see the role adaptation plays in this ambition. Adaptation criticism frequently focuses on the rearrangement of events from the source text to the final cinematic version, comparing this transformation to the Russian formalists' distinction between *fabula* and *syuzhet* (although it is important to emphasize that what is actually being compared are two different *syuzhets*, one literary and one cinematic).[19] Comparing the order of narrative incidents in adapted films and their literary sources in the early silent era, I have noticed that early filmic adaptations frequently retell the events in strictly chronological order, converting literary back-story into the early narrative events. For instance, Vitagraph's 1911 adaptation of Dickens's *A Tale of Two Cities* actually begins with the murder of the Marquise's commoner lover by her aristocratic family, an event served up late in the novel as a back-story revelation. Whereas Hauptmann's novel begins with Kammacher catching the *Roland* on its voyage out, the film begins by showing his family life in Germany, revealing both his wife's mental illness and the failure of his paper on bacteria. Thus, early in the film we see Mrs. Kammacher's attempt on her husband's life that leads to her confinement to an asylum. In the novel, this event is only described much later (in my copy of the translation it occurs on page 315!).[20]

The film then chronicles Kammacher's journey, the opening traumas of his wife's incarceration and his professional failure providing a motivation for his trip. Stressing the motivation for the doctor's wandering allows the film to portray this voyage as an objective correlative of Kammacher's depression and restlessness. Successively the film presents his trip to Berlin and encounter with Ingigerd, as Kammacher witnesses both her performance and her flirtatious narcissism. The film then follows him briefly to Paris, where he retreats after feeling shunned by Ingigerd (following an inter-title saying "I feel unwanted"), then catches the pilot boat to board the *Roland* when he learns Ingigerd is on board (the point, more or less, where the novel begins).

A couple of observations are worth making about this textual transformation in terms of what Gerard Genette would call "order," the actual arrangement of events in a the telling of a story as opposed to their chronological order.[21] Discussions of the relation between film and literary narration often stress film's ability to rearrange time achronologically, as if this were more natural to film narrative than to literary practice. In fact, the importance of the flashback to early film narration has often been overstated. In cinema before 1913, flashbacks remain quite rare, and even after this point flashbacks, as in the work of Griffith and other American directors, initially tend to supply only brief glimpses of memories, rather than a narrative structure (thus the term *flash*back, emphasizing the brevity of the reversal in time).[22] Although a few early films (often those using court trials as a narrative frame) do employ a recursive narration structure, it is really only with the avant-garde experiments of the 1920s, such as Jean Epstein's *La Glace à trois faces* (1927), that flashback narrative structure emerges. Rather than an inherently cinematic device, it would seem filmic narrative derived the concept of a reordered temporality from literary models, and indeed resisted it for some time.

In *Atlantis*, unraveling the novel's fictional events into a more chronological linear form, while it may partly simplify the conveying of story information, also strengthens the film's dominant chronotope of the voyage (to use Mikhail Bakhtin's term for a narrative figure that combines a temporal and spatial order).[23] As a key text in the history of film's adaptation of literary texts, *Atlantis* represents more than a failed encounter between a sophisticated, modern, interiorized novel and an exteriorized, "primitive," filmic discourse, although its success may be relative.[24] As a precocious attempt at the appropriation of the modern novel's subject of a character's psychological odyssey, *Atlantis* provides an object lesson in the way cinema could be transformed by an encounter with literary modes that forced it to both draw upon already established filmic techniques and yet redefine their use and meaning.

Hauptmann's own evolution as an author, both a dramatist and a novelist, moves from his youthful naturalism to a late style strongly influenced by Decadence and Symbolism, perhaps even displaying a proto-Expressionism. Thus *Atlantis*, like J. K. Huysmans's transitional novel *En Rade*, which rerouted his style from Naturalism to Symbolism, interweaves detailed accounts of its protagonist's dreams with the daily routine of his ship voyage, his conversations with friends and erotic encounters with women. The dreams take up less time in the film, with the oneiric realm of the Toilers of Light only appearing in one extended sequence. However, this sequence, although even more enigmatic than its equivalents in the novel, occupies a key point in the structure of the film and presents one of the film's most visually striking sequences.

In the film, Kammacher's dream coincides with the collision of the *Roland* with the derelict ship that will cause it to sink. It shows a series of allegorical scenes invoking the realm of the Toilers of Light, a dream-world that in Hauptmann's novel represents a reality beyond the surface of things, a hash of visions of the afterlife and utopian world harmony. In Blom's film the dream scenes are superimposed over the sleeping figure of Kammacher in his cabin in the *Roland*, which we have just seen spring a leak from its accident. After an inter-title that explains that Kammacher is entering the sunken city of Atlantis (lying in the depth of the ocean he is sailing over), a mobile shot follows Kammacher standing on a boat that pulls into a dock where the caped figure of his dead friend Dr. Schmidt greets him. The image of the sleeping Kammacher aboard the *Roland* appears in the lower left of the frame, superimposed on the back of his dream figure, and the mobile shot vividly conveys the process of merging into a dreamscape. The few shots that make up the dream sketch a trajectory as Kammacher is led by his dead friend, first through a city street, then a field, then to a garden gate that magically opens on its own, and finally to a flowerbed tended by gardeners. In varying degrees of clarity, Kammacher's figure (sleeping in his shipboard bunk) remains visible through all these shots, which continue to be superimposed over him. These images derive from an extensive dream described in the novel, forming part of a longer voyage into the realm of the Toilers of Light where the metaphysical nature of this otherworldly realm is explained. In the film, the significance of this otherworldly voyage never becomes fully explicated, and the images of the dream convey only a sense of mysterious and enigmatic significance, while the viewer remains aware that the dream is embedded within the real world through the persistent superimposition of the sleeping dreamer. Dream and reality collide much more dramatically than in the novel, as in the last shot of the dream when the gardener makes a pointing gesture that visually blends into the super-imposed ship's cabin and dramatically introduces the ship's steward, who rushes into Kammacher's cabin to announce the ship's danger and to order him to abandon ship.

In its accelerated appropriation of literature around 1913, the cinema's relation to the fantastic, long embodied in the trick and *féerique* genres, played an important role. The first German *Autorenfilms*, such as *The Student of Prague* and *Der Andere* (both from 1913) featured themes of the fantastic. Georg Lukács in his succinct, yet brilliant, essay on film written the same year *Atlantis* was filmed, 1913, indicated that an affinity to the fantastic constituted one of cinema's greatest strengths, claiming "an Arnim or Poe of our days would find [in the cinema] an instrument ready for his scenic yearnings."[25] Paul Wegener, star of *The Student of Prague,* declared fantasy to be the natural language of the cinema.[26] But *Atlantis,* while its very title announces its relation to the mythical and oneiric, places the fantastic firmly within the contemporary real world, contrasting with the *märchen*-inspired German films of the same year. Expending great effort (and spending much money), Blom shot most scenes on real locations (including filming aboard a real ocean liner, rather than a constructed set). He devoted a surprising amount of the film to displaying these locations, such as the cities Kammacher visits, often using strikingly mobile shots, aboard trains, automobiles, boats, and trolleys. Even more than the dream sequences, these mobile location shots play a vital role in the film's appropriation of the novel, even though they have no obvious literary equivalent (Hauptmann does not engage in long descriptions of Berlin or Paris, for instance).

Lukács's essay stressed that the fantastic aspect of cinema did not contradict its relation to photographic reality: "the fantastic is not the opposite of living life," he claims in his 1913 essay, "it is only a new aspect of it."[27] In fact, Lukács believed the cinema revealed the fantastic aspect to modern life: "Only in the 'cinema' has the automobile—to cite only one example—become poetic, such as in the romantically exciting event of a chase in racing autos. In this manner even the normal activity of streets and markets here acquires a strong humor and an extremely powerful poetry."[28] In Blom's film, the recurrent imagery of travel and traveling shots creates, I believe, a central merging of psychological metaphor and exterior reality. The sequence of Kammacher's trip to Berlin, part of the back-story in the novel, becomes vivid in the film through its extraordinary sequence of location shooting in that city, in which the film not only presents actuality views of Berlin city streets, but features a particularly striking shot from a moving taxi, juxtaposing Kammacher in the foreground with the mobile background of the cityscape. Mobile shots abound in the film. As Kammacher boards the *Roland* at sea, Blom shows him standing on a pilot boat as it pulls ever closer to the ocean liner (anticipating the later shot in the dream sequence of his boat pulling up the pier of the realm of the Toilers of Light). Once Kammacher arrives in New York City, the city is introduced by a mobile view of the skyline taken from a boat edging the coast, and later Blom manages a technically difficult shot inside a moving trolley. Even Eva Brown's trip to an improbably mountainous Connecticut to care for Kammacher toward the end of the film includes a mobile shot from the outside of the train as it moves through a snowy viaduct.

What role do these recurring mobile shots play in this film? I would claim they relate less to direct textual transformation of literary description than to the cinema's desire to appropriate a psychological novel in 1913 by making use of film's own devices of moving imagery. I have both a moderate and a more extreme interpretation of this issue, and I admit my readings shade into each other. Following the logic of fashioning a feature film out of the elements available from earlier cinema, *Atlantis* offers a sort of compendium of earlier film genres: the trick film in the dream sequences; society dramas in the interaction between characters; dance film in Ingigerd's performance of "The Spider's Victim"; vaudeville turns in the sequence (complete with close-ups and address to the camera) made up of Stoss's "Armless Wonder" routine; and finally actuality films of street scenes and phantom rides familiar from travelogues in these sequences in Berlin and New York City. No question this accumulation of diverse genres with a range of styles reflects an eclectic "cinema of attractions" aesthetic, an aspect that marks *Atlantis* as a transitional film in the establishment of the narratively integrated feature film. However, we must also acknowledge that these actuality sequences do more than introduce discontinuity and variety into the film's style. The more innovative and remarkable aspect of *Atlantis,* particularly as a literary adaptation, lies in the degree of coherence that the psychological narrative and its focus on a central character impose on these diverse scenes and styles.

If we approach *Atlantis* as an attempt to appropriate the sophisticated range of tones that the psychological novel employed in the early twentieth century, portraying a variety of psychological states (from rational discourse to extreme melancholia to dreams and hallucinations), yet rooted very firmly in a recognizable modern realistic world, then the range of styles and genres the film exhibits may seem less like a holdover from early cinema than a bold experiment triggered by the challenges of literary adaptation. Thus, these moving shots of city locations root the action of the film in a believable and complex environment and relate to the mastery of realist techniques that marks Blom's cinematic style generally, such as composition in depth and careful construction of sets. But the film also aspires to more than a naturalistic treatment of the locations of Kammacher's voyage. How can Blom join a sense of psychological interiority with cinema's already-established ability to capture realistic images of the exterior world?

The film's lack of equivalents for the novel's interior monologues, or even extended conversations expressing Kammacher's thoughts and reactions, limits our access to Kammacher as a psychological character, even as the construction of the film appropriates the focalization on a central consciousness that the psychological novel allows and demands. Thus, I claim these moving shots of urban environments (usually centered on Kammacher) present not simply a touristic view, but the impression of voyaging for *this particular* tourist, the film's main character. In other words, shots of Kammacher moving through these locations convey not only a view of the sights, but an interior sense of his wandering, his loneliness. Blom portrays Kammacher's alienation, not simply through the actor Olaf Fonss's recurrent (and rather clichéd and tiresome) gesture of placing his head in his hands, but by using the mobile camera to make us share his detached *flâneur* relation to the world. One could claim that *Atlantis*, combining a legacy from early cinema with an ambitious attempt to appropriate the contemporary psychological novel, ends up somewhere between Antonioni and a travelogue (and, one could add, between Deleuze's Movement-Image and Time-Image).[29]

While one could view my interpretation skeptically and deny the psychological effect of these traveling shots, there is no question that *Atlantis* stands as a bold early experiment in appropriating the subject matter of the modern novel. A traditional approach to the question of adaptation might ask whether *Atlantis* supplies a successful cinematic version of the novel, or even whether its works as a film, offering a successful work in cinematic terms. One might answer negatively on both counts, and from the viewpoint of a coherent unified work, one might be right. But this dismissal would lose the exciting sense the film conveys of wrestling with new energies, exploring new horizons in narrative form, often at the price of coherence. Approached historically, *Atlantis* reveals that the most interesting thing about a filmic adaptation might be the expansion of both subjects and means that the literary work poses to filmmakers, the ambition of its appropriation of a literary model that challenges film style. And the clearest indication of this might lie precisely in the film's incoherence, its push-pull between different models of narrative form. I myself find the way *Atlantis* makes visible the tension between modern literary form and a cinematic form in transition quite compelling, an indication of the way adaptation may be approached less in terms of a coherent end-product than as a process of adjustment and change with the course of film history.

NOTES

1. I have found the most useful treatments of the issue of adaptation to be the essays included in *A Companion to Literature and Film*, ed. Robert Stam and Alessandra

LITERARY APPROPRIATION AND TRANSLATION IN EARLY CINEMA 55

Raengo (Malden: Blackwell, 2004) and *Film Adaptation*, ed. James Naremore (New Brunswick: Rutgers University Press, 2000).

2. Forgive the biological and seemingly traditional nature of the metaphor, but let me emphasize that offspring take many forms—as does intercourse.

3. Tom Gunning, "The Intertexuality of Early Cinema: A Prologue to *Fantômas*," in *A Companion to Literature and Film*, ed. Stam and Raengo, 127–43.

4. The most complete treatment of the complex cultural intertexuality of early cinema remains William Uricchio and Roberta E. Pearson, *Reframing Culture: The Case of the Vitagraph Quality Films* (Princeton: Princeton University Press, 1993).

5. Kemp R. Niver, comp., *Biograph Bulletins 1896–1908*, ed. Bebe Bergston (Los Angles: Locare Research, 1971), 82.

6. Charles Musser, *Before the Nickelodeon: Edwin S. Porter and the Edison Manufacturing Company* (Berkeley and Los Angeles: University of California Press, 1991), esp. 340–53.

7. I discuss the process of narrative integration in early cinema in my book *D. W. Griffith and the Origins of American Narrative Film: The Early Years at Biograph* (Champaign-Urbana: University of Illinois Press, 1991).

8. Gunning, *D. W. Griffith*, 175–82.

9. André Bazin, "Adaptation, or the Cinema as Digest," trans. Alain Piette and Bert Cardullo, in *Film Adaptation*, ed. Naremore, 19–27.

10. The most complex consideration of the *Autorenfilm* has been given by Leonardo Quaresima in "*Dichter heraus!* The *Autorenfilm* and German Cinema of the 1910s," trans. Paul Bayley, *Griffithiana* no. 38/39 (1990): 101–20; and "L'Autorenfilm allemand: Un cinema national produit par des societes estrangeres," in *Cinema sans frontiers/Images Across Borders 1896–1918*, ed. Roland Cosandey and Francois Albera (Lausanne: Editions Payot, 1995), 237–48. Helmet H. Diederichs, "The Origins of the *Autorenfilm*," in *Before Caligari: German Cinema 1895–1920*, ed. Paolo Cherchi Usai and Lorenzo Cordelli (Pordenone: Edizioni Bilblioteca dell'Immagine, 1990), 380–97, gives an excellent account of the movement, including Hauptmann's relation to it. Deniz Gokturk has dealt with *Atlantis* in relation to the *Autorenfilm* in her essay "*Atlantis* oder: Vom Sinken der Kultur—Nobilitierung des fruhen Kinos in Autorenfilm?" in *Schwarzer Traum und Weiss Sklavin: Deutsch-danische Filmbeziehungen 1910–1930*, ed. Manfred Behn (Munich: text+kritik, 1994), 73–86, which unfortunately I have not been able to consult.

11. The best treatment of early Danish cinema available in English is Casper Tybjerg's dissertation, "An Art of Silence and Light: The Development of the Danish Film Drama to 1920" (University of Copenhagen, 1996). He deals with *Atlantis* (195–206). Both Quaresima in the essays cited above and Danish film historian Marguerite Engberg indicate that Nordisk's announced policy in 1912 of hiring famous contemporary authors, such as Hauptmann and Arthur Schnitzler, inspired the German *Autorenfilm* movement. See Engberg, "The Influence of Danish Cinema on German Film 1910–1920," *Griffithiana* no. 38/39 (1990): 128.

12. See Quaresima, "*Dichter*," 104.

13. David Bordwell, "Nordisk and the Tableau Aesthetic," in *100 Years of Nordisk Film*, ed. Lisbeth Richter Larsen and Dan Nissen (Copenhagen: Danish Film Institute, 2006), 80–95.

14. Unfortunately, my lack of Danish prevents me from carrying out a full study of the discourse surrounding *Atlantis*, which would certainly specify the literary appropriation involved in the production and reception of the film. However, Tybjerg supplies a fine summary of its reception in Denmark (201–4), as Quaresima does for Germany in "*Dichter*," 107–8.

15. Gerhardt Hauptmann, *Atlantis*, trans. Adele and Thomas Selzer (New York: R. W. Huebsch, 1912). Although currently out of print, the novel was translated and published in the United States soon after its German publication.

16. Tybjerg, "Art of Silence and Light," 198.

17. Tybjerg, "Art of Silence and Light," 198.

18. Tybjerg, "Art of Silence and Light," 205.

19. This distinction is used by several of the formalists and is nicely summarized by Victor Erlich in *Russian Formalism: History/Doctrine* (New Haven: Yale University Press, 1981), 240; David Bordwell in his neoformalist period applied the concept to film, especially in *Narration in the Fiction Film* (Madison: University of Wisconsin, 1985).

20. Hauptmann, *Atlantis*, 315.

21. Gerard Genette, *Narrative Discourse: An Essay in Method*, trans. Jane E. Lewin (Ithaca: Cornell University Press, 1980), 80–85. Tybjerg also notes the film's rearrangement of events in chronological order ("Art of Silence and Light," 200).

22. The only book-length treatment of the flashback is Maureen Turim, *Flashbacks in Film: Memory and History* (New York: Routledge, 1989). I discuss the flashback in early cinema in *D. W. Griffith*, 117–18.

23. Mikhail Bakhtin, "Form of Time and the Chronotope in the Novel," in *The Dialogic Imagination*, ed. Michael Holquist (Austin: University of Texas Press, 1981), 84–258.

24. The aesthetic failure of *Atlantis* has been claimed by both critics of the time (see Tybjerg, "Art of Silence and Light," 204) and contemporary historians, including the redoubtable historian of Danish silent cinema Marguerite Engberg, who agrees however that the film remains a fascinating experiment. See Engberg, "1913, A Crucial Year for Danish Cinema," in *Griffithiana* 50 (1994): 11.

25. Georg Lukács, "Thoughts on an Aesthetics of Cinema," in *German Essays on Film*, ed. Richard McCormick and Alison Guenther-Pal (New York: Continuum, 2004), 15.

26. Paul Wegener's lecture, "Die kunsterlischen Moglichkeiten des Film," delivered in 1916, is extensively quoted and analyzed by Kristin Thompson in her essay, " 'Im Anfang War…' Some Links Between German Fantasy Films of the Teens and the Twenties," in *Before Caligari*, ed. Usai and Cordelli, 138–61. Quaresima also emphasizes the importance of the fantastic to the *Autorenfilm*, in "*Dichter*," 113–14.

27. Lukács, "Thoughts on an Aesthetics of Cinema," 13.

28. Lukács, "Thoughts on an Aesthetics of Cinema," 15.

29. Gilles Deleuze, *Cinema 1: The Movement-Image*, trans. Hugh Tomlinson and Barbara Habberjam (Minneapolis: Minnesota University Press, 1986); *Cinema 2: The Time-Image*, trans. Hugh Tomlinson and Robert Galeta (Minneapolis: Minnesota University Press, 1989).

Heart of Darkness (Welles, 1939, not completed)
Photograph courtesy of Lilly Library, Indiana University, Bloomington

3

Hearts of Darkness

Joseph Conrad and Orson Welles

James Naremore

As I have argued elsewhere, there are several reasons why Joseph Conrad's *Heart of Darkness* (1899) could be regarded a distant ancestor of the film noir.[1] Conrad employs a form of "impressionistic" narration that, like many such films, places emphasis on subjective focalization and involves a good deal of shifting back and forth in time; he calls attention to the narration by nesting it within a dramatic scene, in a manner roughly analogous to the openings and closings of movies like *Double Indemnity* (Wilder, 1944), *Murder My Sweet* (Dmytryk, 1944), or *Detour* (Ulmer, 1945), and he gives a great deal of attention to a shadowy, somber mood, so that the meaning seems to lie on the atmospheric surface—or, in the narrator's famous words, on "the outside, enveloping the tale."[2] Notice also that even though Conrad's plot has a family resemblance to nineteenth-century adventure stories about British imperialism, his style is hallucinated, oneiric, greatly concerned with the psychology of the narrator, who says at one point, "It seems to me I am trying to tell you a dream" (46). Hence, no less than any of the classic film noirs, which often contain dream sequences or take place on the margins of dreams, *Heart of Darkness* invites psychoanalytic interpretation. Perhaps the novella's most general affinity with noir, however, is that although it belongs to the genre of bloody melodrama, it strives to seem un-melodramatic. It does so through a familiar device of gothic fiction that can be seen in *Laura* (Preminger, 1944), *Shadow of a Doubt* (Hitchcock, 1943), *Strangers on a Train* (Hitchcock, 1951), *Blue Steel* (Bigelow, 1990), *Basic Instinct* (Verhoeven, 1992), and many other dark thrillers: everyone is a bit guilty, and the ostensibly "good" character representing reason and ordinary decency is in some ways a double of the manifestly evil or guilty character. This "secret sharer" theme, especially when combined with Conrad's foregrounding of style and pessimistic view of Western "progress," gives *Heart of Darkness* a liminal position in modern culture: like most noirish fiction and film, it blends popular adventure with certain traits of modernism. As Fredric Jameson says, it belongs in a zone somewhere between Robert Louis Stevenson and Marcel Proust, and therefore enables us to sense "the emergence of what will be contemporary modernism...but also, still tangibly juxtaposed with it, what will variously be called popular culture or mass culture, the commercialized cultural discourse of what, in late capitalism, is often called media society."[3]

Not surprisingly, *Heart of Darkness* became a sort of ur-text for Anglo-American modernism, influencing T.S. Eliot's "The Hollow Men," Scott Fitzgerald's *The Great Gatsby,* and the novels of William Faulkner. In the realm of popular fiction, it had a similar influence, especially among sophisticated writers of thrillers and their Hollywood adapters. Raymond Chandler's first-person narrator is named Marlowe; Graham Greene's "entertainment" novels, all of which became film noirs, were inspired by his reading of Conrad's novella; and Greene's script for *The Third Man* (Reed, 1949) not only borrows its narrative structure from *Heart of Darkness* but also contains a minor character named "Kurtz." (Where later movies are concerned, the novella also became an intertext for pictures about U.S. imperialism in Vietnam: Francis Coppola's *Apocalypse Now* [1979] was modeled on *Heart of Darkness,* and Stanley Kubrick's *Full Metal Jacket* [1987] has distant echoes of the same source.) Surprisingly, however, very few filmmakers have been interested in adapting the novella itself. A canonical work known by virtually every college student in the English-speaking world, *Heart of Darkness* constitutes a "pre-sold" commodity, and by virtue of its brevity might seem to present fewer problems for a screenwriter than the novels of Jane Austen or Charles Dickens, which have been adapted many times. Yet to my knowledge only one film is based directly on the story: Nicholas Roeg's adaptation for Turner Network Television, starring Tim Roth as Marlow and John Malkovich as Kurtz, which was filmed in Central America and broadcast in the United States in 1994. This picture was nominated for a Golden Globe by the international press, but it rarely achieves the haunted, dryly ironic quality of its source, and in most other ways is a disappointment.

Perhaps *Heart of Darkness* hasn't been filmed more often because of its formal properties: it has no heroic action, not much dialogue, and a great deal of what F. R. Leavis called a merely "adjectival insistence" on horror.[4] Leaving aside its racist and patriarchal implications, which create another set of problems that I will address later, it holds our attention largely through a kind of spellbinding trickery, the literary equivalent of smoke and mirrors. But I also suspect that any cinematic adaptation of the novella is likely to be overshadowed by a legendary film that was never made: Orson Welles's 1939 *Heart of Darkness,* which was developed at RKO, the most noir-like of the Hollywood studios, in the period immediately before Welles began work on *Citizen Kane* (1941). The very idea of such a project is enough to fascinate cinephiles and create an anxiety of influence in later directors. We can never know if Welles's adaptation would have succeeded, and we have every reason to be grateful for *Kane;* nevertheless, Robert Carringer's *The Making of Citizen Kane* provides some tantalizing details about the aborted earlier production, and Jonathan Rosenbaum and Guerric DeBona have each written essays that provide further information. Welles's script and production-company records have survived, giving us a good sense of his specific plans. His version of *Heart of Darkness* would have been an intriguing picture by any measure, of interest not only for its political and aesthetic qualities but also, in secondary ways, for what it suggests about the problem of fidelity in adaptation.

In 1938, when Welles was offered a three-picture contract at RKO, a Gallup poll conducted by the studio determined that audiences most wanted him to appear in a "man from Mars" film related to his infamous *War of the Worlds* broadcast of that same year. Welles countered with an offer to film *Heart of Darkness* and a couple of Hitchcock-style thrillers on contemporary political themes. The studio agreed, and Welles brought most of his Mercury Theater organization to Hollywood to prepare for the Conrad production. He had already directed a moderately successful one-hour radio adaptation of the novella, starring Ray Collins as Marlow and Welles as Kurtz, which aired on CBS only a week after the Mars-invasion show, and he seemed enthusiastic about a film version. His associate, John Houseman, was paid $15,000 to assist in developing a script, but was frustrated by the job. "I never understood why Welles had chosen such a diffuse and difficult subject," Houseman wrote in his memoirs. "Joseph Conrad had used all sorts of subtle literary devices; the evil that destroyed [Kurtz] was suggested and implied but never shown. In the concrete medium of film no such evasion was possible."[5] Under the circumstances, Houseman grew increasingly frustrated and withdrew from the job.

Welles wrote the script alone, and despite Houseman's reservations there were several reasons why *Heart of Darkness* was a logical choice for his initial film. His theatrical reputation was based on spellbinding, somewhat gothic stagecraft; his radio show, "The Mercury Theater of the Air," was initially subtitled "First Person Singular" and was devoted to experiments in subjective narration; and in the Conrad novella he saw a good opportunity to do something rather like his famous stage production of Shakespeare's *Julius Caesar,* which had been performed in modern dress and transformed into an antifascist parable. Notice also that many of Welles's most important stage projects, including the Harlem *Macbeth* in 1936 and *Native Son* in 1940, were concerned with the theme of racial blackness; indeed one of the actors he planned to use in the film of *Heart of Darkness* was Jack Carter, who had played Macbeth in Harlem. Besides all this, *Heart of Darkness* was well suited to what Michael Denning has identified as the "middlebrow" cultural project of the Mercury Theater—a project shared in slightly different ways in the 1930s by the Book-of-the-Month Club, the Modern Library, and NBC's radio symphonies, all of which attempted "to popularize and to market high culture."[6] Denning, somewhat like Pierre Bordieu, mounts an effective defense of middlebrow art, at least where Welles's Popular-Front activities are concerned, pointing out that under the right circumstances it can serve as a vehicle of class struggle and social progress. Thus, just at the moment when Theodor Adorno and Max Horkheimer were developing their savage critique of the culture industry, Welles tried to use the mass media as a democratic weapon, popularizing high culture on behalf of left interests, mixing Shakespeare with thrillers and science fiction, blurring the boundaries between the classic and the vanguard.

Having caused a nationwide panic with a radio broadcast, Welles also saw the autobiographical resonance of stories about demagogues who manipulate the masses. *Citizen Kane* was designed to suggest certain ironic parallels between Welles and Charles Foster Kane, and the film version of *Heart of Darkness* would have contained similar parallels between Welles and Kurtz. To some extent, the parallels were already present in Conrad's novella, where Marlow describes Kurtz as "very little more than a voice," capable of "the unbounded power of eloquence—of words—of burning noble words" (66). Most people in America associated Welles with just such a voice; and, like Kurtz, he had recently shown what Marlow calls "the power to frighten rudimentary souls" (67). An idealist and a liberal, Welles was often regarded by the press as a Byronic type; perhaps for that reason, he was attracted to stories about the Faustian temptations of political power, and he sometimes used these stories as a form of indirect self-criticism. In his preliminary notes on the film script for *Heart of Darkness,* he describes Kurtz as "the Byron of a totalitarian state, what Byron would be if he had become president of Greece." On a more covert level, according to John Houseman, he also considered modeling Kurtz's fiancée, "the Intended," on the Chicago socialite Virginia Nicholson, to whom he was married. In his notes for the film he names this character "Elsa Gruner" and describes her as a woman with "a tremendously appealing and lovely kind of gravity.... She is not militantly honest, she is simply without guile. There is probably only one thing she doesn't know about Kurtz, who is her lover, and that is how little any woman must mean to such a man."[7]

Welles's method of writing the script was similar to the one he and his staff had used in adaptations for the Mercury Theater radio show: he found a copy of the novella in a pocket-sized anthology, cut out the pages, pasted them onto sheets of typing paper, and began deleting material, retaining a good deal of narration but changing a phrase here and there in marginal notes. On the first few pages, for example, he eliminated Marlow's listening audience—the unnamed narrator, the lawyer, the accountant, and the director—and altered certain lines in Marlow's opening speech. An important passage in the original reads, "The conquest of the earth, which mostly means taking it away from those who have a different complexion or slightly flatter noses than ourselves, is not a pretty thing when you look into it too much. What redeems it is the idea only. An idea at the back of it; not a sentimental pretense but an idea; and an unselfish belief in the idea—something you can set up, and bow down before, and offer a sacrifice to" (21). Welles changed "flatter noses" to "slightly different noses" and rewrote the last sentence to give it a more skeptical, less imperialistic tone: "What redeems it is the idea at the back of it; sometimes it's a sentimental pretense, something you can set up, and bow down before, and offer a sacrifice to."

In his book-length interview with Peter Bogdanovich, Welles said he believed his adaptation of *Heart of Darkness* might have been a success because it made considerable use of Conrad's language, mostly as offscreen narration. "I haven't got anything at all against a lot of words in movies," he explained. "I don't see how you can do Conrad without all the words."[8] Nevertheless, Welles always took liberties with his sources, giving the auteur equal status with the author, and his adaptations were interesting precisely because they weren't slavishly faithful. *The Magnificent Ambersons* (1942) transforms Booth Tarkington's genteel fiction into a Freudian melodrama; *Chimes at Midnight* (1965) amounts to what André Bazin called a "digest" of several Shakespeare plays; and *The Trial* (1962) conducts a sort of quarrel with Kafka. *Heart of Darkness* was no exception. Some of the changes Welles made were motivated by his political aims, some by his desire to make the novel more dramatic or "cinematic," and others by the need to make a popular Hollywood entertainment. One of his most significant decisions was to set the film in the present day and to make Marlow an American, thereby translating the novella into what he called a "political parable," an "attack on the Nazi system," and a "psychological thriller" about a representative man thrown into the midst of "every variety of Fascist mentality and morality."[9] The screenplay opens in New York on the Hudson River, with Marlow's voice speaking of a "monstrous town marked ominously on the sky, a brooding gloom in the sunshine, a lurid glare under the stars," while a series of lap dissolves show lights being turned on across Manhattan at dusk—the bridges, the parkways, the boulevards, the skyscrapers. The camera tours the length of the island accompanied by a montage of sounds—snatches of jazz from the radios of moving taxis; dinner music from the big hotels; a "throb of tom-toms" foreshadowing the jungle music to come; the noodling of orchestras tuning up in the concert halls; and finally, near the Battery, the muted sounds of bell buoys and the hoots of shipping. Next we enter New York harbor, where we find Marlow leaning against the mast of a schooner, smoking a pipe and directly addressing the camera. "And this also," he says, "has been one of the dark places of the earth" (19).

In the process of changing Marlow into an American, the script deletes his chauvinistic remark that in the British colonies "some real work is done" (24) and gives his story a more thoroughgoing anticolonial implication. Marlow's politically well-positioned aunt is also deleted. Aimless and romantic, Marlow applies for a job in what the script describes as a "Central European seaport town," at a trading company that occupies a vast building "in the best Bismarck style." The company doctor examines his cranium in the interests of confirming the superiority of the Aryan race, and sends him off to an unnamed, generic "Dark Continent," where the landscape and tribal customs derive from a mélange of African, Stone Age, and indigenous American cultures, all of which had been elaborately researched by Welles's staff at RKO. The exploitation and murder of the black population is carried out by obvious proto-fascists. "This shouldn't surprise you," one of them says to Marlow. "You've seen this kind of thing on city streets." Kurtz, the most successful of the fascist types, has been installed in the jungle by his political opponents, who want him removed from Europe, and as a result of his unlimited authority and will to power he has become a ruthless demagogue. "I have another world to conquer," he says when Marlow finally meets him. "Five more continents and then I'll die." When Marlow asks, "Is that all you want?" Kurtz replies, "I want everything."

A good deal of dialogue has been invented for the screenplay, and its rhythms are carefully stipulated, to the point in many scenes of specifying the precise words on which the actors are supposed to interrupt or speak over another. The result is a distinctive style of rapid, fevered, almost-musical overlapping of voices, similar to what we hear in *Citizen Kane* and most of Welles's other films. In keeping with the political allegory, the array of characters Marlow meets on his journey along the river has also been altered and elaborated. Most of them join Marlow on the riverboat in search of Kurtz. At the outer station, Marlow encounters Eddie (Robert Coote), an effete British citizen who has brought a piano and several cases of champagne to the jungle, where he acts as an ineffectual spy on the European interlopers. "They'd like to own the country, I guess," Eddie says to Marlow. "It's ours, you know…England's. That's why I'm here. To keep my eyes open. Never can tell, you know, when they might take a plebiscite among the cannibals." At the next station Marlow comes across de Tirpitz (John Emery), a Germanic aristocrat with a club foot, who harbors an intense hatred of Kurtz because, as Welles wrote in background notes for the production, "Kurtz is to him the perfect example of the ascendant lower-middle class which has stolen his inheritance." Aboard the riverboat, Marlow's steersman and assistant is called simply "the half-breed" (Jack Carter) and is described as "an expatriate, tragic exile who can't remember the sound of his own language."

One of the major differences between the screenplay and Conrad is in the character of Elsa, "the Intended," who in the novella makes her only appearance in the climactic scene and is presented as a figure on a pedestal—guileless, naïve, and, like most women in Conrad, incapable of facing the stern truths known to men. Partly to give the film the suggestion of a romantic interest, Welles transforms her into a more active woman who goes to the jungle in search of her lover. Marlow first meets her at the outer station of the Dark Continent, where she smiles and remarks on a striking physical resemblance between him and Kurtz. While Eddie plays his piano she uses a pencil and a rough pine board to draw a crude map of the river journey Marlow is about to take, marking all the stations along the way, explaining what he can expect to find, and creating a mood of suspenseful foreboding. Despite everyone's protestations, she insists on traveling down the river aboard Marlow's steamer. During the trip she and Marlow have a conversation in the pilot house, and from Marlow's perspective we see his face and hers partly reflected in the front window, mingled with the changing patterns of the jungle. She explains that she waited in Europe four months without letters from Kurtz: "I was afraid. He was almost too popular. There was no good reason for sending him to the Dark Country—except to get him out of Europe…I didn't like him at first. I thought he was—I don't know *what*. Cruel—ruthless. First Impressions. I wasn't very intelligent or grown up…It's not easy to refuse him anything. He wanted to know me—I got to know him." She remains on the boat until it almost reaches its destination, but when scores of headless dead bodies are discovered in the jungle Marlow sends her back in a canoe manned by a couple of his crew members. She then reappears in a climactic scene like the one in Conrad's story, with Kurtz's ghostly image hovering behind her as Marlow tells her a lie.

In addition to using a great deal of offscreen narration, Welles wanted to create a cinematic analogue for Conrad's narrative technique, and to this end he planned a radical innovation: the story would be told almost entirely from Marlow's point of view, with a first-person camera. The device had been used intermittently in previous Hollywood pictures—the first ten minutes of Rouben Mamoulian's *Dr. Jekyll and Mr. Hyde* (1932), for example, are told entirely through the eyes of Jekyll—but Welles appears to have been the first director to attempt it for virtually an entire film. Given this unorthodox approach, he intended to begin *Heart of Darkness* with a brief prologue "designed to acquaint the audience as amusingly as possible with the [subjective camera]." The prologue has been discussed and completely reproduced in Jonathan Rosenbaum's *Discovering Orson Welles*,[10] so I will describe it here only briefly. It opens with Welles's voice heard over an entirely black screen. "Don't worry," he announces, "There's just nothing to look at for a while. You can close your eyes if you want to." He explains that he is about to "divide this audience into two parts—you and everybody else in the theater. Now then, open your eyes." Iris into the subjective viewpoint of a bird looking out of a cage at Welles's hugely magnified chin and mouth. "You play the part of a canary," Welles says. "I'm asking you to sing and you refuse. That's the plot." Welles's chin moves down until his fiercely glaring eyes become visible. "Here is a bird's eye view of me being enraged," he says. "I threaten you with a gun." He slides the muzzle of a pistol through the bars of the cage until it looks like Big Bertha. "That's the way a gun looks to a canary," he says. "I give you until the count of three to sing." He then goes on to create a series of other dramatic situations, some of them wish-fulfilling, as when the audience is granted the ability to fly, others nightmarish, including one in which "you" play a condemned man strapped to the electric chair. Finally, looking straight into the lens, he says, "Now, if you're doing this right, this is what you ought to look like to me." Dissolve to the interior of a theater seen from the point of view of the screen: the camera pans around the room and we discover that the audience is made up entirely of motion-picture cameras. "I hope you get the idea," Welles says. Fade to black. A human eye appears at the left of the screen, an equal sign appears next to the eye, and at the right appears the first-person pronoun. The eye winks and we dissolve to the beginning of the picture.

This witty and sadistically entertaining opening, which would have contained a few shots in color, such as a "blinding red stain" that flows over the lens in the electrocution scene, creates a very different effect from the script proper—more like the "cinema of attractions" than the immersive, hypnotic experience of Conrad's story. Running beneath its playful tone, however, is an implicit commentary on the potentially authoritarian nature of the film medium. By putting us in the position of passive subjects, Welles gives us a cinematic analog of the manipulation and demagogic deception practiced by Kurtz; but at the same time he occasionally gratifies our fantasies of power, subtly prefiguring a link the film will later establish between us and a fascist demagogue. As Rosenbaum puts it, "the multiple equations proposed by the introduction, whereby I = eye = camera = screen = spectator, are extended still further in the script proper, so that spectator = Marlow = Kurtz = Welles = dictator" (31).

The equations would have been reinforced by Welles's plan to play both Marlow and Kurtz. His voice, and by this time his face, were so well known to the public that when the camera came eye to eye with a homicidal dictator in the jungle, a mirror-image effect would have been created. Welles intended to stage the scene in darkly humorous, somewhat anticlimactic fashion: Kurtz is discovered at the shadowy end of a vast wooden temple filled with skulls; as the camera/Marlow/spectator moves in to a close-up of his face, he looks back and asks, "Have you got a cigarette?" (Welles did makeup tests in costume as Kurtz, looking unusually gaunt and wearing a scraggly beard.

He told Bogdanovich that just when the film was about to begin shooting he changed his mind and decided to have the character played by someone else, preferably an actor who was cast against type, thereby creating the kind of surprise and irony that the discovery of Kurtz generates in the novella; there is, however, no evidence that he followed through with this idea, and he confirmed to Jonathan Rosenbaum that, had the picture actually gone into production, he would have played the dual role as originally planned.)

One of the most important questions posed by the unfilmed production is whether the subjective camera would have been dramatically effective. Historians often argue that Robert Montgomery's adaptation of Raymond Chandler's *Lady in the Lake* (1946), in which the camera becomes Phillip Marlowe, offers proof positive that the first-person device inhibits identification, eliminating the suturing effect of ordinary continuity editing and making the audience excessively aware of the apparatus. This argument may be correct, but it doesn't take into account Montgomery's leaden direction, nor the fact that Chandler's private eye is a very different sort of character from Conrad's sailor. Marlow in *Heart of Darkness* is largely an observer rather than a participant—at any rate he is never punched in the face or kissed by a beautiful woman—and his narration creates the feeling of a waking dream. Welles's plan for the subjective camera was therefore more technically and affectively complex than Montgomery's straightforward literalism. The technique, he explained to Bogdanovich, was ideal for Conrad's story, which consists largely of a man piloting a boat down a river; the film could minimize "that business of a hand-held camera mooching around pretending to walk like a man" (31). As Jonathan Rosenbaum has pointed out, the screenplay's more flamboyant or gimmicky uses of the subjective camera are reserved for the early scenes, such as the one in which Marlow has his skull measured by a doctor; elsewhere, the camera seems relatively unobtrusive. Equally important, and despite both Welles's and the Mercury publicists' repeated claim that "the *audience* plays a part in this film," Welles appears to have wanted to create a tension between identification and estrangement. His script is often moody and hypnotic in the manner of Conrad, but when it describes characters facing the camera, it feels as if Welles wanted to undermine the "keyhole" effect of conventional cinema; in strategic and somewhat Brechtian ways, it turns the audience into guilty participants rather than absorbed viewers.

Photographer Stanley Cortez later used a subjective camera for one of the long sequences in *The Magnificent Ambersons,* in which George Amberson Minifer walks through every room of the shuttered Amberson mansion and then kneels to pray at his dead mother's bedside; RKO cut everything but the concluding image from this sequence, but Welles told Bogdanovich that he wasn't troubled by the cuts because he was unhappy with the results Cortez had obtained. He thought *Heart of Darkness* was a more suitable story for the technique, and before production he shot one experimental sequence (involving Robert Coote as Eddie) that convinced him he had made a correct decision. "It would have worked, I think," he said in the Bogdanovich interview. "I did a very elaborate preparation for [*Heart of Darkness*], such as I've never done again—never could. I shot my bolt on preproduction on that picture. We designed every camera setup and everything else" (31).

Indeed, Welles's screenplay, which was composed with the technical assistance of RKO script supervisor Amalia Kent, is one of the most camera-specific ever written, containing a detailed plan of the decoupage and even indicating the arrangement of figures in the frame for several of the shots. Only one sequence, involving multiple characters and chaotic action, is left for the director to work out on the set. To photograph a few scenes, Welles proposed that studio engineers equip a camera with one viewfinder for the operator and another for himself; but for many shots he wanted a handheld Eymo equipped with a gyroscope, rather like the present-day Steadicam—a device he claimed had been employed during the silent era. He planned to construct most of the film out of long takes, the longest of which he estimated would run twelve minutes. This would have required the kind of deep-focus photography later used in *Citizen Kane,* but with a great deal more tracking, craning, and panning. Temporal ellipses would be signaled with dissolves, which would occasionally shift us back to Marlow in New York harbor; but most of the subjective shots would be imperceptibly linked with what Welles described as a "feather wipe." In shot A, Marlow's "head" would turn and the camera would a pan across a wall or a stand of trees, ending at a precisely measured spot; in shot B, the camera would be repositioned at the same distance from the designated spot and the panning movement would resume. As Robert Carringer points out, one of the most elaborate and difficult series of these linkages occurs when Marlow arrives at the First Station: "Marlow as the camera was to proceed up the hill from the docks, pass the excavations, discover the dying natives, enter the settlement..., go to the British representative's quarters [where he meets Elsa], have a conversation, retrace his steps through the settlement to the manager's office, and have another conversation there—all continuously and without an apparent cut."[11]

Welles's experiments with duration and invisible editing would probably have delighted André Bazin, but his camera would also have been highly expressive and self-reflexive. In the script, it occasionally shows things from an omniscient perspective, such as brief shots of Marlow's boat moving down river; and like Conrad's prose it shifts focalization within a scene, moving without a visible cut from a literal point of view shot to a poetic or symbolic image—as when it tracks backward with Marlow out of the manager's office at the First Station, tilts down to look at a sick man dying on the floor, passes through the front entrance, cranes over the roof to show the jungle beyond, and tilts up to a starry sky. In many sequences, grotesque faces bob in and out of Marlow's view (one of the most eerie scenes involves a search for Kurtz across a marsh in heavy fog, with faces suddenly looming up out of a white limbo), and disorienting effects are created by offscreen sounds, especially when Marlow hears voices and turns to look at them or when he overhears scraps of heated conversation from another room. Mild shocks are administered whenever any of the characters look at the lens, and, significantly, many of these characters are black. At the First Station Marlow walks past a "big, ridiculous hole in the face of a mud bank, filled with about thirty-five dying savages and a pile of broken drain pipes.... Into some of these pipes the natives have crawled, the better to expire.... As Marlow looks down, CAMERA PANS DOWN for a moment, registering a MED. CLOSEUP of a negro face, the eyes staring up at the lens. The CAMERA PANS UP AND AWAY." Elsewhere, Marlow is confronted by the "half-breed" steersman, by the dark woman who is Kurtz's lover at the Central Station, and by the anonymous black man who announces, "Mister Kurtz, he dead." The film as a whole could in fact be described as a hallucinated white dream about blackness (Marlow suffers literal hallucinations toward the end, when he becomes ill with a fever), or, in terms of a Freudian critic such as Norman O. Brown, it could be viewed as a symptom of how white anxiety about blackness is sublimated into artistic discourse. Whatever interpretation we might offer, Welles's *Heart of Darkness* would have been the first and only time in the history of classic Hollywood when a white gaze would have been troubled by a returning black gaze.

As plans for the film advanced, Welles had models constructed for the sets in order to determine camera angles, and he screened a number of films so that he could become familiar with technical matters. Studio records indicate that he watched John Ford's *Arrowsmith*, a 1931 film set in the tropics and photographed by Ray June—a film which, despite its date, contains several wide-angle, deep-focus shots exactly like the ones Welles and Gregg Toland later used in *Kane*. Welles also viewed Ford's *Stagecoach* (1939), Jean Renoir's *Grand Illusion* (1937) (useful for the study of long takes), and Julien Duvivier's *Pépé Le Moko* (1937) (filled with atmospheric North African exoticism and grotesquerie). Meanwhile, RKO designers and special-effects technicians began preparatory work on the film. Marlow's journey was originally designed in six stages involving six different kinds of jungle atmosphere. Welles wanted to send a photographic crew to the Florida Everglades for background imagery, but eventually he decided to use stock footage from jungle movies, with which he planned to create a back-projected collage of increasingly strange scenery. Among the films from which he planned to appropriate images were *Chang: A Drama of the Wilderness* (Cooper, 1927), *The Four Feathers* (Korda, 1939), *Sanders of the River* (Korda, 1935), *Suez*

(Dwan, 1938), and a couple of low-budget shorts called *Congorilla* (Johnson, 1932) and *Baboona* (Johnson, Talley, 1935). He also screened such oddities as *Jungle Madness, Crouching Beast,* and *Hold that Wild Boar*. Much of this may sound risible, but there is every reason to believe he would have used the appropriated material brilliantly. The matte photography in *Citizen Kane* is consistently fascinating (as in the nocturnal party in a Florida swamp, which involves sinister prehistoric birds from *The Son of Kong* [Schoedsack, 1933]), and Welles's other films are noteworthy for the way they employ the process screen as a poetic rather than a realistic device—for example, in the surreal exoticism of the San Francisco aquarium scene in *The Lady from Shanghai* (1947).

The complex choreography of camera and players required what Welles described in a note to the studio as "absolute perfection of preparation before the camera turns." He brought composer Bernard Herrmann into the process quite early and wanted the Mercury players to record the entire script so that Herrmann would have a guide for the composition and placement of music. (Besides the actors already mentioned, other members of the cast included John Hoysradt, Vladimir Sokoloff, Gus Schilling, Everett Sloane, George Coulouris, and Erskine Sandford.) In a memo to RKO, he argued that this careful preplanning would save time and money, but studio executives probably raised their collective eyebrows when he also noted that because of the camera technique he wanted to use, the completed film couldn't be shortened except by cutting whole sequences. As if in compensation, he offered them a great deal of spectacle: a giant snake landing on the deck of the steam boat; cannibal natives firing metal arrows and pinning one character's hand to the boat rail; a severed head on a pole; hundreds of blacks bowing down to Kurtz and forming long serpentine lines to haul ivory out of the jungle; a temple erected on stilts in the midst of a jungle lake; a cloud of bats scurrying down from the ceiling of the temple; Kurtz's throne surrounded by a wall of human skulls similar to the bizarre wall of human faces in Welles's 1938 stage production of George Buchner's *Danton's Death*; Kurtz crawling on all fours into the jungle; Kurtz's frail body lifted from the ground by servants and silhouetted against a campfire as he murmurs "I was on the verge of great things"; a tremendous conflagration in the jungle; and a climactic lightning and rain storm inspired by Conrad's *Typhoon*, during which Kurtz keeps repeating "The horror! The horror!"

One of the most amusing documents in the Mercury files is a somewhat disingenuous list of these spectacular elements and enticing "story angles," probably written by Mercury Theater publicist Herbert Drake, which was intended to be used in selling the film to RKO executives and ultimately in publicity by the studio marketing department:

The story is of a man and a girl in love…There is a hell of an adventure going up the river. There is an unhappy ending which we won't need to mention…There are cannibals, shootings, native dances, a fascinating girl, gorgeous, but black, a real Negro type. She has an inferred, but not definitely stated, jungle love-life with our hero. There is a jungle in flames and heavy storms of a spectacular nature…We don't know who [will play the white girl] but she is going to be a great beauty…sexy without waving her hips around. She is to have a calm, half-smiling face, perhaps over a full bosom, for instance…Theory of the story is two moderns who have a hell of an adventure in the dark places of the earth. The idea is, more or less by implication, that this is the God-damnedest relation between a man and a woman ever put on the screen…Everyone and everything is just a bit off normal, just a little oblique…in surroundings not healthy for a white man.

RKO probably had doubts about all this, but it kept faith until December 5, 1939, when a detailed budget and day-to-day production schedule was submitted. The picture would have taken thirty weeks to complete at a cost of approximately $1,058,000, which was considerably more than RKO intended to pay. After a week of intense work, the Mercury organization offered cost-cutting suggestions that reduced the budget to $985,000. This was not beyond the means of the studio (*Citizen Kane* cost approximately $750,000), but it was too much for a picture that, from their point of view, had other problems. It was still unclear who would play Elsa. (Welles tried to obtain Ingrid Bergman, who had yet to appear in a U.S. film; he eventually decided to cast Dita Parlo, whom he had seen in *Grand Illusion,* but she encountered difficulty getting out of France). There were few close-ups, no shot/reverse shots, and the director/star would only briefly appear on screen. An even bigger problem for RKO was that Welles wanted to photograph lots of black people. He resisted the studio's proposal that extras in blackface could be used in crowd scenes, and he planned to suggest a sex relation between Kurtz and a black woman—this despite the fact that miscegenation was strictly forbidden by the Production Code.

The end came on January 9, 1940, when *Variety* reported that *Heart of Darkness* had given the studio cold feet and that Welles's organization had been paid $160,000 to shelve it. Conrad's novella nevertheless remained one of Welles's preoccupations for long afterward. In 1945, he produced a second adaptation for the radio and announced during the broadcast that perhaps he would some day be able to make it into a motion picture. It seems to have influenced various aspects of his later work, including the narrative method of *Citizen Kane,* the Latin American scenes in *The Lady from Shanghai,* and the elaborate tracking camera in *The Trial.* As important as Conrad was for Welles, however, his attempt to adapt *Heart of Darkness* for the movies had brought at least three irresolvable contradictions uncomfortably to the fore.

First was the contradiction between modernism and mass culture, which became apparent when Welles added expensive spectacle and a love interest to an oblique narrative technique that subsumes adventure within an introspective, serpentine monologue. Second was the potential contradiction between Welles's democratic idealism and his fascination, even partial identification, with Byronic individualists such as Kurtz. Third, and most significant, was the contradiction between Welles's often-courageous opposition to fascism and racism and his interest in a story that expresses what Chinua Achebe has correctly identified as a conservative and racist ideology.

Conrad's *Heart of Darkness* is an implicit attack on Rousseau; although it shows the cruelty of Belgian exploitation in the Congo, it approves of a "good" colonialism that represses Africa's putative savagery and controls the ancient bestiality in the human heart. As Patrick Brantlinger has observed, it offers "a powerful critique of at least certain manifestations of imperialism and racism, at the same time that it presents that critique in ways that can only be characterized as imperialist and racist."[12] Welles's adaptation completely rejects colonialism, places the action in a Dark Continent of the mind, and tries to become a commentary on fascism, but it doesn't avoid Conrad's primitivism. From the opening moments, when jazz drums in Manhattan foreshadow jungle drums in the "dark places of the earth," the politics of the film become confused. The effort to retain aspects of Conrad's rhetoric only adds to the problem. Welles was a liberal activist, but like many white liberals of his era (and our own) he sometimes equated black culture with a kind of atavistic energy. His script seems to take melodramatic relish in Conrad's references to a "black and incomprehensible frenzy" (51) and a "night of first ages" (51–52), and the film's treatment of women would have been quite close in spirit to Conrad's misogyny.

We might recall that in the 1897 preface to *The Nigger of the Narcissus*, Conrad described art as "a single-minded attempt to render the highest kind of justice to the visible universe," and his own task as "before all, to make you *see*." D. W. Griffith adopted that last phrase as a motto, and Welles gave it a potentially subversive implication through his plans for a subjective camera. Welles's *Heart of Darkness* was in many ways a brilliant visual experiment, especially when it updated the action of the novella, introduced cinematic effects homologous with Conrad's prose, and suggested a link between European fascism and U.S. racism. In my own view, however, even had the film reached the screen, it would have been caught on the horns of a dilemma, forced to be either too faithful to Hollywood or too faithful to Conrad. There is of course no reason why fidelity should always be a primary concern in film adaptations, but in this case neither a mass-cultural nor a high-modernist rendition of the original text, no matter how revisionist, could have avoided the ideological contradictions of Conrad's novella. Any attempt to expurgate, condense, or modernize the narrative is faced with the choice of retaining these contradictions or of becoming some other kind of thing entirely. Orson Welles embraced the contradictions, which were part of his own artistic history. To borrow a metaphor from Conrad's *Lord Jim,* we might say that he chose to immerse himself in the potentially destructive element of both Hollywood and *Heart of Darkness.* The results on screen would likely have been problematic at the level of politics, but there is no doubt they would have been cinematically fascinating.

Notes

1. James Naremore, *More than Night: Film Noir in its Contexts,* rev. ed. (Berkeley and Los Angeles: University of California Press, 2008), 47–48, 237–39.

2. Joseph Conrad, *Heart of Darkness,* ed. Ross C. Murfin, 2nd ed. (Boston: Bedford-St. Martin's, 1996), 20. All subsequent references are to this edition, and page numbers are indicated parenthetically in the text.

3. Frederic Jameson, *The Political Unconscious* (Ithaca, N.Y.: Cornell University Press, 1981), 206.

4. F. R. Leavis, *The Great Tradition: George Eliot, Henry James, Joseph Conrad,* new ed. (Harmondsworth: Penguin Books: 1993), 119.

5. John Houseman, *Run-Through: A Memoir* (New York: Simon and Schuster, 1972), 435.

6. Michael Denning, *The Cultural Front: The Laboring of American Culture in the Twentieth Century* (London: Verso, 1996), 392–94.

7. *Heart of Darkness* screenplay (November 30, 1939), Orson Welles collection, Lilly Library, Indiana University, box 14, folder 17. All subsequent quotations of dialogue and description are from this screenplay.

8. Orson Welles and Peter Bogdanovich, *This is Orson Welles,* ed. Jonathan Rosenbaum (New York: Harper Collins Publishers, 1992), 31. All subsequent references are to this edition, and page numbers are indicated parenthetically in the text.

9. Orson Welles collection, Lilly Library, box 14, folder 19.

10. Jonathan Rosenbaum, "The Voice and the Eye: A Commentary on the *Heart of Darkness* Script," in *Discovering Orson Welles* (Berkeley and Los Angeles: University of California Press, 2007), 28–48. All further references are to this edition, and page numbers are indicated parenthetically in the text. For additional commentary on the screenplay, especially on the prologue, see Guerric DeBona, O.S.B., "Into Africa: Orson Welles and *Heart of Darkness," Cinema Journal* 33, no. 3 (Spring 1994): 16–34.

11. Robert Carringer, *The Making of Citizen Kane* (Berkeley and Los Angeles: University of California Press, 1985), 10.

12. Patrick Brantlinger, "*Heart of Darkness*: Anti-Imperialism, Racism, or Impressionism?" in *Heart of Darkness,* ed. Ross C. Murfin (New York: St. Martin's Press, 1996), 364–65.

Madame de . . . (Ophuls, 1953)

4

Max Ophuls's Auteurist Adaptations

Laura Mulvey

I would like to start with some points about the particular importance of adaptation for Max Ophuls before discussing three of his films in detail, namely *Madame de...*(France, 1953), adapted from Louise de Villmorin's 1952 novella; *Letter from an Unknown Woman* (Hollywood, 1948) from Stefan Zweig's 1922 novella; and *Lieberlei* (Germany/Austria, 1933) from Arthur Schnitzler's 1895 play. An original work, very often of literary value or interest, was central to Ophuls's filmmaking process. To mention a selection: his second film was written by Erich Kästner, who adapted the script from his own children's story; Ophuls later worked with Collette on *La Tendre enemie* (France, 1936). He adapted Goethe with *Werther* (France, 1938) and Molière with *L'Ecole de femmes* (France, 1940). His disastrous project with Preston Sturges in 1946, *Vendetta,* was an adaptation of Prosper Mérimée's *Colomba. La Signora di Tutti,* made in Italy in 1936, was adapted from a novel by Salvatore Gotta. Elisabeth Sanxay Holding's novel *The Blank Wall* became *The Reckless Moment* (Universal, 1948). After his return to Paris, another Schnitzler play was the basis for *La Ronde* (France, 1950), and three Maupassant short stories were adapted for *Le Plaisir* (France, 1952). And, as I said, this is only a selection; so far as I can see, adaptation was the basis for twenty out of his twenty-five films. Thus, my opening premise is that Ophuls was a "director of adaptation," sometimes writing the script himself but always very closely involved in script development across his whole body of work, including the films he made in Hollywood.

Lutz Bacher's invaluable book *Max Ophuls in the Hollywood Studios* describes Ophuls's intimate involvement with the adaptation of all four of his Hollywood films and five scripts (including *Vendetta,* from which Ophuls was sacked by Preston Sturges early in production).[1] That Ophuls was himself conscious of this is born out by a remark quoted by Georges Annenkov (the costume designer on all of Ophuls's French films in the 1950s) in relation to their first conversation about *Madame de...*: "Do you really think that I should make this film? Don't you think that after having done Goethe, Maupassant, Schnitzler, Stephan Zweig, it might be rather thin? However, it's true that I've also done Colette and Maurice Dekobra."[2] However, I should also point out that none of the three stories I am discussing here were actually chosen by him; all three fell, as it were, into his lap by fortunate coincidence.

Secondly, there is the question of fidelity: the three films I have chosen here vividly illustrate a tension between the original stories and their molding in adaptation. In all three cases, the originals allow Ophuls to work with material and develop the situations that most consistently characterize his films as whole: people tied together by emotion, love caught in constraint, the melodrama of romantic failure. In this sense, a certain fidelity to the originals is guaranteed, as they serve the director's purpose. Central to the originals, and clearly of intrinsic interest to Ophuls, is the huge gap that lies between the worlds of passion and convention. As these stories tend to be ruled not by human rationality but by a kind of novelistic destiny (both benign and malign), they lead into the protagonists' unconscious and then out into their social milieux in which a different kind of "unconscious," of class and gender, holds sway. The confrontation between the two brings chaos and tragedy. On the other hand, although he used stories that were about his preferred themes, Ophuls is not a "faithful" adaptor. The adapted scripts diverge from the originals in absolutely key ways: in all three of the films I am addressing, extra "Ophulsian" scenes are imposed and, more significantly, aspects of character and narrative are radically changed to give the films their own meanings.

Of interest to me in this essay, the reason for my emphasis on "auteurist adaptation," is that the films' divergence from their original texts has a consistency. The films alter the relationships that exist in the originals to create contrasting iconographies of masculinity. Ophuls, at three very different points in his career, tells the story of a romantic triangle characterized by three emblematic figures: a central woman, her husband (a military man), and her lover, whom I characterize as a "womanizer." The triangle creates, in the first instance, an antinomy between the two iconographies of masculinity, a structural opposition between a man dedicated to the rigidity of the military, its authority in the name of patriarchal and traditional values, and a man dedicated to sex, and thus to women, to the erotic and the reckless. At best, the young Fritz in *Lieberlei*, a "ladies' man," as he is known to his fellow officers, has been having an affair with an aristocratic married woman, from which he tries to escape when he falls in love with Christine. Or at worst, the aging Stefan in *Letter from an Unknown Woman*, a "libertine" whose lifetime of compulsive seductions renders him incapable of seeing Lisa in terms other than a latest conquest, another "one-night stand." And Donati in *Madame de...* shares something of the character of both the others. The triangular relationships are by no means exactly repeated, but they do enable the confrontation between two kinds of masculinity within differing narrative circumstances: the young man doomed by an old affair, the aging libertine who has forgotten a former one…the temporalities and ages and memories change.

The three original stories I am discussing here are altered in adaptation to maintain this pattern. All three films are set in the late nineteenth century: *Madame de…* in a vaguely belle époque Paris; *Letter from an Unknown Woman* opens with the title "Vienna 1900"; and Vienna again in *Lieberlei*. All three end with a duel: as the military man kills (in many ways a legalized execution) the womanizer, illicit passion is erased and patriarchal law and order restored. In the original stories, however, only *Lieberlei* ends in a duel. It serves, in this sense, as the prototype for the adaptation of the other two stories to which the duel ending has been added. The fact that Ophuls chose to end *Madame de…* with a duel, in 1952, throws a retrospective light back on the ending of *Letter from an Unknown Woman* in 1947. All this is to say that, in these three cases, Ophuls's lack of fidelity as an adaptor follows a distinct pattern: the duel ending is imposed on the later films and, in all three, the husband is transformed into a "military man," sharpening his iconographical role and his binary opposition to the womanizer.

The womanizer, a once-emblematic figure personified by Don Juan, is a man whose presence conjures up the contradictory, paradoxical discourses of sexuality under patriarchy, the simultaneous centrality and repression of sex and gender under its rules. These discourses, in many ways as archaic as the womanizer himself, are familiar from psychoanalytic theory and have found fertile ground in feminist, psychoanalytically influenced film theory. Tania Modleski has written about the significance of Stefan in *Letter from an Unknown Woman* as a "feminized" man, pointing out that this figure cannot be detached from the figure of the woman: "Although he is a womanizer, this activity paradoxically womanizes him for it immerses him in a sensuous existence, a stereotype associated with the feminine and running counter to the self-denial espoused by Lisa's husband."[3] Her argument has been taken up and debated by Stanley Cavell.[4] In some ways, this opposition around the womanizer is ideological and serves to condemn the death-dealing rigidity of aristocratic patriarchy, particularly that of the thoroughly anti-Semitic Hapsburg elite. In other ways, it creates an emblematic opposition between eros and thanatos. This antinomy can also be displaced onto narrative structure: the principle of desire that "fires" and drives forward a story while death brings it to closure and stillness. But in the context of adaptation, and for this essay, I am leaving these implications aside and concentrating on tracing the way that Ophuls distorts the original stories in order to extract this confrontation between the womanizer and the military man. These plots, themes, and iconographies have a bearing on their translation to the screen, the main purpose, after all, of their adaptation. While his adapted stories reflected his thematic interests, the recurring themes also allowed him to create cinematic space for the choreography of emotion, overflowing into ecstatic and extended moments and delaying the development of the story. This stylistic space emerges out of, and acts as a figuration for, moments of passion. As their rendition on the screen is focused intensely on people (performance, star presence, is of the essence) and focused intensely on their emotion, the two work together in a choreography that finds its ideal moments, literally, in dance sequences. In these ultra-cinematic moments in which music and dance take over, fidelity, plot, and thus any relation to the literary original falls away.

Across this essay lies the theme of repetition. Many commentators on Ophuls have discussed the centrality of repetition as an aesthetic device in his films, most of all in relation to *Letter from an Unknown Woman* (hereafter *Letter* for short). But in the context of adaptation, the question of repetition takes on added significance. As James Naremore pointed out at the adaptation conference in Pittsburgh that inspired this volume (this is not an exact quotation): "The study of adaptation needs to be joined with recycling, remaking, and every other form of retelling in the age of mechanical reproduction. . . . By this means, adaptation will become part of a general theory of repetition." In the case of Ophuls, not only did he adapt, repeatedly, but he also repeated his own deviations from originals in the three films discussed here. Furthermore, the womanizer's iconographical attributes are defined by serial conquest, the restless move to something new. In *Letter,* the repetition compulsion of the seducer fuses with the repetitive activity of the pianist and washes over the aesthetic of the film itself, with its own repeated motifs that both echo *Lieberlei* and prefigure *Madame de. . . .* By the time Ophuls made *Madame de . . .* in 1952, repetition (in the form of the cyclical circulation and exchange of the earrings) had, indeed, become the central theme of the film, the aspect of the story that appealed to and interested Ophuls. Finally, in the dance sequences that I will discuss below, the repetition of movement conjures up the repetitive nature of the cinema itself: film as a mechanical animation of life, transforming the human figure into an automaton, destined to repeat forever in projection the limited range of actions originally performed in production.

The Schnitzler play, *Lieberlei,* is about class, refracted mainly through two parallel romances of two upper-class young students with two young girls from the "Vorstadt." The relationship between Mizzi and Theodore is flirtatious, with Mizzi's role being to insist to her friend, Christine, throughout the play, on the necessary short-term nature of these kinds of affairs between working or petit bourgeois girls and men of a higher class. On the other hand, Christine has fallen passionately in love with Fritz, embarking on the affair in terms of the exclusivity and eternity of her love. Fritz becomes increasingly entranced with his "sweet maiden" as the play develops. These experiments in cross-class romance, with a hint of modernity, are abruptly disrupted by the return of the past. Fritz tells Theo at the beginning of the play that he has decided to end his affair with a married woman of his own class. However, later in the first act, the husband (der Herr/the Gentleman) intrudes into the party that the two young couples are enjoying and challenges Fritz to a duel. Fritz's gradually less guarded feelings for Christine emerge in the second act (the day after the party) under the shadow of his certain death. Some days have passed by the third act, which is very short and dominated by Christine's reaction to the news that Fritz has been dead for two days "because of another woman" and has already been buried by his grieving family who, of course, know nothing of her existence. In an impassioned outburst, she recognizes and condemns the way she has been excluded from these events, leaving to find Fritz's grave. Her father collapses saying the last words of the play, "I know she'll never come back." Throughout the play, the close relationship between Christine and her father, who plays in the orchestra at the opera, is a significant theme.

Ophuls, who wrote the screenplay himself, stayed quite close to the outline of this plot but deviates from fidelity to the original in a way that establishes the first stage of the pattern I am tracing. He accentuated the play's political implications by giving it a military and more aristocratic setting, so that the affair, which returns from Fritz's immediate past, brings with it the presence of the past personified by the politically conservative Hapsburg elite. Fritz and Theo are no longer students but lieutenants in the cavalry. The "Gentleman" becomes the Baron von Eggersdorff, the brother of their commanding officer, so that the duel is placed rigorously in an aristocratic tradition with its military rituals, conventions, and codes of honor. Ophuls added crucial scenes that allow these military resonances to occupy an important place among the film's motifs. It is when the Baron's brother, Major von Eggersdorff, overhears gossip from his fellow commanding officers over dinner about the Baronin's affair that he calls on the Baron, confirming his suspicions and pointing out that family honor is at stake. Subsequently, a scene in a shooting gallery establishes that the Baron is a perfect marksman and that the duel will be, in effect, an execution. Ophuls also introduced a further antimilitary element to the "militarized" plot: Theo protests against the injustice of the duel and against the army's refusal to condemn the tradition. He says, "This is an old affair; the man involved has met someone else. They love each other. This duel should not take place." In the face of his officer's intransigence, Theo leaves the army and does not, in the film, act as Fritz's second as he does in the play. He and Mizzi watch from the distance (their poignant cry, "Why no second shot?" will be echoed by Louise in *Madame de...*). On hearing the news of Fritz's death, Christine commits suicide, and her reaction to the situation is less clearly articulated than in the play. This means that, through Theo, the film's political position is slanted toward a condemnation of the military and the aristocracy and away from Christine and the class and gender themes of the play.

It is tempting to see in this adaptation of *Lieberlei* something both of Ophuls's own background and the immediate context in which the film was made. He was born in 1902 in Saarbrücken, a small state switched throughout its history between France and Germany. He has described in his autobiography the successive occupations of the city by the German and then the French armies during World War I.[5] Ironic in tone, he describes witnessing the transformation of the German army, which arrived as a confident imperial force, only to disintegrate as deserters and war resisters were hunted down and shot by offers, until finally it retreated in humiliation. But in 1933, as a Jewish intellectual embarking on his career as a film director in Berlin, to critique, even through a detour into the late nineteenth century, the values upheld by tradition, the aristocracy, and the military would have amounted to something like a political statement.[6] But in terms of my argument, the introduction of the military presence in *Lieberlei* generates a more extreme, inflected, binary opposition between the Baron and Fritz that moves away from the specifics of class—central though they are to both the original and the film's story—to create strongly contrasted masculinities. Ophuls injects psychoanalysis into Schnitzler's *Lieberlei* through the sinister role of the phallic, patriarchal military man, played to the full by the monocle-wearing Gustav Gründgens. Although the affair with the Baronin, which then gives way to his discovery of love through Christine, might not turn Fritz into a fully fledged womanizer, he is associated with women, romance, and seduction. To emphasize the point, a fellow officer comments ironically on Fritz's success with women. On the other hand, he is unable to refuse the duel, and an indictment of the code of dueling is displaced onto Theo's rejection of a military career that had been in his family for generations. While these twists are of intrinsic interest in Ophuls's adaptation of *Lieberlei,* they also establish the pattern repeated in the two later films.

In *Lieberei,* Ophuls also elaborates the restricted space of the play to create founding instances of locations that came, through repetition in later films, to be characteristically "Ophulsian." Howard Koch has described how Ophuls, when working with him on the script of *Letter,* would repeatedly say "this script needs more air," a phrase which Koch came to understand as signifying specific locations that would fill out the dialogue and, presumably, give him space and relevant opportunity for his own cinematic style.[7] In giving "air" to Schnitzler's *Lieberlei,* Ophuls adds the two café scenes, the millinery shop where Mizzi works, the young officers on maneuvers, and Fritz and Christine's sleigh ride at the height of their romance. He also realizes scenes that are described in the play but inassimilable to its dramatic structure, particularly filling in scenes between Fritz and the Baronin. But he establishes some scenes and locations, highly connotative social settings, the Opera and the railway station, that necessarily bring with them certain kinds of emotions or situations that were to recur within his cinematic "vocabulary."

In *Lieberlei,* the two young couples meet at the Opera at the beginning of the film (how they have met is not clear in the play), when the girls drop their opera glass from the balcony almost onto the two young men in the more aristocratic stalls below. Ophuls also introduces opera scenes, missing in the originals, to both later films. In *Letter,* the setting for Stefan and Lisa's final chance meeting (a nightclub in the story) is a performance of *The Magic Flute* and the site of one of Ophuls's most spectacular camera movements up the grand staircase. In *Madame de...,* Louise announces the loss of her earrings as she and her husband arrive at the Opera (a ball in the original story), and the general's fruitless search for the missing earrings is played with an emphasis on repetition that prefigures the aesthetic of repetition that will come to dominate the film. Not only did Ophuls include an extended and complex opera scene, but he also needed to save the ball as the setting for Donati and Louise's serial romantic encounters at the center of the film.

Before the duel in *Lieberlei,* the Baron's brother sees the Baronin off at the railway station. This is not a significant scene and contributes little to the plot (except to further confirm an unbending male and military iconography). The railway-station farewell, perhaps its first appearance in an Ophuls film, features twice at significant moments in *Letter:* during Lisa's parting from Stefan after their first night of love and when his final words "two weeks" are echoed as Lisa sees off her son on his last, tragic journey. In *Madame de...,* the general gives Lola the earrings as they say goodbye at the station on her way to Constantinople (Latin America in the novella); later, in a similarly staged railway-station scene, he sees Louise off on her journey to the Italian lakes, thus firmly establishing the importance of these locations for Ophuls.

Ophuls made *Letter* in a very different context: as a nearly penniless refugee in Hollywood, where his films were barely known, where work was humiliatingly difficult to get, and where his personal cinematic style was often seen as both an affront to other industry professionals and a recipe for alienating audiences. *Letter* was his second Hollywood film. Perhaps strangely, as it is his best-known and most-written-about film—it is often said to typify his themes and style—*Letter* was not initiated by him. The adaptation of the Stefan Zweig novella was the long-cherished project of William Dozier, vice president of Universal International, and the first picture he wanted to produce for his wife, Joan Fontaine, through their independent production company Ramparts. It was Howard Koch, already engaged as screenwriter, who persuaded Dozier and Fontaine to take on Ophuls as director. In his 1957 interview with Jacques Rivette and François

Truffaut, Ophuls says that a script already existed but he managed to "rework it completely, together with Howard Koch, to make it the way I saw it."[8] Koch particularly mentions the Prater scenes as Ophuls's contribution, but given the "auteurist" pattern of his adaptations, it seems likely that he contributed the more radical plot revisions that I am discussing here.[9]

The Stefan Zweig novella *Letter from an Unknown Woman* takes the form of a letter addressed to a successful, nameless writer by a nameless woman who had loved him since childhood. It is a story of two diametrically opposed erotic compulsions: hers to dedicate her whole life to her love for a man she encounters twice in her adult life, while his life is dedicated, symmetrically and completely incompatibly, to compulsive seduction. She remembers every detail of their two encounters; he remembers absolutely nothing. The first time they meet, for three nights of passion, she had hoped that he would remember his young former neighbor. The second time, ten years later, she hopes he will remember the young virgin, who is now the mother of his child. Having given birth, after the first meeting, in conditions of horror and degradation, she had made up her mind never again to suffer from poverty and embarked on a career as a successful courtesan, surrounded by friends and many admirers. Although occasionally their social circuits overlap, the writer's polite look never shows the slightest sign of recognition while her existence continues to revolve around his. She cares for their son, refuses offers of marriage, and sends him white roses on the anniversary of their previous meeting, which is also his birthday. Ten years later, in a nightclub, she feels him watching her with admiration and leaves with him immediately in response to his gesture. During this second encounter, she feels once again the compulsive seducer's dedication to and understanding of women's sexuality. She silently examines every detail of his behavior, searching for an awakening of recognition. After another night of passionate love, he leaves a large sum of money in her clothes, taking her, once again, for an unusually beautiful and charming prostitute. Driven to despair by this gesture, and his inability to respond to her, despite her hints, with anything but attentive charm and politeness, she leaves. (As they pass on the stairs, Johann, his servant, recognizes her immediately.) Her letter tells him that their son has just died of fever from which she herself was already suffering and will certainly also die. The writer finishes the letter and tries to remember the woman whose life had been dedicated to him, arousing an indistinct memory, "like a stone shining under water, its shape trembling and unformed." In the last few sentences, the compulsive Don Juan feels a sudden wave of emotion and an overwhelming recognition of love, even though its actual object still eludes him.

Once again, in a key deviation from the original, the story as told in the film is "militarized." Once again, a rich, aristocratic military man is introduced as the husband of the "unknown woman" (now Joan Fontaine as Lisa Berndle), replaying the opposition of iconographies Ophuls had initiated in *Lieberlei*. From a practical point of view, a change along these lines was needed: one problem of adaptation was the explicitly sexual content of the original story, and the Breen office continued to ask for revisions in an already-censored script. Lisa's status in the second part of the story would have had to be "respectable" both for censorship purposes and for the image of the star. In the central male character (the writer in the novella; in the film, the pianist Stefan Brandt, played by Louis Jourdan), the iconography of the "womanizer" is fully realized so that the married woman, military husband, and lover triangle, which forms the deadly subplot in *Lieberlei*, is at the center of the story in *Letter*. As in the novella, the film begins with the male protagonist returning home where his servant hands him a thick envelope. In the film, Stefan has just received a challenge to a duel that he has no intention of accepting and is preparing to leave Vienna for an extended journey. The main body of both works is the story of the female protagonist's extraordinary and silent love that can finally be told on her deathbed. The novella ends with the writer's abstract sensations. The film ends as Stefan leaves to confront his opponent, whom he now realizes is Johann Stauffer, Lisa's husband and the stepfather of his child.

One important difference between the two endings is that Stefan, when he finishes the letter, remembers Lisa in a montage sequence that recapitulates iconic moments of their time together. Lutz Bacher describes in detail the difficulties and the disagreements over the ending of *Letter*, a difference of opinion between Ophuls, who tried to tone down Stefan's remembering, and Dozier who inserted the shot of fourteen-year-old Lisa: as Stefan leaves the house for the last time, he "re-sees" the little girl who opened the door for him many years before, the moment that Lisa had described in her letter as definitive for her love. Dozier recalls that it was he who "insisted that it be in there. John [Houseman, the producer] didn't want to do it; Max didn't want to do it because they thought somehow it was a little corny. I admitted that it was. But I said 'I think it will be very telling and very touching.'" Dozier goes on to describe "the long harangues" that finally ended when Houseman said: "Ok, we'll put it in but we'll call it the President's shot."[10] As Bacher recounts, the ending continued to cause problems that led to reshoots in postproduction:

> The principle change in [Dozier's] new ending was one that Ophuls had resisted until now: the unequivocal shift from an evocation of the spirit of Zweig's ending to a strong dramatic motivation for Stefan's decision [to accept the duel] in the form of an emphatic assertion of *visual* remembrance of Lisa.[11]

In *Madame de...*, a love affair between a grand lady of fashion and an aristocratic ambassador (nameless, in the novel, like the heroine and her husband Monsieur de...) comes to revolve around a pair of beautiful diamond earrings. Gradually, the earrings take on a symbolic significance in the erotic exchange between the heroine, her husband, and her lover. At first they simply circulate: Madame de...had received them as a gift from her husband the day after their wedding but sells them to pay some debts she has carelessly accumulated. The jeweler brings them back to Monsieur de..., who buys them for a second time and gives them as a parting present to his mistress as she leaves Paris for South America. To conceal her action, Madame de...embarks on an elaborate lie, with which her husband indulgently plays along, about the loss or possible theft of the diamonds. To pay her gambling debts, the former mistress sells them, and the ambassador happens to buy them on a whim. Soon after, the ambassador arrives in Paris. He meets and becomes entranced with Madame de..., and their romance moves from flirtation to grand passion, the first love that she has ever felt. Just as they are about to begin an affair, he gives her the diamonds as a secret token of his love. This is the turning point of the story, and the significance of the earrings begins to change. Failing to understand that the earrings symbolize sexual possession for both her husband and her lover, Madame de...tells different lies to each. To her husband she says that she has just "found" them; when her lover protests that she cannot wear such an expensive and flamboyant gift in public, she says that their origin will be "their own private secret," and she will tell her husband that they are a present from a rich, eccentric relative. Monsieur de..., on hearing his wife's flagrantly ridiculous lie, realizes that, by some strange coincidence, they have returned as a gift from the ambassador. He simply explains to the ambassador the circumstances of the original gift (the "day after their wedding"). The ambassador is devastated to realize this emblem of mutual love had already been emblematic of a husband's sexual possession of his wife. He returns them to the original jeweler and Monsieur de...buys them for a third time. This time he forces his wife, distraught by the ambassador's changed manner, to give the earrings to a favorite but impoverished niece. On Madame de...'s advice, the niece sells them back to the family jeweler who, for the fourth time, sells them back to Monsieur de.... The story ends with a final misunderstanding between the ambassador and Madame de...: when she appears at a ball wearing the earrings, he interprets her gesture, one that she had intended to signal their earlier love, as one of contempt for it and he whispers to her, "I'll never forgive you." She falls into a terminal decline, and on her deathbed she summons the ambassador; she dies, reaching out to him and to her husband, each hand holding an earring.

Once again, Ophuls introduced a contrast between the man dedicated to the erotic and the "military man" into the film version as Monsieur de...is transformed into General de.... Georges Annenkov describes a discussion between Danielle Darrieux (who was to play Louise), himself, and Ophuls about the casting of Charles Boyer as Monsieur de... The two actors had starred together in a film once before, in 1936, when the very young Darrieux had played opposite Boyer in *Mayerling,* directed by Anatole Litvak (who had, incidentally, been instrumental in introducing Ophuls to the cinema in early 1930s Berlin), and for which Annenkov had been the costume designer. Annenkov pointed out to Ophuls that Boyer had played a lieutenant in the film and Ophuls had responded, "Then this time, we'll make him a General."[12] In spite of the poignancy of the anecdote, the return of the military iconography clearly forms part of Ophuls's wider plan, for the adaptation and the film, once again, ends with a fatal duel. The circulation of the earrings also changes from novella to film. In the original story, Monsieur de...returns the earrings to his wife in exchange for her agreeing once more to go out into society with him, as, in her despair at losing the ambassador's love (Donati in the film), she had refused all social engagements. In this sense, her appearance with her husband at a ball wearing the earrings signified a return to normality between the couple. In the film, the general refuses to buy back the earrings for a fourth time. Louise sells everything she has of value in order to buy them herself from the jeweler and dedicates them to her favorite saint on the morning of the duel, praying for Donati's survival. In the film, the general's challenge to Donati is provoked by his wife's refusal to return to normal relations, or even respond to his sympathy with her, and her fetishization of the earrings as a substitute for her lost love.

According to Annenkov, Ophuls declared himself interested in the story of *Madame de...* purely because of the earrings, objects that begin to affect the destiny of those involved with them, ultimately bringing tragedy. However, in the briefing that he gave Danielle Darrieux on the character of Louise, he emphasizes her vacuity, the pointlessness of her life and those of rich aristocrats more generally. Here the ideological inflection that Ophuls gave the plot turns more on this trait, and the character of the General has less of the patriarchal inflexibility of his predecessors. Boyer plays the part with enormous charm, energy, and some sympathy for his wife's dilemmas. His final exasperation, leading him to challenge Donati to the duel, is aroused by Louise's relentless fetishization of the earrings so that, in the absence of her great love, she seems to cling to him erotically through the diamonds that she ceaselessly caresses. Ophuls had already "sexualized" Louise's relationship to the earrings in a scene (not in the book) where she and Donati meet secretly, and as they kiss she reaches for them, whispering repeatedly, "*mes boucles d'oreilles.*" Through this inflection, Ophuls connects the emptiness of the woman's life, the impact that a first experience of love has on her, and the irrationality of her passion as invested in the earrings. He also introduces superstition and religion into her character, in the repeated scene with her favorite saint and her belief in her old nurse's fortune-telling cards. Louise's irrational passion links back to the irrationality of Lisa's passion in *Letter...* and also throws light on Ophuls's version of *Lieberlei*. Christine's suicide shifts her love for Fritz into that kind of overwhelming dedication that characterizes the other two women so all three reflect, as it were, on the female unconscious and the tragedy of female sexuality.

In the triangle, the woman's fetishization of love caricatures her role, to use the Lacanian term, as marginal to the Symbolic Order and the Law. The womanizer directly confronts the icon of the Symbolic Order, the military man, because he understands the woman's significance within in it and, following the alternative interpretations of the Don Juan story, either liberates her or exploits her love of love.[13] The husband is lost in the face of the womanizer's dedication to sex, which flaunts in front of him not only "what the woman wants," but also the essentially castrated, de-sexualized nature of the Symbolic Order. As for the womanizer, while he might lack potency in the realm of traditional exhibitionist military masculinity, his relentless erotic obsession, phallic in a sexual sense, is a challenge to the Phallic masquerade by which the military man signifies his authority. Ultimately, this man who appeals so deeply to "women who love love" cannot succeed against a system founded on legitimized violence and the right to kill in the name of honor. The final duels with which, in all three films, the military man reasserts both his authority and that of the Law are reminiscent of Don Juan's fateful meeting with the commendatore. In the process, the woman at the center of the triangle is rendered irrelevant. The drama returns to the world of men.

Across the three films, the psychoanalytic implications of these masculinities come more to the fore and become increasingly invested in performance and screen presence. In *Lieberlei*, as the confrontation is between two men in uniform, the Baron and Fritz are contrasted particularly in relation to rigidity and mobility. Although the two men in *Letter* never occupy the screen simultaneously, Lisa's decision to go to Stefan against her husband's prohibition is realized emblematically in the contrast between the two men's clothing and stance. In *Madame de...*, the opposing masculinities that have confronted each other often on the screen are fully played out when the general challenges Donati to a duel. Donati is lounging in a chair, a cigarette in the corner of his mouth (with a kind of loucheness that is reminiscent of Leonardo in *La Signora di Tutti*), while the general is fully erect in his uniform and military accoutrements. The Phallic rigidity of the Symbolic Order on the one side; on the other, a lack of it.

Such lack of rigidity, however, shifts, in relation to the woman, into a mobility of the erotic and the womanizer materializes emotion through the characteristic Ophulsian dance sequences. These privileged moments slow down the narrative, leaving it, as it were, on the side of the Symbolic, and bring into being another kind of temporality, or, rather, a timelessness in which erotic passion grows with the insistent beat of the music. Here, *in* the womanizer's mobilization of desire, *out of* his ability to open up a space for its expression, the cinema finds a kind of embodiment of its own. The rhythmic movements of the couple draw attention to the rhythmic movement of the "motion picture," that is, both the human (illusion of) movement on the screen and the mechanical movement of the celluloid that enables the illusion to materialize. This concept of succession, essential to the cinema's basic functioning, creates a bridge between the screen, its glamorous illusion, and the hidden, sequential movement of the projector. While succession relates to the movement of the film frame (the actual projector), "projection" relates rather to illusion. In the dance sequences, mirrors break up the screen space so that reflection and screen image merge. The simple combination of rhythmic movement, the repeated framing of the dancers, and the beauty of the stars, costumes, setting, lighting, and so on seem to construct a metaphor for the fascination of the cinema.

The prototype for this kind of sequence is Fritz and Christine's dance to the little mechanical jukebox: their movement is caught by successive mirrors, in which they repeat the days of the week to each other as they plan future repetitions of their dance. In *Letter,* Ophuls includes a dance sequence during Lisa and Stefan's evening at the Prater, but was unable to invest it with this particular extended and emotional resonance due to technical problems; here, reference to the cinema emerges more specifically in the sequence of the train panorama. In *Madame de...,* Ophuls uses mirrors once again in a montage of dance sequences to chart the process of Donati and Louise's love, again in an echo of *Lieberlei,* with repeated words reflecting the nuances of their growing passion. At the end of the sequence, the news that the general will be returning the next day brings this episode in Louise and Donati's romance to an end. Simultaneously, the musicians stop playing (in a repetition from *Letter*) and a flunkey gradually snuffs out the candles. The cinematic and erotic repetition, embodied by the dancing couple, the "self-reflexivity" of their double presence on the screen and in mirror image, is interrupted by the mundane, the everyday, embodied by the musicians and the servants. The General's return ends the romantic and cinematic utopia of the dance sequence and is marked by the following scene, the hunt, which brings the movie out of this timelessness back into the military man's realm of action.

In her article "The Concept of Cinematic Excess," originally published in 1977, Kristin Thompson reflects on Roland Barthes's concept of "obtuse meaning" and Stephen Heath's use of the term "excess." She draws attention to the opposition between moments of cinematic excess and narrative motivation: "Excess does not equal style, but the two are closely linked because both involve the material aspects of the film."[14] And: "Excess is not only counternarrative; it is counterunity."[15] She goes on to suggest that excessive aspects of cinema tend to get lost under conventions of storytelling, motivation, cause and effect, and conventions of viewing, "following" the narrative. These points relate very closely to Ophuls in two ways. First of all, his approach to cinema was paradigmatically "excessive," not only quite obviously, as in the dance sequences that I have discussed above, but also in his sense of his personal style, his insistence on shooting in long camera movements and resisting the cut-away and the insert. Second, many of the Hollywood professionals that he worked with, particularly editors, objected to Ophuls's style, cutting off any unnecessary length of movement that could be spared and inserting the cut-aways that had often been shot at the insistence of the front office. Bacher comments that while the "long take" might be finding acceptance in Hollywood,

> Ophuls other stylistic "trademark" had increasingly been drawing studio criticism. Not using close-ups meant not only his reluctance to supply shot coverage but also implied having stars turned away from the camera, in shadow, or hidden behind set elements. His penchant for "natural," less than perfect, sound also drew fire. In his later French work, it is those stylistic qualities and a return to the frequent use of rhythmic long takes, together with innovations in narrative structure, that marked Ophuls as a modernist and helped his films to succeed on the American art cinema circuit.[16]

These excessive, "counternarrative" moments in Ophuls's cinema form a crucial component of his auteurist adaptations. I have been arguing that Ophuls uses stories and settings to create an opposition between a military man and a womanizer; furthermore, as he opens up the narrative to emotion, the womanizer disrupts the conventional flow of narrative to carve out sequences of movement, particularly with dance, in which the cinema itself finds visibility. The womanizer might thus also be a figure for Ophuls's own desiring engagement with the mobile camera and the extended shot in contradistinction to the rigidity of studio style. But Ophuls also flourished in the Hollywood environment, with the opportunities offered by the crews, the cranes, the sets, the moving walls, the staircases and so on—the *mechanisms* of the cinema. His films, emerging at the last gasp of modernity in the early 1930s, often looking back to its early appearance at the turn of the century, celebrate the excitement of the machine itself and its metaphoric relationship to desire. For me, this fusion is represented above all by two moments:

first, in his adaptation of *Lieberlei* when Fritz and Christine dance to a little mechanical jukebox, surrounded by mirrors and caught by the movement of the camera; second, in Stefan and Lisa's journey on the fairground train in *Letter*. Both moments involve linking a mechanism of modern popular culture to love and to the cinema.

NOTES

1. Lutz Bacher, *Max Ophuls in the Hollywood Studios* (New Brunswick, N.J.: Rutgers University Press, 1996).
2. Georges Annenkov, *Max Ophuls* (Paris: Le Terrain Vague, 1961), 63.
3. Tania Modleski, "Time and Desire in the Woman's Film," *Cinema Journal* 23, no. 3 (Spring 1984): 19–30.
4. Stanley Cavell, "Postscript (1989): To Whom It May Concern," *Critical Inquiry* 16, no. 2 (Winter 1990): 248–89.
5. Max Ophuls, *Souvenirs*, trans. Max Roth (Paris: Cahiers du cinéma, 2002).
6. It might be worth remembering that Schnitzler himself had been demoted from officer to private in the Vienna Military Hospital for a novella (written in 1900, a few years after *Lieberlei*) entitled *Leutenant Gustl*, his attack on ritual dueling in the army. He was to be cited by Hitler as an example of "Jewish filth."
7. Howard Koch, "From Script to Screen with Max Ophuls," *Film Comment* 6, no. 4 (Winter 1970–71): 40–43.
8. Ophuls, "Interview with Max Ophuls," by Jacques Rivette and François Truffaut, in *Ophuls*, ed. Paul Willemen (London: BFI Publishing, 1978), 22. Originally printed in *Cahiers du cinéma* 72 (June 1957): 7–25.
9. Koch, "From Script to Screen with Max Ophuls."
10. William Dozier, quoted in Bacher, *Max Ophuls*, 190.
11. Bacher, *Max Ophuls*, 194.
12. Annenkov, *Max Ophuls*, 68
13. In his *Cahiers du cinéma* interview, Ophuls tells Rivette and Truffaut that he had adapted a Don Juan story that had never come to fruition (29).
14. Kristin Thompson, "The Concept of Cinematic Excess," in *Narrative, Apparatus, Ideology*, ed. Philip Rosen (New York: Columbia University Press, 1986), 132.
15. Thompson, "Concept of Cinematic Excess," 134.
16. Bacher, *Max Ophuls*, 320.

To Have and Have Not (Hawks, 1944)

5

To Have and Have Not

An Adaptive System

Kathleen Murray

Humphrey Bogart
with his kind of woman
in a powerful adaptation
of Ernest Hemingway's
most daring man-woman story!

—Tagline for the film's original release

"I can make a film out of the worst thing you ever wrote...That piece of junk, *To Have and Have Not*." Sitting in a fishing boat, Howard Hawks is trying to convince Ernest Hemingway to come to Hollywood, write for the movies, and make some money.[1] This rather apocryphal anecdote is invoked in nearly every discussion of the Hawks adaptation of Hemingway's novel. In 1944, Hawks did produce and direct *To Have and Have Not,* but the film's narrative has very little to do with Hemingway's novel, at least on the surface.

Hawks studiously avoided high-concept and political pictures; *To Have and Have Not* could be considered both. The opening credits read in their entirety: "Warner Brothers Presents...Humphrey Bogart in...Ernest Hemingway's *To Have and Have Not*...a Howard Hawks Production." The imprint of Hemingway's name in the opening credits is more than window dressing; it is not "based on a story by..." or "from the novel of..." four or five screens into the credits as was frequently done for less prestigious authors.[2] The film not only starred Humphrey Bogart, but also Walter Brennan and Lauren Bacall in her first role. The result is a wonderful film that challenges any easy notion of adaptation. With the screenplay written by Jules Furthman and William Faulkner, and the film released and distributed by Warner Brothers, *To Have and Have Not* is a remarkable confluence of names and talent.

Several drafts of the adaptation from the novel by both Furthman and Faulkner remain preserved, but the actual film is dramatically different from any existing text. Hawks would end up making a film about how Harry Morgan, the protagonist of the novel, and his wife, Marie, met—before the action of Hemingway's novel occurred. From the very beginning of the process, Hawks was making a film with very loose plot ties to the original text. Hawks even claims, "There wasn't anything in the picture that was in the book."[3] However, there is an obvious rapport and friendship between Hawks and Hemingway that, I would argue, tie the two texts very closely. While superficially the novel and film are extremely divergent, to the point where it is difficult to recognize the similarities of setting, plot, character, dialogue, or even theme (that is, the elements we normally consider as transferable from one medium to another), there are deeper and intriguing connections between the two in terms of approach, style, and attitude.[4]

TOWARD A USEFUL ADAPTATION

Quite a few of Hawks's movies are adapted from plays and novels, and all of them are dramatically reworked: *Twentieth Century* (1934), *His Girl Friday* (1940), *The Big Sleep* (1946), *Red River* (1948), and *The Big Sky* (1952). Hawks's manner of filmmaking, itself, challenges the normative rules of adaptation. By all accounts, his process of transforming a written text into a filmic language was intensely collaborative on all levels of production: from screenwriting, to on-set elaboration and improvisation.[5] If, as Gerald Mast writes, "Hawks produces narratives that not only differ in emphasis and tone from their originals but also are essentially new narratives altogether," then how can we consider this "new narrative" an adaptation?[6] Why is the whole notion of adaptation so tied up in narrative? What are the other means available to a filmmaker, or rather, what are the elements, besides narrative, that are "adaptable"?

When critics write about adaptation, they tend to address the notion of transferring the basic narrative elements from one medium to another. Even the best take this as their starting point. For example, in his book, *Novel to Film: An Introduction to the Theory of Adaptation*, Brian McFarlane creates a workmanlike approach to the notion of adaptation using all the tools of narrative theory. But, of course, this already shows a prejudice for narrative. While McFarlane discusses the specifically filmic elements of point of view and mise-en-scène, the bulk of his work is spent on detailed plot and narrative analysis. This type of analysis reveals many intriguing elements; there are others, however, that are not so clearly addressed. Every theorist has a unique approach that carefully addresses the specificity of the texts with which he or she is working. There is no satisfying general theory about adaptation.

The failure of much work on film adaptation is a narrow or, conversely, a nonspecific definition of the word. The sense of adaptation in Roy Rappaport's book, *Ritual and Religion in the Making of Humanity*, provides a firmer and more fecund ground on which to work. Rappaport was an anthropologist and an ecologist, interested in both biological evolution and the way in which language plays a part in human adaptive behaviors. He uses the term adaptation "to designate the processes through which living systems of all sorts maintain themselves, or persist, in the face of perturbations, originating in their environment or themselves, through reversible changes in their states, less reversible or irreversible transformations of their structures, or actions eliminating perturbing factors."[7]

This conception of adaptation provides several important elements. The first is the word "system." System implies a circuit. Adaptation does not simply work one way. The original text is transformed by the film version. It cannot be read in quite the same way again. Indeed, this is exactly what is at stake when a critic uses a term like "infidelity," as if the differences a film introduces actually hurts the original. Rappaport's definition accounts for this reciprocal aspect of adaptation. In addition, the layering of possible changes can be useful in considering adaptation. The second key term is "state," which refers to surface or superficial responses in the face of change. Through this particular conception of adaptation, we have the beginning of a way to talk about surface and depth, form and content, and a reciprocal system that is formed through both biology and language. Thinking of adaptation in these terms can get us out of the rut of case-studies to a larger notion of how we can think about the process.

The work in semiotics by Charles S. Peirce and in ecology and cybernetics by Gregory Bateson play a large role in Rappaport's thinking. The strength of Peirce's sign system is that it is not strictly linguistic, although it can be applied to language. Peirce's semiotics has been used in various ways in film theory, most notably by Gilles Deleuze in *Cinema 1: The Movement-Image*. Using a definition of adaptation that comes from this ground provides an interesting focal point for thinking about film adaptations. Because it is systemic and arises out of the images of both novel and film explicitly, the concept is large enough to encompass a variety of texts that work in a variety of ways. That is, it allows us to think of the different ways films might adapt existing texts without holding the dichotomy of fidelity to/betrayal of an originary text as the singular critical approach.

Much of the recent work on adaptation has, in one way or another, been an active attempt to escape the stranglehold of this kind of thinking, as Imelda Whelehan writes in her introduction to *Adaptations: From Text to Screen, Screen to Text*:

These commentators [Bluestone, Richardson, Wagner, Spiegel, Cohen, Miller, Giddings and Reynolds] have already charted the problems involved in such an exercise and the pitfalls created by the demands of authenticity of fidelity—not least the intensely subjective criteria which must be applied in order to determine the degree to which the film is "successful" in extracting the "essence" of the fictional text. What we aim to offer here is an extension of the debate, but one which further destabilizes the tendency to believe that the origin text is of primary importance.[8]

However, as Thomas Leitch notes in his article "Adaptation Studies at a Crossroads," the desire to make value judgments about the success of a film based on the idea of fidelity to the source material persists even if it is coded in more complex taxonomies.[9] Rappaport's definition of adaptation is able to provide a way of thinking about different sorts of adaptations simultaneously and perhaps to avoid the pitfalls to which adaptation studies are prone.

This definition of adaptation inevitably points to, allows for, and even embraces change and flexibility: "Flexibility is central to adaptive processes, and the enormous flexibility of the human species rests, of course, largely upon a property universal to and unique to humanity, namely language."[10] And of course, language is a behavior. This model allows for choice as well as inevitable change. Adapting a film from a novel is an artistic enterprise as well as a technical one of transposing two different media; it is a process of both responding to an entire system of expectations and attitudes about the process of filmmaking and responding to the novel's plot, theme, characters, and style.

Jacques Rivette writes in his influential article in *Cahiers du cinéma,* "There seems to be a law behind Hawks's action and editing, but it is a biological law like that governing any living being: each shot has a functional beauty, like a neck or an ankle. The smooth, orderly succession of shots has a rhythm like the pulsing of blood, and the whole film is like a beautiful body, kept alive by deep resilient breathing."[11] This rather poetical reading leads us to consider film, and specifically Hawks's films, in biological and aesthetic terms simultaneously.

THE FILM AND ITS HISTORICAL CONTEXT

The plot of the film, *To Have and Have Not,* is relatively simple, but I will outline it here in some depth, as its details are important for later discussions. It opens in the town of Fort de France in Martinique. Harry Morgan (Humphrey Bogart); his friend the alcoholic (or "rummy" as he is referred to in the film), Eddy (Walter Brennan); a man to cut and bait fish, Horatio (Sir Lancelot); and their client, Mr. Johnson (Walter Sande) set out for a day's fishing on Harry's boat, *The Queen Conch*. This is the sixteenth day of such ventures. Mr. Johnson hooks a marlin, but it gets away because he does not follow Harry's instruction. He catches another, but he loses it as well, along with Harry's tackle. Disappointed, they head back for shore where Johnson and Harry agree to the details of Johnson's bill, agree that Harry will be paid the following day "when the bank opens," and head back to the Hotel Marquis where they are both staying (and where most of the action of the film happens). Frenchy (Marcel Dalio), the owner of the hotel, approaches Harry in his room with a request to transport some "friends of friends" (who are fighting on the side of the Free French against the Vichy government in Martinique). Harry refuses, not wanting to get involved in politics. During their discussion, Slim (Lauren Bacall) appears in the doorway and famously asks if anybody has a match, easily catches the box Harry tosses to her, and disappears again.

Down in the hotel bar, Harry sees Slim with Johnson and catches her stealing Johnson's wallet. Having some stake in the contents of Johnson's wallet (Johnson still owes Harry $825 for the fishing expedition), Harry follows Slim upstairs and confronts her about her grab. She admits to stealing it because she needs the money to leave Martinique and because she simply does not like the man. This is logic that Harry can understand. Examining the contents of the wallet, Harry realizes that not only did Johnson have the money he owed Harry, but he also had a ticket to go back to the States at dawn. In the middle of their conversation, there is a knock on the door and Frenchy, with his Free French friends, enter to ask Harry for his help. Harry again refuses and they leave. Harry takes Slim and the wallet back down to the bar to confront Johnson. Johnson reluctantly agrees to sign over his traveler's checks, but as he begins the process the Free French leave and get shot outside the bar. A stray bullet kills Johnson before he can sign a single check.

After the shooting, the Vichy Prefect of Police, Captain Renard (Dan Seymore), arrives and takes Slim, Harry, and Frenchy down to the station for questioning. At the station, the captain takes all of Harry's money, allows Slim to get slapped in the face by one his officers for being insolent, and sends them on their way again. Harry and Slim go to a bar before realizing that neither of them has any money. Slim decides to hustle for a bottle and Harry leaves. Bottle in hand, Slim returns to Harry's room, and they get to know each other better. The bottle passes back and forth between their rooms several times as they get angry with each other and leave and return again. By the end of the evening, they are a couple. In order to provide Slim with enough money to leave Martinique, Harry takes Frenchy's job. Because the trip might be dangerous, Harry comes well armed.

When Harry and Eddy (who has stowed away on board despite Harry's refusal to carry him) get to the appointed place to pick up these "friends of friends," Harry discovers that he is picking up Paul de Bursac (Walter Szurovy), an important resistance leader, and his beautiful wife. On their way back to Martinique, they are discovered by a patrol boat. While Paul cowardly tries to turn himself in, Harry shoots out their searchlight and they get away, but in the process Paul is wounded. Frenchy hides Paul and his wife, Helene de Bursac, in the basement of the hotel. Again asked for help, Harry initially refuses to aid the wounded man, and again finally accepts and successfully operates on Paul with the able assistance of Slim. She has not left Martinique, but instead has a job singing at the hotel in order to be near Harry.

The next morning, Slim is solicitous of Harry, assuming a relationship, or rather, continuing and deepening their burgeoning one. He tells her that "there's no strings" on him. This avowal is barely out of his mouth when Harry is summoned to the aid of Eddy, who has been picked up by the police. They are trying to get Eddy drunk, but he keeps telling bigger and bigger fish stories (literally). Harry talks to the police, frees Eddy from their clutches, and Renard offers him quite a bit of money for information about the de Bursacs. Harry tells Renard he will think about it. Slim and Harry make plans to go away; their only worry is the absence of Eddy. Renard and two of his goons come up to Harry's room and inform him that they have picked up Eddy again, but instead of getting him drunk they are going to withhold alcohol from him, knowing that this might kill him. This bit of cruelty is the last straw for Harry. He shoots one of Renard's men, ties up Renard and the other officer, and beats them until they agree to release Eddy. Harry decides that looking out for himself alone is no longer enough. While he has Renard in his power, Harry makes him not only release his friend, but sign papers allowing the de Bursacs to leave the country. His political transformation can be summed up in his line to Frenchy, "Well, I like you and I don't like them." The final scene shows us Slim, Harry, and Eddy, happily leaving the bar to embark on their journey as independent fighters for the Free French.

As we will see, the plot of the film diverges dramatically from Hemingway's novel. Based on the assumption that even what is sometimes considered Hemingway's worst novel still somehow deserves to be respected, Robin Wood writes that "a feeling that Hemingway's novel had been betrayed" was one of the reasons for the film's "unflattering critical reception in this country in 1945."[12] Betrayal is a common-enough term in adaptation.[13] But before we explore its relationship with Hemingway's work, I would like to situate the film within its cinematic moment and in relation to some other films.

By 1945, there were a variety of prestige pictures based on a pantheon of highbrow authors, as well as very successful films based on the novels of decidedly middlebrow authors—Margaret Mitchell's *Gone with the Wind* (1939), for instance. The Academy Awards seemed to favor these sorts of productions. *All Quiet on the Western Front* (1930), *Mutiny on the Bounty* (1935), *Rebecca* (1940), *How Green Was My Valley* (1941), and *Mrs. Miniver* (1942) all won Best Picture and all were adaptations. In fact, in the twenty-five years from the inception of the Academy Awards until the year of the release of *To Have and Have Not,* there were only four Best Picture winners that were not based on a play, novel, or short story. Even the famous *Casablanca* (1943) was based on a play, *Everybody Comes to Rick's.* The case of *Casablanca* highlights a vivid double standard. In order to really be considered an adaptation, even a poor one, the original text has to be of a certain cultural standard, the author of a certain stature. As Leitch notes in "Adaptation Studies at the Crossroads," this reveals an inherent hierarchy not just of film but other popular forms.

> Because "literature," unlike "cinema," is already an honorific, however, any discussion of literature on screen, as opposed to journalism or comic books or video games on screen, will begin willy-nilly with a bias in favour of literature as both a privileged field (literary texts are what movies normally adapt) and an aesthetically sanctified field (literary texts have already been approved by a jury whose verdict on their film adaptations is still out).[14]

No one treats *Casablanca* as an adaptation.

It was the success of *Casablanca* that made Bogart into a romantic leading man. Until this point in his career, while he certainly had starring roles, he largely played character parts—gangsters and tough guys, mostly. The genius of *Casablanca* was to combine this tough-guy persona with the frustrated-romantic role. The screen persona that Bogart solidified and Hawks exploited was of a tough guy of extreme competence and confidence with a loving heart and romantic nature. The plots of *Casablanca* and *To Have and Have Not* certainly run along similar lines. An unflappable and competent loner in an exotic locale, who sticks his neck out for nobody, gets involved in the good fight through the love of a good woman.

Above the similarity of plot, there are a remarkable amount of similarities on the level of casting and character. Dan Seymour, who plays the fat prefect of police, Captain Renard, seems like he is doing an extremely poor Sydney Greenstreet impression. Greenstreet played opposite Bogart in both *The Maltese Falcon* and *Casablanca.*[15] (This similarity does not seem like a coincidental casting choice.) The name of his character even sounds awfully similar to the prefect of police in *Casablanca,* Captain Renault. Marcel Dalio, who plays Gerard/Frenchy, bears a passing resemblance to Peter Lorre. The character of Paul de Bursac shares much in common with Victor Laszlo as well as there being a vague likeness between the men who played them, Walter Szurovy and Paul Hienreid. These very specific similarities are worth pointing out because they are all elements created by the screenwriters after the success of *Casablanca*, and there can be no doubt that Warner Brothers was exploiting the unexpected success of the earlier film.

The screenplay was originally set in Cuba, but when the script was submitted to the Office of the Coordinator of Inter-American Affairs, it was rejected because it seemed to portray then-ally Cuba in a negative light. Rejection would have meant that the film could not have received an export license. The response nearly closed down production on the film. Hawks asked if the Office could suggest another location, and they offered up French Martinique. Bringing in William Faulkner, Hawks transformed the political context into the conflict between the Free French and the Vichy government.[16] This change made the comparison between *To Have and Have Not* and *Casablanca* even more explicit.

There is even a marked similarity between the opening of *Casablanca* and *To Have and Have Not*. But it is worthwhile as well to examine the very distinct differences between the two films. Both begin with a map. While *Casablanca*'s map is intensely flat, showing all of Europe and North Africa marked with movement that follows the voice-over (as the voice-over mentions the trip across North Africa, lines appear on the map marking the route), the map in *To Have and Have Not* is an extremely detailed map of Martinique. Hawks's map is topographical in appearance as opposed to the cartoonish outlines of the other. There is no context for thinking about Hawks's world. Martinique sits lonely in the ocean, not connected to Europe. While both films have a similar opening sequence, Hawks does not rely on a voice-over like the fairly extended one in *Casablanca*, despite the availability of Hemingway's text to set the tone and exposition. Instead, there is just a brief intertitle. The importance of this difference is that Hawks is not trying to establish a grand narrative of politics and romance. Rather, he creates a very small specific world that does not require outside context.

The lighting and the camera work are also remarkably different. *Casablanca*'s camera is in almost-constant motion and the lighting is showy as well. *To Have and Have Not*, on the other hand, has very distinct lighting, some very high-key elements, but they are always diegetically motivated. For example, every time someone lights a match (and someone is always lighting a match) Hawks puts a very subtle spotlight on their face, so they seem to glow in the light of the flame. There is no recourse to obvious soft-focus shots of Lauren Bacall (as there are of Ingrid Bergman), but she does light a lot of matches. The lighting has more in common with noir than with *Casablanca*. Often the characters weave in and out of the horizontal slats of light through Venetian blinds. While there is high contrast in the lighting, it is not the dramatic black-and-white world of *Casablanca,* but rather a world with more subtle gradations.

But it is on the level of character that the differences really come to light. One could never imagine Slim telling Harry Morgan that he has to do the thinking for both of them, as Ilsa implores Rick. Slim does not cry. She gets angry. She is independent. She offers him money. She gets a job. She is just as competent in the surgery scene as Harry himself, shown up in sharp contrast to the fainting Helene du Bursac. One could never imagine Slim telling Harry that she is frightened. Her moments of domesticity—as when she tries to help Harry off with his shoes, to draw his bath, to bring him breakfast—are clearly in line with Marie's character in the novel. These offers are genuine and while not accepted, they do not denigrate her in any way. She, too, wants to be of service. She might not understand all the politics of the region, but she clearly does understand the politics of personal relations. It is her perfectly timed match that prevents Harry from punching out Johnson and creating a row. Her perfect understanding of Harry's plan to shoot the police in his room, and her perfect execution of providing the weapon is proof of this.

Mast proposes that *To Have and Have Not* is, in fact, a direct riposte to *Casablanca:* "Contrary to the schematic opposition in *Casablanca* of love and honor, of tough pragmatism and noble idealism, of selfishness and sacrifice, or private and public morality, *To Have and Have Not* synthesizes these oppositions, which Hawks finds facile and deceptive."[17] The synthesis is where the alignment between Hawks and Hemingway is clearest. While *To Have and Have Not* shares such a considerable amount of narrative with Casablanca that it could be considered an adaptation of it (and was considered so by contemporary critics), *To Have and Have Not* is rather an adaptation of the novel despite the fact that the two texts share virtually no narrative elements.

HEMINGWAY AND HIS NOVEL

The biography of Ernest Hemingway has passed into American cultural mythology. His progression from cub reporter to a participant in World War I to his time in Paris in the 1920s, defining and exemplifying the Lost Generation, is the stuff of fantasy to a certain type of college student. He is a man's man, interested in sport and shooting. He ran through several wives, but still betrays a certain lost romanticism. Phillip Young, in his book *American Fiction, American Myth,* evokes "an old *New Yorker* cartoon of the hairy-chested writer clutching a single rose in a big fist" to express this "incongruous truth.

Fist and rose, both were real."[18] Firmly behind the Republicans in the Spanish Civil War, he makes a great deal of effort on their behalf, and is staunchly antifascist in whatever guise it might arise. In 1954, he wins the Nobel Prize for literature. After a long and debilitating depression, Hemingway kills himself with his own double-barreled shotgun in 1961.

Hemingway publishes *To Have and Have Not* in 1937. It is the depths of the Depression in the United States and the Spanish Civil War is waging, with repercussions that reach throughout Europe and decisively through Hemingway's literary and cultural milieu. In 1940, Hemingway publishes *For Whom the Bell Tolls* about Americans' involvement in Spain's Civil War. His resistance against fascism is not only on the level of foreign politics, but manifests against any system that takes away the dignity of the "common man."

To Have and Have Not began as a short story, "One Trip Across," and a companion piece, "The Tradesman's Return." Both stories feature the character of Harry Morgan and loosely make up the first two sections of the novel.[19] The novel is divided into three sections. The first is about 60 pages, the second, only 20, and the third a sprawling 180 pages. I point this out to indicate that the architecture of the book is uneven, to put it mildly. The opening section (Part One—Harry Morgan—Spring) is narrated from the first-person point of view of Harry Morgan. It takes place in Cuba, and the action begins in a café as Harry is being offered a job of landing three Cubans on the Florida Keys for some Cuban revolutionaries for $3,000, a job that Harry refuses. As the revolutionaries leave the café, they get shot down by unknown assailants. Johnson, who had hired Harry's boat for the previous two weeks, enters the cafe and they, with the "rummy" mate Eddy and Horatio, a black man who cuts bait, leave for the day's fishing. Johnson hooks and loses two marlins and Harry's fishing tackle. Johnson decides that he is done and will fly home the next day after paying Harry for the days of fishing and the tackle. Johnson skips town without paying Harry, leaving him broke. Not even having enough money to run some liquor back to the States, he agrees to pick up a dozen Chinese men for $1,200 and basically drown them. Planning on taking the trip alone, Harry refuses to take Eddy on as mate. Eddy sneaks on anyway. When they rendezvous with Mr. Sing, who had hired them, Harry picks up the men, takes the money, and then kills Mr. Sing, taking all the men close enough to land that they can walk to shore. He then goes back home to his wife, Marie, in Key West.

The second section is told in the third person and tells the story of Harry and his mate Wesley who are both shot after a skirmish with the law while running liquor. They are trying to dump the liquor when they are spotted by "one of the three most important men in the United States today" (as he describes himself) on a boat chartered from a friend of Harry's.[20] While the other captain tries to steer them away from the sight of the rumrunners, the end result is that Harry loses his arm to a bullet, and his boat to the excise men.

"Part Three—Harry Morgan—Winter" begins with a chapter that notes "Albert Speaking" (91). Albert is a regular guy working on relief. Harry gets a proposition from a lawyer, who Harry refers to as Beelips, to carry some different revolutionaries from Key West to Cuba for 200 dollars, and Harry convinces Albert to come along to make some extra money. Harry narrates the second chapter while he thinks about the plan, and the rest of the novel is told in the third person. This final section is rather a muddle as the narrator switches attention from Harry's story to those of a series of "Have's" referred to in the novel's title and back again. For our purposes, Harry's story is the most important, so I will not go into the details of the other narrative elements that Hemingway introduces at this point. The novel itself does not particularly hold together. Hemingway switches narrators and points of view throughout. For a large chunk, Harry Morgan is the first-person narrator, then Hemingway mixes omniscient and first-person narrators, then Morgan's friend Albert takes it up, describing his own life and Morgan's.

Hemingway's prose has been described as an iceberg, one-eighth above the surface and the rest hidden below. It is always the unsaid, the hinted at, the glancingly touched upon that form the meat of a Hemingway novel, and *To Have and Have Not* is no exception. Hemingway describes his own process of writing in terms of billiards: "I always try to do the thing by three cushion shots rather than by words or direct statements," and this movement is a "metaphor for pictorial discourse, the cinematic language of reality."[21] While much of the novel is made up of first-person narration, a great deal is portrayed in dialogue. Hemingway's reliance on dialogue would seem to make him ideally suited for the transition to film, and certainly many of his works were adapted. In addition, his descriptions have a visual clarity that also translates well into film. In fact, many of the stage directions in the screenplay are lifted directly from the novel.

HAWKS AND HIS PROCESS

There are deep stylistic similarities between Hawks and Hemingway. Hawks even claims to have learned his style of dialogue from Hemingway: "Well, Hemingway calls it oblique dialogue. I call it three-cushion. Because you hit it over here and over here and go over here to get the meaning. You don't state it right out."[22] With two such inveterate storytellers, it is impossible to say who came up with the phrase "three-cushion" first. Nor is it particularly important. As Mast points out, "both developed a style—either verbal or visual—which was distinguished for its spare, bare, understatement. Interestingly enough, while literary critics praised Hemingway's authority for the idiosyncrasies of it bareness, to many film critics Hawks's functional style seemed simply styleless—'uncinematic' or typically Hollywood."[23] This is an ideal starting point to begin a discussion of Hawks. His films seem so effortless as to be artless. But in fact, Hawks's work reveals a distinct style. As my earlier discussion of the intersection between *To Have and Have Not* and *Casablanca* shows, Hawks was a different sort of filmmaker than many of his cohorts in Hollywood.

Hawks made movies in nearly every popular genre: westerns, screwball comedies, war movies, even a musical. Hawks criticism is equally divergent: from Joseph McBride's wonderfully intimate and hilarious series of conversations and anecdotes with Hawks, to Gerald Mast's loving and attentive reading, to Robin Wood's political interpretations. James Agee and Hawks's contemporary critics and scholars thought Hawks was a hack or simply dismissed him as typical Hollywood. But through the years he has been read and interpreted by feminists, Marxists, and even Jungians. But a transformative moment in the history of Hawks criticism was the French New Wave's embrace. In 1953, Jacques Rivette's influential article in *Cahiers du cinéma*, "The Genius of Howard Hawks," proposes Hawks as an auteur. Hawks can stand as an example of the strengths and limits of auteur theory. He was an intensely collaborative director and producer, and yet he left a distinctive mark on every movie he directed. While I am not particularly interested in making the auteur argument, it provides us with a place to begin thinking about Hawks's styles and themes.

Hawks has a "uniquely clean, efficient, entertaining, and classical style."[24] For all of his sparseness and lack of tricky photography, Hawks is a master of subjective camera work. He disdains a first-person point-of-view shot, but at the same time, he always follows his main characters. They are rarely not in a shot, and we, the audience, exist in the same space with them, being where they are and perceiving their reactions to things we see. He walks the line between subjective and objective camera work. As Mast explicates, "Howard Hawks's films define space not physically but psychologically. Space is neither two- nor three-dimensional but saturated with the feelings, perceptions, attitudes, and values of the storyteller. Hawks's control of point-of-view makes his images represent not physical seeing but psychological feeling—and in so doing, he fuses the two senses of cinema point-of-view (as a character's seeing and a storyteller's judging) into one."[25] Hemingway attempts this exact process in his novel—s witching between points of view to create a world that is whole in all of its complication.

Hawks says that he likes to play violence fast, so fast that you are not really sure what happened.[26] In this novel, Hemingway takes a similar approach.

This might seem counterintuitive as he spreads Morgan's death over the last ninety pages of the book. But the action—the gunfight that leaves five men dead—only lasts for a page and a half (170–72). Hawks is continually described as a director devoted to action, to physicality. He seems a good match for Hemingway's muscular, straightforward prose where the psychological perception is present, but left unsaid.

Throughout his work, Hawks pays a great deal of attention to objects: the last bits of things scraped up from the runway in *Only Angels Have Wings* (1939), the naughty pictures and guns in *The Big Sleep*. But Hawks's camera never lingers on the objects, but rather on the faces of those who interact with them. There is never a moment in Hawks's films when you get the idea that a mere object is significant all on its own. And this markedly differs from other comparable films. Michael Curtiz lingers on the letters of transit in *Casablanca* and also endows songs with an object-like quality of a memento, both "As Time Goes By" and "The Marseillaise." (And certainly John Huston spends a great deal of time examining the Maltese Falcon.) Objects are not important in themselves for Hawks, but rather for what they mean and for what function they serve to the characters. Take the wonderful bit of business with the bottle in *To Have and Have Not*. It gets passed back and forth between Slim and Harry three times, and each time serves to both clarify and intensify their relationship. The last handoff ends in a kiss that seals their relationship.

Hawks said that he liked to make every film into a comedy if he could. His transformation of Hemingway's novel certainly proves this desire. The difference between the novel and the screenplay and then the difference between the screenplay and the film confirms it. Compared to the novel and earlier versions of the screenplay, the film is quite spare when it comes to plot. It is the richness of the relationships that comes through. But even the relationships are simplified and clarified during the transition from the screenplay to what was actually filmed.

A critical aspect of Hawks's filmmaking process is the screenwriting praxis he fostered. Jules Furthman worked with Hawks on several screenplays and wrote the first several versions of the script. Hawks always insisted on good writers and he got them, but he always worked with them throughout the process.[27] He asked Furthman, "Do you suppose we could make a girl who is insolent, as insolent as Bogart, who insults people, who grins when she does it, and people like it?"[28] In addition, Hawks would do extensive rewriting on the set, molding lines to suit an actor, even though he would dismiss such claims: "You're not really re-writing it, you're just saying it in different words, with a different attitude."[29] Even working on a film with two Pulitzer Prize–winning authors, Hawks wrote the most famous line in the film, "You don't have to do anything. Not a thing…Oh maybe…just whistle.…"

Hawks and his other screenwriter, Faulkner, were good friends, as well as colleagues. Hawks even claims to have brought Faulkner to the attention of the New York literati. They worked on several screenplays together. Hawks said of their collaboration, "We seemed to talk the same language. He knew what I wanted... Bill loved working on it [*To Have and Have Not*] because it was Hemingway's. He wanted to change it."[30] All of the produced screenplays that Faulkner got screen credit for were for Hawks except one.[31] Bruce Kawin calls Faulkner "the most cinematic of novelists."[32] By this he means that André Bazin's notion of "ideal cinema" is reflected in the greatest novels and stories of Faulkner but only pops up occasionally in the films he helped to write—that Faulkner at his best was thinking not in terms of movies but in tropes that are most convincingly explicated in cinematic terms.[33] Interestingly, Kawin says of Faulkner what Eugene Kanjo says of Hemingway—that they used this "cinematic style," drawn heavily from montage, in their work.[34]

Ironically, some to the best lines in the film are written by neither Furthman, Hemingway, nor Faulkner, but lifted from other films entirely. When Slim is asked by the police why she came to Martinique, she says, "To buy a new hat," a line lifted from *The Grand Hotel* (Goulding, 1932). And another, "I'm hard to get, Steve. All you have to do is ask me," was said by Jean Arthur in *Only Angels Have Wings*, which did have Furthman as a screenwriter, but it is anyone's guess where the line originated.

This sort of collaborative process not only challenges the notion of the auteur, but of adaptation itself. The idea that adaptation consists of one person working to translate another's work into a different medium still carries weight in the writing around adaptation. However, as we are beginning to see, this is complicated by the sheer number of people involved in making a movie. I do not want to discount the strength of Hawks's abiding vision that pulls the variety of elements together, but nor is it possible for me to discount the distinct work done by others and even the exigencies of the medium. This is where my notion of adaptation being systemic and reciprocal becomes critical.

Hawks is making this film for Warner Brothers. That is one system to which he belongs. It is produced as the United States is entering the Second World War—a larger system. The changes necessitated by those systems have profound effects on the final version of the film. In addition, the screenwriters, both Furthman and Faulkner, help to transform the plot, adapt to those systems, and choose narrative strains and dialogue to retain and to discard. One could think of the various drafts of the script as "states" in Rappaport's terms, as responses to the environment. In a very loose sort of way we could consider Hawks the primary environment that affects those states, and the texts, novel and film taken together, as the living system that is changed. The actors play their role in the transformation as do the lighting, camera work, and sound. Rappaport's definition is broad enough to address all these disparate elements and begin to put them together.

TRANSFER, PLOT, AND CHARACTER

One can clearly see from my description of the plots that the two texts are significantly different. However, it is worthwhile to compare them at specific lines of intersection and difference in order to explore their thematic congruencies. One of the most interesting changes is the amount of money Harry is offered for the rather risky venture of illegally transporting people. In the novel, he is offered $5,000, a tempting offer for a man in his situation. In the film, he is only offered 50 bucks. While his acceptance of the offer is attributed to getting enough money to help Slim leave the island, it is clear that there is more at work in his acceptance. It is a move toward political commitment rather than monetary interest. This shift is also apparent when Frenchy asks him to doctor the wounded de Bursac. While he initially refuses Frenchy's request ("Not a chance, Frenchy"), when the cashier comes up with the bill and offers to dismiss it in exchange for his assistance, he laughingly gives in but says, "I'll still owe you that bill." While money remains important for Harry's character, it is not what involves him in the political action. As Mast writes, "Harry's 'sympathies' for the people he likes, however, will require his political 'sympathies' to evolve as well."[35]

This is a key difference because the proposition by the revolutionaries is one of the explicitly shared plot points between the novel and the film. While the setting is different, and the opposition fighters are less ambiguous in the film, it is the turning point in both. In the novel, Harry's involvement ends in a bloodbath and his own long, agonizing death. While he has some sympathy for the Cubans fighting Machado, he neither trusts them nor approves of their methods. In their escape from the bank robbery, Albert objects to carrying them on the boat and he is summarily shot. One of the revolutionaries apologizes and tries to explain: their purpose is to help workers in Cuba, and the terrorist activity, the killing, the bank robbery is just in service to the revolution. Harry thinks to himself, "What the hell do I care about his revolution. F——his revolution. To help the working man he robs a bank and kills a fellow works with him and then kills that poor damn Albert that never did any harm. That's a working man he kills. He never thinks of that. With a family... The hell with their revolutions. All I got to do is make a living for my family and I can't do that. And then he tells about his revolution. The hell with his revolution" (168). But in a curious way the two stories are linked; it is his wife and family that serve as his motivation in the novel, in the same way that Slim and Eddy serve as Harry's in the film.

In Hemingway's novel, it seems that what Harry is carrying is immaterial. It is the activity of transporting that is important, not the stuff on board (be it men or liquor). Neither Hawks nor Hemingway has much patience with exposition. Neither of them linger on action, but rather invest their energy in their characters. Hawks's lack of concern over the details of his plots is why he had such an easy relationship with the censors. Because so much is invested in the characters, what actual things happen, where they happen, or even what can be shown becomes less important to him. His ease with the censors allowed him to film some of the raciest dialogue in Hollywood at the time.

While it remains true that Hawks is a director of action, the action is centered firmly on the characters and their figures. By looking at the characters, their relation to the characterization in the novel, and finally at the reciprocal circuit that exists in this film between the star personas of Bogart, Brennan, and Bacall and their characters in the film, we can see the strength of Rappaport's definition of adaptation. *To Have and Have Not* provides an apotheosis of this relationship.

It is the characters that form the most intriguing and explicit transfer and adaptation of the novel into the film. The character of Eddy in the novel is described as tall and sloppy. "He walked with his joints all slung wrong" (9). While this line is not present in the final screenplay, it does aptly describe Walter Brennan's wonderful gait in his portrayal of Eddy, all loose and jerky. There is another bit of stage direction lifted word for word from the novel to describe Eddy: "standing there, tall and hollow cheeked, with his mouth loose and that white stuff in the corners of his eyes and his hair all faded in the sun...dead for a drink" (18–19).[36] Likewise, the description of Horatio in the screenplay is directly from the novel's description of the man who cut bait while out fishing with Mr. Johnson.[37] It is intriguing that the two, both spare and direct in description, should so exactly align.

The lingering traces of Hemingway that did not get eliminated from the screenplay are often startling. In the film, Harry refers to the police chief, Renard, as "Beelips," which at least makes some sort of sense as the actor does have full red lips. In the novel, it is a lawyer that is called "Beelips," and it is completely unexplained. The nicknames that the two characters in the film inexplicably have for each other, Steve and Slim, are from Hawks's own marriage.[38] Their mutual love for the unexplained nickname is another example of the deep similarity between Hawks and Hemingway.

The most obvious difference between the novel and the film lies in the change of time frame. In the novel, Harry Morgan is forty-five and his wife is two years older: they have been married for years. The film takes place at an earlier time in their history—before they married, before everything went bad. Harry is a far more sympathetic figure in the film. Talking about why he decided not to make Harry one armed as he was in the novel, Hawks said it was just too technically difficult. Furthermore, the only thing it adds to the story is a dimension of Marie and Harry's relationship, "the girl made that one arm into as asset. She received the one arm and got a physical kick out of it. He poked it in her. That was a great relationship—a girl that would do that. So that gave us a lot of ideas about the relationship."[39] The women in *To Have and Have Not* are remarkably loving for a Hemingway novel. The importance of the change of the time frame is the change in characters it allows.

One of the most dramatic changes is the control of point of view in the film. Hemingway's wanders throughout his novel. In the film, however, as Mast writes, "Harry Morgan's perceptions exclusively control the film's narrative point-of-view; there is not a single scene in which Harry is not present."[40] However, Hemmeter and Sweeney note that Harry and Slim's "scenes of conflict often feature a rigorous crosscutting between equal combatants" and that "we get point-of-view shots from her perspective...and from his perspective."[41] This combination of subjective camera work and multiple points of view mirrors Hemingway's (less successful) work in the novel.

But finally, the point of view of the film is focused on the actions of the main characters. As the couple develops, Slim gets more and more camera time, and more shots from her own perspective. Mast writes, "Slim is tough enough, wise and clever enough, witty and sensible enough, to conquer the smaller tasks, which eventually will allow her to conquer the bigger ones."[42] One of the crucial shots in the film is exclusively from her perspective. In the climactic scene when Harry and Slim are confronted by Renard and his men, Harry gets angrier and angrier, and, while still keeping his laconic cool, more and more ready to act. Harry asks Slim to get him a cigarette that he keeps in the drawer of his desk. As she opens the drawer we get a shot that only she could see: the gun in the drawer. She, calmly and intuitively understanding, leaves the drawer open so the Harry can grab the gun and shoot one of Renard's men. Not only is her help, her calm, her cool, needed to complete the action, but it is her view that allows us, the viewers, to know what is happening. Hawks is fully aware of the importance of this shot. As he tells Robin Wood, "The success of the action...depends on a spontaneous, split-second timing and the partnership between man and woman. The sudden violence of the bullet ripping through wood to secure the characters' freedom is at once the explosion and the relief of the accumulated tensions of the whole film."[43]

In many ways, Slim has two roles to play. She is not only the love interest, but also the trusted friend that we often see in Hawks's films.

The dynamics of sexual play and the love interest is often secondary to this friendship. While Harry does have a friend, Eddy, he is more of a burden, a "string" tying Harry down, than a helper. And yet Eddy will unexpectedly help out the action, if not Harry. Eddy's rescue becomes a device around which the plot turns, rather than the more frequently seen love interest that serves this function. The fact that Slim has this dual function gives her a fierce weight in the film, and makes their love affair, and of course Bacall's portrayal, unique among Hawks's films, and unique in Hollywood. While Bacall is wonderful in many other films, never does she recapture the raw magnetism she has in this role.

Richard Dyer claims that Hawks divides the "female world into manipulative feminine women and likeable masculine (or non-feminine) women."[44] The whole assumption that a woman must somehow be like a man to be likeable in Dyer's universe, or at least his portrayal of Hawks's universe, is deeply problematic. Significantly, there is no mention of Lauren Bacall in this discussion. She is *both* feminine and likeable. Mast, on the other hand, sees Hawks as somehow undoing cultural stereotyping through his portrayal of women by showing that women were not "somehow less feminine if they were smart, shrewd, talented, and tough."[45]

If one thinks of women in Hawks's films, they are always strong, interesting, attractive, and assertive. But they are not quite like Lauren Bacall's portrayal of Slim. Think of Jean Arthur in *Only Angels Have Wings*. She is tough, or at least has the sense to hide her weaknesses, and she is a performer. But she will not stop talking. Even Rosalind Russell in *His Girl Friday* is not sexy the way that Bacall is. I could go on with the list of wonderful female characters, but there is no denying that there is something different about this role and about this actress. Bacall has a sort of trembling stillness and vulnerability coupled with that insolence for which Hawks was reaching. It is stunning. This is Bacall's best and defining role.

Mast writes that "*To Have and Have Not* gets it depth, complexity, and vitality from its characters as performers and its performers as characters."[46] This reciprocal understanding of the relations between performer and character is a critical one, both for an understanding of the film and as another element of the adaptive system. Actors loved working with Hawks because he would manipulate the text so that it fit the personality of the actor.[47] Humphrey Bogart is a Hemingway man. Harry Morgan is irresistible to women, as incomprehensibly as Bogart himself. And yet there it is. Incontrovertible. Unflappable. While originally lined up for roles like those of Edward G. Robinson, Bogart created the cynical romantic and above all competent persona that still resonates. Bogart as Rick in *Casablanca* is not honest, but he is good. In *To Have and Have Not*, Bogart as Harry is honest to a fault, but not particularly good. There is no role he plays as leading man where he is ever at a loss. This competency is an important theme in both Hemingway and Hawks.

THEMES

One of the most striking and touching aspects of the novel is Harry and Marie's relationship, but it is secondary to the plot of the novel. While an avowed intention of Hemingway's was to write a political novel, Hawks's reading of it as a love story is really the meat of it, even if this is not the love story that is articulated in the novel. In the novel, Harry and Marie love each other in a straightforward way that is obviously appealing to Hawks. Marie supports Harry in all of his ventures, and in return he does all his work for her. They are without judgment in their loving. None of the other relationships in the novel have this quality. They describe bad marriages and bad relationships, which throws Harry and Marie's into sharp relief. Linda Welshimer Wagner writes in *Hemingway and Faulkner: Inventors/Masters* that *To Have and Have Not*, "The Snows of Kilimanjaro," and "The Short Happy Life of Francis Macomber" share a sub-theme: "the possible relationship between husband and wife, here too used as an objective correlative for man's relationship with life."[48] According to Gerald Mast, it was "The Short Happy Life" that Hawks had always wanted to make, but somehow it was a project that always got delayed.

Interestingly, Philip Young claims that the theme of the novel is really desperation, "a profound loss of hope for the lot of man" and more interestingly, that this theme is voiced by Harry's wife, Marie.[49] The importance Young places in Marie is the opposite of that posited by Thomas Hemmeter and Kevin W. Sweeney in their article "Marriage as Moral Community: Cinematic Critiques of Hemingway's *To Have and Have Not*." They argue that Harry's relationship with his "passive" wife, Marie, is not particularly important in the development of the novel as opposed to its filmic adaptation.[50] While Marie (Slim) carries a more important function in the film (she certainly get more time and attention), their easy dismissal of her positioning in the novel is misjudged, as it is for her that Harry gets into trouble. She is the motivation of his actions. This relationship between life and love is critical to Hawks. Throughout his films it is something he is always working out. And as I have explored above, Slim is a critical to the action of the film.

Of equal significance is the notion of work, which again puts the film into a very interesting relationship with Hemingway. *To Have and Have Not* is Hemingway's proletariat novel. Harry Morgan is the protagonist, but he is not learned, bookish, or even particularly educated. But he can work and wants to work but refuses to get on the assistance program that he feels dehumanizes workers, takes away their pride. He goes it alone. He realizes that this refusal to be helped, to work with others, is his undoing. Harry Morgan's last words were "No matter how a man alone ain't got no bloody fucking chance" (225). This is the tragedy and the irony of the novel. Work finally kills Harry, but at least he dies working. Hawks's themes in general, as Robin Wood notes, circle around "the assertion of basic human qualities of courage and endurance, the stoical insistence of innate human dignity."[51] In Hawks's film, Harry Morgan is also a worker, and it is through work that both love and politics are worked out. And it all works out.

Finally, it is their politics, or rather politics as an extension of a personal morality, that bring Hemingway, Faulkner, and Hawks into alignment. In a letter, Hemingway writes that he would not produce propaganda for the Second World War, but rather: "There is plenty of stuff that you believe absolutely that you can write which is useful enough without having to write propaganda...If we are fighting for what we believe in we might as well always keep on believing what we believed, and for me this is to write nothing that I do not think is the absolute truth."[52] This comment not only attests to the relationship Hemingway had with the war, his belief in its principles, but also reveals his own personal credo: a commitment to the integrity of his own beliefs and a sort of professionalism, a notion that his work should be "useful," an idea clearly in line with both Hawks's and Faulkner's attitudes. Faulkner gave a high school commencement address for his daughter Jill in which he told the graduates never to be afraid "to raise your voice for honesty and truth and compassion, against lying and greed. If you...will do this, you will change the earth."[53] Again, the themes of honesty and use shine through. His acceptance speech for the Nobel Prize points to the universal truths that need to come through storytelling: "love and honor and pity and pride and compassion and sacrifice."[54] While Hawks claimed not be interested in "political intrigue," he insists on a personal code of ethics. Robin Wood even claims that *To Have and Have Not* "embodies one of the most basic anti-Fascist statements the cinema has given us...The protest is against any authoritarian interference with the rights of the individual."[55] In the adaptation of *To Have and Have Not,* we can see the personal and political ethos of these three important figures of the time come into direct alignment.

SYSTEMATIC AND RECIPROCAL CREATION

I have discussed adaptation in two ways throughout this paper, both in the conventional sense of transforming a text into a different medium, and as systemic and reciprocal practice of creation. I think finally it is the second that yields more fruit. Exploring the intersection and differences between the texts provides a clear reading of a process of creation. And that process is far more complex than any simple transference of plot and character from novel to screen. By having the flexibility to explore all the different states and structures that created the transformation of one text into another, we open up any closed notion about adaptation. The film and the text have a rich alignment, as do all the people who were part of their development. *To Have and Have Not* stretches the limits of conventional notions of adaptation. Through exploring it in depth, we have arrived at a more flexible model. It needs to be thought of as a Warners picture, a Hawks film, a Hemingway adaptation, a Faulkner screenplay, a response to *Casablanca,* and a Bogart/ Bacall vehicle simultaneously. It is only through holding all of these in our heads at once, juggling them around to see how they fit, thinking of them as a system, that the true richness of the text emerges.

NOTES

1. Howard Hawks, interview by Joseph McBride, *Hawks on Hawks*, ed. Joseph McBride (Berkeley and Los Angeles: University of California Press, 1982), 94–95.
2. The opening credits of *The Big Sleep* (1946), for instance, list Raymond Chandler after the actors, on the same screen as the screenwriters.
3. Hawks, *Hawks on Hawks*, 94.
4. This concern for the aesthetic instead of the functional is shared by Robert Stam. Indeed, we both engage in what used to be known as "close-reading" of the texts under discussion. However, as we shall see, the contexts of those readings are markedly different. He addresses the issues he sees the "filmic adapter" facing; historical and social concerns are understood in terms of changing styles. Stam, *Literature through Film: Realism, Magic, and the Art of Adaption* (Malden, Mass.: Wiley Blackwell, 2004), 17–18.
5. Linda Hutcheon explores the conundrum of collaborations and adaptation and broadens the elements normally considered adaptable by tackling not just the usual suspects of directors and screenwriters, but also the actors, editors, music, and costume designers. This broadened approach is critical to a rich understanding of process of adaptation. See Hutcheon, *A Theory of Adaptation* (New York: Routledge, 2005) 80–83.
6. Gerald Mast, *Howard Hawks, Storyteller* (Oxford: Oxford University Press, 1984), 38.
7. Roy A. Rappaport, *Ritual and Religion in the Making of Humanity* (Cambridge: Cambridge University Press, 1999), 408.
8. Imelda Whelehan, "Adaptations: The Contemporary Dilemma," in *Adaptations: From Text to Screen, Screen to Text,* ed. Deborah Cartmell and Imelda Whelehan (New York: Routledge, 1999), 3.

9. Thomas Leitch, "Adaptation Studies at a Crossroads," in *Adaptation* 1, no. 1 (2008): 64.

10. Rappaport, *Ritual and Religion*, 414.

11. Jacques Rivette, "The Genius of Howard Hawks," in *Focus on Howard Hawks*, ed. Joseph McBride (Englewood Cliffs, N.J.: Prentice-Hall, 1972), 73.

12. Robin Wood, *Howard Hawks* (Garden City, N.Y.: Doubleday, 1968), 24.

13. Robert Stam offers a robust list of synonyms and their connotations: "Terms like 'infidelity,' 'betrayal,' 'deformation,' 'violation,' 'bastardization,' 'vulgarization,' and 'desecration' proliferate in adaptation discourse, each word carrying its specific charge of opprobrium. 'Infidelity' carries overtones of Victorian prudishness; 'betrayal' evokes ethical perfidy; 'bastardization' connotes illegitimacy; 'deformation' implies aesthetic disgust and monstrosity; 'violation' calls to mind sexual violence; 'vulgarization' conjures up class degradation; and 'desecration' intimates religious sacrilege and blasphemy." Stam, *Literature and Film: A Guide to the Theory and Practice of Film Adaptation,* ed. Robert Stam and Alessandro Raengo. (Malden, Mass.: Blackwell Publishing, 2005), 3.

14. Leitch, "Adaptation Studies at a Crossroads," 63.

15. Seymour's wild overacting and pronunciation, as hammy as they are, are rather charming in the film.

16. For further historical details, see Bruce Kawin, "Introduction: No Man Alone," in Jules Furthman and William Faulkner, *To Have and Have Not: The Screenplay*, ed. Bruce Kawin (Madison: University of Wisconsin Press, 1980), 9–54; and Gene D. Phillips, *Hemingway and Film* (New York: Frederick Ungar Publishing Co., 1980).

17. Mast, *Howard Hawks, Storyteller*, 286.

18. Philip Young, *American Fiction, American Myth: Essays by Philip Young* (University Park: Pennsylvania State University Press, 2000), 89.

19. Phillips, *Hemingway and Film*, 49.

20. Ernest Hemingway, *To Have and Have Not* (New York: Scribner, 2003), 80. All further references are cited parenthetically by page number in the text.

21. Hemingway, quoted in Eugene Kanjo, "Hemingway's Cinematic Style," in *A Moving Picture Feast: The Filmgoer's Hemingway*, ed. Charles M. Oliver (New York: Praeger, 1989), 3.

22. Hawks, *Hawks on Hawks*, 32.

23. Mast, *Howard Hawks, Storyteller*, 246.

24. Kawin, "Introduction: No Man Alone," 41.

25. Mast, *Howard Hawks, Storyteller*, 44.

26. Hawks, *Hawks on Hawks*, 65.

27. Hawks, *Hawks on Hawks*, 30–32.

28. Hawks, *Hawks on Hawks*, 100.

29. Hawks, *Hawks on Hawks*, 34.

30. Hawks, *Hawks on Hawks*, 56–57.

31. Gene D. Phillips, *Fiction, Film, and Faulkner: The Art of Adaptation* (Knoxville: University of Tennessee Press, 1988), 27.

32. Bruce Kawin, "The Montage Element in Faulkner's Fiction," in *Faulkner, Modernism, Film: Faulkner and Yoknapatawpha, 1978*, ed. Evans Harrington and Ann J. Abadie (Jackson: University of Mississippi, 1979), 105.

33. Kawin, "Montage Element," 105.

34. Kanjo, "Hemingway's Cinematic Style," 3–5.

35. Mast, *Howard Hawks, Storyteller*, 262.

36. Furthman and Faulkner, *To Have and Have Not: The Screenplay*, 72–73.

37. Furthman and Faulkner, *To Have and Have Not: The Screenplay*, 73.

38. Hawks, *Hawks on Hawks*, 34.

39. Hawks, *Hawks on Hawks*, 79.

40. Mast, *Howard Hawks, Storyteller*, 251.

41. Thomas Hemmeter and Kevin W. Sweeney, "Marriage as Moral Community: Cinematic Critiques of Hemingway's *To Have and Have Not*," in *A Moving Picture Feast*, 66–67, 69.

42. Mast, *Howard Hawks, Storyteller*, 266.

43. Wood, *Howard Hawks*, 30.

44. Richard Dyer, *Stars*, new ed. with supplementary chapter by Paul McDonald (London: BFI Publishing, 1998), 156.

45. Mast, *Howard Hawks, Storyteller*, 61.

46. Mast, *Howard Hawks, Storyteller*, 252.

47. Mast, *Howard Hawks, Storyteller*, 54–55.

48. Linda Welshimer Wagner, *Hemingway and Faulkner: Inventors/Masters* (Metuchen, N.J.: The Scarecrow Press, 1975), 77. In this full-length study of Faulkner and Hemingway, no mention is made of Faulkner's work on the screenplay of Hemingway's novel, nor indeed, any of Faulkner's work in Hollywood at all.

49. Young, *American Fiction, American Myth*, 95.

50. Hemmeter and Sweeney, "Marriage as Moral Community," 66–67.

51. Wood, *Howard Hawks*, 23–29.

52. Hemingway, quoted from a 1942 letter to Maxwell Perkins in *Hemingway on War*, ed. Sean Hemingway (New York: Scribner, 2003), 399.

53. Faulkner, quoted in Gene Phillips, *Fiction, Film and Faulkner*, 183.

54. Faulkner, quoted in Gene Phillips, *Fiction, Film and Faulkner*, 183.

55. Wood, *Howard Hawks*, 26.

The Virgin Suicides (Coppola, 1999)

6

HAPPIER WITH DREAMS

Constructing the Lisbon Girls through Nondiegetic Sound in
The Virgin Suicides

Stephanie McKnight

From the opening shot of Sofia Coppola's *The Virgin Suicides* (1999), the hypnotic musical score, originally produced, composed, and performed by Air, is coupled with dreamlike images; the first is that of teenaged Lux Lisbon (Kirsten Dunst) bathed in hazy golden light, sucking on a popsicle. This Lolita-esque image of Lux, together with a mesmerizing instrumental excerpt from Air's "Highschool Lover," sets the tone of the film and establishes Lux Lisbon as not only frozen in time in our collective male narrator's memory, but also as the narrator's fantasy. A hazy montage of idyllic, 1970s upper-middle-class Michigan suburbia begins as Air's music continues to play: images of beautiful homes, manicured lawns, sprinklers, and white people leisurely milling about their neighborhood flash on the screen. But within this montage is a shot of workers in orange suits nailing a "Notice for Removal" sign to a tree. Thus, the image track immediately informs us of the inevitability of death. Moreover, the sound of sirens and the haunting "Highschool Lover" further complicate any simplistic pleasure or sense of innocence we might derive from the image track alone.

Air's music then halts abruptly, but the sound of sirens remains combined with the ominous slow drip of a faucet. We see a blue-filtered close-up of a lifeless Cecilia Lisbon (Hanna Hall) lying face up in a bathtub filled with blood-tinted water. A male voiceover (Giovanni Ribisi) overlays Cecilia's image: "Cecilia was the first to go." Air's music resumes as we return to the golden-filtered suburban world with a medium shot of several boys—whom we will soon identify as part of the collective adult male narrator performing the voiceover—watching Cecilia being loaded into an ambulance. The music halts again with an abrupt cut to a bluish-green-filtered hospital room. We see Cecilia lying in a hospital bed, and in the film's first instance of diegetic dialogue, the faceless doctor asks her: "What are you doing here honey? You're not even old enough to know how bad life gets." To which Cecilia replies: "Obviously, doctor, you've never been a thirteen-year-old girl."

Air's music kicks in again, this time with "Clouds Up"—a similarly haunting instrumental piece—as we abruptly cut back to images of the upper-class tree-lined suburbs rolling by, as if from the perspective of a passenger looking out a car's side window. The camera pushes upward through the trees, the sun filtering through the diseased-looking leaves and branches, as we continue to hear "Clouds Up," the nondiegetic music receiving an emphasis equal to that of the image track. The image of the sun peering through the trees slowly dissolves into a cloud-filled, hazy blue sky, slowly superimposed with multiple "The Virgin Suicides" title graphics, each in a handwritten style of a young girl, reminiscent of playful doodling in a diary, further complicating the opening sequence through elements of frivolity combined with sexuality and death (conveyed through both the image and sound tracks). The title graphics dissolve into a close-up of a smiling Lux Lisbon looking seductively into the camera, briefly superimposed on the cloud-filled sky. We hear the nondiegetic sound of a bell chiming as Lux winks at us like a fairy, then her image disappears, leaving us with a wispy impression, and only the sky and Air's music remain.

The voiceover resumes: "Everyone dates the demise of our neighborhood from the suicides of the Lisbon girls." The voice is coupled visually with the cloud-filled sky and continues as a sound bridge to a shot of the same 1970s suburban neighborhood that we've already seen, overlaid with a "Michigan 25 years ago" handwritten-style graphic. The two nondiegetic sound elements—Air's music and the voiceover—work not only as sound bridges between the dreamy Lux close-up and the shot of the suburban neighborhood, but also as narrative bridges between the subjective, fantasy/memory framework of the film (represented by the image of Lux), and the actual events surrounding the suicides, which a group of adult males, twenty-five years later, are trying to piece together (represented by the shot of the neighborhood).

Air's music combined with images of the Lisbon girls—Lux and Cecilia in the opening sequence—heightens the subjective male view of the girls as otherworldly beings, while Ribisi's voice maintains the presence of that male view, and the adultness of the voice reminds us of the collective narrator's distance from the 1970s world on the screen. The audience is kept at a distance from the Lisbon girls just as the grown men looking back at them through their clouded memories and pieced-together investigation are also kept forever at a distance from them. The opening sequence exemplifies what I will show occurs throughout the film: it uses nondiegetic sound to place the film's focus on the mere impression, as opposed to the reality, of the Lisbon girls that the men are left with at the end of Jeffrey Eugenides's *The Virgin Suicides* (1993), the source text for Coppola's adaptation.

In a film adaptation, there are many dynamic ways to translate and transform the source text. As Robert Stam writes:

> The shift from a single-track, uniquely verbal medium such as the novel, which "has only words to play with," to a multitrack medium such as film, which can play not only with words (written and spoken), but also with theatrical performance, music, sound effects, and moving photographic images, explains the unlikelihood—and I would suggest even the undesirability—of literal fidelity. Because novels do not usually feature soundtracks, for example, should the filmmaker deprive him or herself of music as an expressive resource?[1]

The expressive resources that Coppola most effectively employs in her transformation of Eugenides's source text are elements of nondiegetic sound coupled with an image track that emphasizes the Lisbon girls as distant spectacles. My aim in what follows is to demonstrate how Coppola achieves this shift in focus through cinematic means, namely the use of nondiegetic sound.[2] To demonstrate Coppola's shift in focus, I will contrast the use of nondiegetic sound elements in the opening sequence of the film (described above) with the beginning of Eugenides's novel. Then I will turn to a broader discussion of nondiegetic sound in the film, focusing on the original score composed by the French electronica duo Air, appropriated 1970s popular music, and Giovanni Ribisi's voiceover, which represents the film's collective male narrator.[3]

The opening lines of Eugenides's novel insert us into the day of the last Lisbon girl's suicide with an almost-journalistic recounting of the details:

> On the morning the last Lisbon daughter took her turn at suicide—it was Mary this time, and sleeping pills like Therese—the two paramedics arrived at the house knowing exactly where the knife drawer was, and the gas oven, and the beam in the basement from which it was possible to tie a rope. They got out of the EMS truck, as usual moving much too slowly in our opinion, and the fat one said under his breath, "This ain't TV folks, this is how fast we got." He was carrying the heavy respirator and cardiac unit past the bushes that had grown monstrous and over the erupting lawn, tame and immaculate thirteen months earlier when the trouble began.[4]

The Virgin Suicides is a remarkably detailed novel—an investigation by a collective narrator (several men) into the lives of five girls who mesmerized them and committed suicide twenty-five years prior, when they were all teenagers. It is a novel filled with minutiae and "evidence": over one hundred interviews with characters revealing some tidbit of information about the girls, a plethora of photos and documents including doctors' records, newspaper clippings, a diary, notes from the girls, miscellaneous personal belongings and so forth. Three paragraphs into the novel, the narrative structure is established as an investigation, an attempt to reassemble the fragments of our collective narrators' memories: "We've tried to arrange the photographs chronologically, though the passage of so many years has made it difficult" (4–5).

By the end of the novel, our narrators have accumulated ninety-seven "exhibits" including: "(#1) Ms. D'Angelo's Polaroid of the house...; (#18) Mary's old cosmetics drying out and turning to beige dust; (#32) Cecelia's canvas high-tops...; (#57) Bonnie's votive candles nibbled nightly by mice; (#62) Therese's specimen slides showing new invading bacteria; (#81) Lux's brassiere." In the end, however, the pile of evidence does not amount to any better understanding of the Lisbon girls or why they committed suicide. Having wandered down a path "of hypothesis and memory"—"a path that led nowhere"—the men are left with only the *unknowability* of the Lisbon girls, "pieces of the puzzle" that won't fit together: "no matter how we put them together, gaps remained, oddly shaped emptinesses mapped by what surrounded them, like countries we couldn't name" (246). Coppola's film adaptation on the other hand ostensibly begins where the book ends, with "pieces" and vague impressions—specifically of Lux, the most sought after and elusive of the Lisbon girls.

In the film, the Lisbon girls are all blonde and pretty, and obviously cast for these qualities to fit to our collective narrator's fantasies, with Lux as their goddess and the others as slightly less perfect copies. But in the novel, we do get some of the girls' flaws:

> Bonnie...had the sallow complexion and sharp nose of a nun. Her eyes watered and she was a foot taller than any of her sisters....Therese Lisbon had a heavier face, the cheeks and eyes of a cow....Mary Lisbon's hair was darker; she had a widow's peak and fuzz above her upper lip that suggested her mother had found her depilatory wax. Lux Lisbon was the only one who accorded with our image of the Lisbon girls. She radiated health and mischief. (26)

The film amplifies the novel's fascination with Lux and transposes her image onto the other Lisbon girls to achieve the effect of the girls as the collective ideal of male dreams, with Lux as the prototype. Coppola's adaptation shifts the focus from the male narrators' investigative process, which is central in the novel, to what they are ultimately left with: fleeting, idealized images.

NONDIEGETIC MUSIC: AIR

According to Claudia Gorbman in *Unheard Melodies*, "The moment we recognize to what degree film music shapes our perception of a narrative, we can no longer consider it incidental or innocent."[5] And Air's score is far from incidental or innocent. It keeps us detached from the 1970s world we see on screen and heightens the dreamlike quality of the Lisbon girls, thereby achieving a distancing and alienating effect. While "most feature films relegate music to the viewer's sensory background,"[6] Air's music is constantly pushed to our sensory foreground, demanding attention equal to that of the image track. Gorbman asserts that music is one inseparable part of what Stam calls film's "expressive resources": "Image, sound effects, dialogue, and music-track are virtually inseparable during the viewing experience; they form a *combinatoire* of expression."[7] Jeff Smith, in "Movie Music as Moving Music," supports Gorbman's contention and asserts that music and visual narrative elements have an additive effect and can shape the meaning of a scene through what he calls "affective congruence," whereby "the matching of musical and narrative affect heightens and intensifies the emotional qualities of the cinematic signifier such that they exceed those of the musical and visual components in themselves."[8] The opening shot of Lux, for example, combined with Air's "Highschool Lover," would not have the same affective meaning as Lux's image on its own. This particular combination of image track and music track hyper-amplifies any dreamlike qualities that could be conveyed either through visual or musical components on their own.[9]

In "Film Music and Narrative Agency," Jerrold Levinson makes what he himself calls a "contentious" observation about *composed* versus *appropriated* musical scores: "Music composed *for* a film...is more likely to be purely narrative in function than preexisting music appropriated *by* a filmmaker."[10] While possibly contentious, I would argue that Air's music composed for *The Virgin Suicides* upholds Levinson's argument that it is more narrative in function than appropriated music would be, primarily because it has no prior, extra-filmic associations. Air's original score is attached *only* to Coppola's adaptation, and the specific images with which it couples. I believe this heightens the affect of the images themselves and thus further bolsters the narrative intention of the images in a way that appropriated music might not. Appropriated music may have extra-filmic associations that could complicate its use in conveying the otherworldly quality that is so essential to Coppola's adaptation and is achieved so effectively with the combination of Air's music and Coppola's imagery. While Eugenides's novel creates a sense of realism in its detailed recounting of events leading up to the suicide, the film chooses instead to focus on the impression of the Lisbon girls that the men are left with at the end of their "real-world" investigation. Instead of the minutiae of souvenirs, doctor's reports, newspaper articles, notes, poems, and second- and third-hand tidbits of information from anyone who had even the smallest contact with the girls, we get Coppola's version of the novel: the Lisbon girls as mere impressions, frozen in time. In other words, Air's music supports the narrative emphasis on the unknowability of the girls as opposed to the detailed process of trying to know them that we get in the novel. To demonstrate this more clearly, I will look at a couple of specific uses of Air's music in the film.

As I showed above, Air's music is used in the opening sequence to establish and heighten the fantasy/memory aspect of the narrative. It is also used in the closing sequence, thereby book-ending the film within this framework. In fact, the use of Air is almost continuous in the last section of the film: from the scene in which the boys go to the Lisbon girls' house and the remaining suicides are committed until the final shot of the film. The effect of this increased use of Air at the end of the film is a heightened sense of unknowability, beginning with the unfathomable suicides of the four remaining Lisbon girls and building until the end of the film, where the men are left with no better understanding of the girls. Additionally, the only time Air's music is heard with lyrics is when the lyrical version of "Playground Love" begins as the closing credits roll, perhaps signaling that we've left the fantasy/memory narrative and can now return to the "real world" once the film has ended. The futile attempt to piece the girls back together is mirrored by the lack of lyrics to provide us with any additional narrative meaning in the film. We are at a loss in understanding the Lisbon girls just as the men are at a loss.

During a scene in which the boys have obtained Cecelia's diary after her second, successful suicide attempt, a shot of the boys reading the diary is intercut with a montage of the girls, starting with Cecelia. The images of the girls have a nebulous quality; they are superimposed on each other and the sky, each of them beautifully sunlit and glowing, lounging dreamily in wheat fields with the wind blowing through their hair. The visual montage is coupled with Air's music, and the combination of visual and sound elements achieves a distant, otherworldly quality—a clear example of affective congruence. In Eugenides's novel, however, when the boys are reading Cecelia's diary—one of the many pieces of evidence they accumulate in their investigation—they think they are beginning to *understand* the Lisbon girls and what it is like to be a girl in general:

> We knew what it felt like to see a boy with his shirt off, and why it made Lux
> write the name Kevin in purple Magic Marker all over her three-ring binder

and even on her bras and panties, and we understood her rage coming home one day to find that Mrs. Lisbon had soaked her things in Clorox, bleaching all the "Kevins" out. We knew the pain of winter wind rushing up your skirt, and the ache of keeping your knees together in class, and how drab and infuriating it was to jump rope while the boys played baseball. (43)

Coppola's adaptation skips much of the specific information contained in Cecelia's diary and focuses instead on the effect it has on the boys/men, which is why we see the fantasy images of the girls on screen, as opposed to the specific instances referred to in Cecelia's diary. This scene in the film heightens the elusiveness and unknowability of the girls, while this section of the book emphasizes the process of trying to accumulate real information about the girls to somehow get inside them. In the novel, we get a sense that our collective narrator is truly coming to know the girls.

Air is also used to emphasize the girls' oppressive environment and the inevitability of the suicides, and thus, the literal and figurative distance they are kept at from the men, forever. Some of the instances of Air's music that convey themes of oppression, imprisonment, and suicide are: immediately after Cecilia has attempted suicide the first time (as part of the opening sequence described above); immediately after Cecelia's successful suicide, coupled with the image of Cecilia impaled on the Lisbon's fence as the automatic sprinkler comes on; during the scene in which Trip Fontaine (Josh Hartnett) leaves Lux alone on a deserted football field after they've had sex (since Lux has failed to make her curfew, we know this image of her alone at dawn is ominous given her restrictive home); during the Lisbon girls' subsequent suburban imprisonment, conveyed as a time-lapse shot of the Lisbon house from the outside as the changing seasons show the neglect and decay of the Lisbon house; during the scene in which the remaining Lisbon girls commit suicide; and finally, during the entire post-suicides "epilogue" sequence, when still images of empty rooms in the Lisbon house flash on screen like a slideshow, and we see the rest of the neighborhood seemingly unaffected by the suicides at a debutante's coming-out party. In the closing shot, we see the boys standing together, staring at the Lisbon house from across the street, and from a medium long shot of the boys we travel up through the trees, toward the sky, and fade out. The closing shot pushing up through the trees recalls a shot from the opening sequence, further linking the use of Air to the subjective fantasy/memory framework in which the film is situated. And the increasing use of Air from the remaining girls' suicide scene onward further emphasizes the girls as growing more distant and unintelligible in death.

NONDIEGETIC MUSIC: 1970S POPULAR MUSIC

Smith's contention that composed nondiegetic music is more narrative in function than appropriated music holds for Coppola's nondiegetic use of 1970s popular music in *The Virgin Suicides*. According to Rick Altman: "By definition, popular song brings previous audience experiences to the table. In a sense, we never hear a popular song for the first time; we are always hearing it *again,* each time with implicit reference to previous hearings."[11] In other words, because the audience has extra-filmic associations with popular music, they bring those associations to the filmic experience. Because it is music composed specifically for the film, Air's score can achieve an ethereal quality that popular music appropriated by the filmmaker may not, simply because Air's music does not have the same extra-filmic cultural associations that appropriated popular music would. Air's original score is not overtly attached to a specific era as 1970s popular music is. Hence, Air's music composed for Coppola's adaptation can be utilized solely for the purpose of emphasizing the fantasy/memory aspects of her translation.

Nondiegetic 1970s popular music by the band Heart is used solely in conjunction with Trip Fontaine—a more "real-world" character than the Lisbon girls. Unlike the Lisbon girls, who only exist in memories and fantasies, Trip is actually alive twenty-five years later, and is interviewed as an adult by our collective narrator. Drying out in drug rehab, Trip has become a pathetic image of a man still mesmerized by the impression Lux has left on him. Heart's music foregrounds the 1970s setting in which we see Trip, depicting Trip as a "real-world" character in a "real-world" setting, in contrast to the otherworldly Lisbon girls who require Air's music for their characterization. Since the film focuses on keeping us somewhat detached from the 1970s world, the use of appropriated 1970s music does not serve the narrative in the way that Air's original score does, in keeping with Levinson's contention. But Heart's music does effectively characterize Trip and situate him firmly in a 1970s high school setting.

Heart's "Magic Man" functions as Trip's "theme song," meaning the song introduces him, characterizes him, and is only associated with him. According to Gorbman: "Rather than participating in the action…theme songs behave somewhat like a Greek chorus, commenting on a narrative temporarily frozen into spectacle."[12] And Trip's entrance is quite a spectacle. In the novel, we get a sense of Trip's legendary high school experience:

Only eighteen months before the suicides, Trip Fontaine had emerged from baby fat to the delight of girls and women alike. Because we had known him as a pudgy boy whose teeth slanted out of his open, trolling mouth like those of a deep-sea fish, we had been slow to recognize his transformation....We weren't on the lookout for handsomeness appearing in our midst, and believed it counted for little until the girls we knew, along with their mothers, fell in love with Trip Fontaine. Their desire was silent yet magnificent, like a thousand daisies attuning their faces toward the path of the sun. (69)

The lyrical language in the passage above is wonderfully translated through Coppola's use of "Magic Man" combined with a sequence that depicts Trip's high school lover-man persona in the way the novel describes so effectively, but also in a way the written word cannot match, through a *combinatoire* of expression. As "Magic Man" is played for the first time to introduce Trip, we hear the sound of a needle on a record, emphasizing the music's nondiegetic quality, and conveying a sense of our collective narrator constructing this scene for us, putting on a record to show us who this Trip character really was in high school.

The nondiegetic use of Heart's music, in combination with Trip walking the high school halls in slow motion with every girl ogling him, shows he is not only a spectacle for his audience of high school girls in the diegetic world of the film, but also a spectacle for the audience of Coppola's film; his "theme song" holds us captive. In Coppola's adaptation, we get a visceral sense of Eugenides's description of Trip. As "Magic Man" continues, we cut from Trip walking down the middle of the hallway like a runway model, to a Trip-as-high-school-stud montage: we see him lying on an air mattress in a pool; girls writing his papers and bringing him brownies; and in his reflection in the side mirror of his red Trans-Am, we see Trip with his eyes closed, looking stoned and blissful. From the montage we cut to Trip grooving down the hallway post-pot-smoking break, and scooting into a classroom to avoid the principal, all while "Magic Man" continues. As Trip slips behind a desk, we see, in hazy focus from his point of view, the back of a girl's head with long, blonde hair. As the head slowly turns around, Lux's face comes into focus and "Magic Man" stops abruptly. The nondiegetic use of "Magic Man" not only characterizes Trip through the lyrics as "high school stud," situating him in the 1970s world with high school and his encounter with Lux as the peak of his existence, but the abrupt halt of "Magic Man," when Lux is revealed to him, demonstrates once again how Air's music—not Heart's music—used only in connection with the Lisbon girls, maintains a narrative focus on the girls as seen through male eyes.

Another instance of nondiegetic 1970s popular music is Heart's "Crazy on You." Again, in keeping with Heart's association with Trip, "Crazy on You" is used in a scene to convey Trip's intense desire for Lux. We see a frustrated Trip sitting outside the Lisbon house in his Trans-Am after he has just spent the evening watching a nature show with the entire Lisbon household, with Mrs. Lisbon (Kathleen Turner) sitting between Trip and Lux on the couch. Again, we hear the sound of a needle on a record as "Crazy on You" begins, emphasizing the music's nondiegetic quality. It also foregrounds the constructedness of the scene by our narrators, who are interviewing Trip throughout the film and are giving us second-hand versions of his recollections. Additionally, through the repeated use of Heart, "Crazy on You" not only again brings extra-filmic audience associations, it also recalls the Trip spectacle conveyed through his "Magic Man" introduction. Heart's repeated use also emphasizes the restrictiveness of the Lisbon household in this scene; the Lisbon parental unit keeps the sexually desirable "Magic Man," Trip Fontaine, from having what he desires: Lux.

"Crazy on You" begins with a soft acoustic guitar rhythm that continues to build in intensity, coupled with a close-up on Trip's profile that reveals seemingly unbearable pain. With his eyes closed, facing upwards, Trip opens his mouth to breathe, and the powerful electric guitar hook suddenly kicks in as Lux bursts into the car and jumps on him in her nightgown, having snuck out for a brief, illicit make-out session. The music's peak intensity is perfectly timed with Lux's explosive entry into the car, and the sexual tension between them is temporarily released in this one moment, in another clear example of the affective congruence of music and image. Furthermore, the use of "Crazy on You" conveys the intense sexual allure that Lux represents not only to Trip, but also to our narrators, who live vicariously through the adult Trip's recollection of the event. Again, the use of nondiegetic appropriated music, instead of nondiegetic composed music, underlines this scene as a characterization of Trip, not Lux. It is a representation of *Trip's* desire, which is all our collective narrator can know. They can never know what Lux felt at that moment, or even if it really happened, as it is Trip's memory, twenty-five years later. As Lux is the elusive object of our collective narrator's desire, she requires Air's unusual, disturbing music to convey her elusiveness.

DIEGETIC 1970S POPULAR MUSIC

Although my aim here is to demonstrate how Coppola's use of nondiegetic sound is employed to show the Lisbon girls through their male admirers' eyes, I would like briefly to touch on the diegetic use of 1970s popular music in contradistinction to the use of nondiegetic music that I have already discussed. In the scenes where diegetic music is used, the boys actually interact with the Lisbon girls. The girls feel closer, more like real girls as opposed to fairies or angels. The instances of 1970s popular music used diegetically in the film include: the party at the Lisbon household thrown for Cecilia (after her first suicide attempt), which the boys are able to attend; the homecoming dance that Trip and three of the boys take the Lisbon girls to; and when the boys communicate with them over the phone by playing records back and forth.

The use of diegetic music to communicate with the Lisbon girls via phone is wonderfully described in the book; a partial list of songs played (evidence for the record) is even presented to try to recreate the event:

> Most of the songs we've forgotten, but a portion of that contrapuntal exchange survives, in pencil, on the back of Demo Karafilis's *Tea for the Tillerman,* where he jotted it. We provide it here....Actually, we're not sure about the order. Demo Karafilis scribbled the titles haphazardly. The above order, however, does chart the basic progression of our musical conversation. Because Lux had burned her hard rock, the girls' songs were mostly folk music....Our songs, for the most part, were love songs. (196–97)

In the novel, the musical exchange is conveyed in detail; there are even song lyrics from the Lisbon girls' final song choice, Bread's "Make it With You": "Hey, have you ever tried / Really reaching out for the other side / I may be climbing on rainbows, / But, baby, here goes: / Dreams, they're for those who sleep / Life, it's for us to keep / And if you're wondering what this song is leading to / I want to make it with you." From this song choice, the boys construe that the girls must have loved them: "We had never dreamed the girls might love us back" (198). While in the novel we know that the boys are just fantasizing that the girls are in love with them, in the film, we *see* the girls as isolated and imprisoned, and this musical phone conversation is just a way of reaching out to the outside world, and clearly *not* about being in love with the boys. In both the novel and the film, the men have tried to hold on to the fantasy of these otherworldly creatures who might have actually loved them. And they have never gotten over that fantasy, as Coppola captures so well in the film. The men have characteristically neglected the "Dreams, they're for those who sleep" lines of the lyrics, and clung to "I want to make it with you."

VOICEOVER

Coppola effectively employs voiceover to maintain the framework of men looking back through twenty-five years of cloudy memories and fantasies.

Just as Air's music keeps the focus on the Lisbon girls as dream images and distant memories, Giovanni Ribisi's voiceover achieves a similar focus by reminding us through the sound of his adult male voice that the boys we are seeing on screen are actually men looking back at these events through the haziness of memory.

Moreover, *one* voice as representative of a *group* of men, and the continual use of "we," achieves a wonderful alienating effect. We are not able to connect the *one* voice we hear on the nondiegetic sound track to any *one* character we see on the image track. As readers of Eugenides's novel, theoretically, we can always imagine "hearing" multiple narrators' voices while reading, but the film selects one voice to represent them all, thereby emphasizing the film's fantasy/memory focus through a voiceover that is effectively distanced from the images we see on screen. In reading the novel, we are not jarred with images of boys in conjunction with an adult male voice. But the film continually focuses our attention on the distance between the 1970s events we see and the voice we hear through voiceover.

The first use of voiceover is during the opening sequence: "Cecilia was the first to go." Stripped down and powerful, it is a condensed version of a passage from the second paragraph of Eugenides's novel: "Cecelia, the youngest, only thirteen, had gone first, slitting her wrists like a Stoic while taking a bath, and when they found her, afloat in her pink pool, with the yellow eyes of someone possessed and her small body giving off the odor of a mature woman, the paramedics had been so frightened by her tranquility that they had stood mesmerized" (3–4). The pared-down voiceover combines with filmic devices to tell the rest of the story that Eugenides's text describes. To make my point, I will return to a portion of the opening sequence already described: Air's music stops abruptly, then there is silence, then the sound of a dripping faucet as the image of a lifeless Cecilia is revealed, floating face up in bloody bath water. "Cecilia was the first to go" is the next nondiegetic sound we hear after Air's music. What this phrase conveys, quickly and grimly, is that there are more suicides to come. This is just one example of how Coppola offers a unique version of the source text through carefully selected and executed nondiegetic sound—in this case, voiceover—combined with visceral images, using all of the expressive resources at her disposal.

As I have demonstrated, Air's music is used in the opening and closing sequences of the film to emphasize the fantasy/memory framework. The use of voiceover in conjunction with Air in the opening and closing sequences further emphasizes this framework by foregrounding the alienating adult male voice. The very first and very last lines of the film are conveyed through voiceover. The last line of the film is: "It didn't matter in the end how old they had been, or that they were girls, but only that we had loved them, and that they hadn't heard us calling, still do not hear us calling them out of those rooms where they went to be alone for all time, and where we will never find the pieces to put them back together." This is nearly identical to the last line of the novel: "It didn't matter in the end how old they had been, or that they were girls, but only that we had loved them, and that they hadn't heard us calling, still do not hear us, up here in the tree house, with our thinning hair and soft bellies, calling them out of those rooms where they went to be alone for all time, alone in suicide, which is deeper than death, and where we will never find the pieces to put them back together" (249). But Coppola leaves out any descriptors of the adult men, like "thinning hair and soft bellies," which prevents us from getting a clear picture of them. The effect is that the voiceover becomes a disembodied voice, placing additional emphasis on the alienating effect of the voiceover. Furthermore, Coppola's use of the last line of the novel as essentially the last line of the film supports my assertion that the film focuses on what the men are left with at the end of a long, detailed investigation: a mere impression. And from the girls' suicide scene until the end of the film, through a combination and intensification of two crucial nondiegetic sound elements—voiceover and Air's music—we are also left with an impression of the Lisbon girls as becoming increasingly distanced and unknowable, especially in death.

While Lux is wasting away in her suburban prison in the novel, the narrators refuse to see her as simply a suffering human being: "none of these signs of malnourishment or illness or grief (the small cold sores at the corners of her mouth, the patch of hair missing above her left ear) detracted from Lux's overwhelming *impression* of being a *carnal angel*" (148, emphasis mine). And that is what Sofia Coppola's film adaptation takes up and amplifies: the fact that the men can never know these girls beyond their own impressions and fantasies. There is one line of Giovanni Ribisi's voiceover that gets to the crux of Coppola's translation: "We were happier with dreams than wives." The film magnifies this aspect of the source text, emphasizing the girls' imprisonment in this impossible male dream, as another of Ribisi's voiceovers exemplifies: "We felt the imprisonment of being a girl, the way it made your mind active and dreamy and how you ended up knowing what colors went together." Underneath the male construction we see on the surface, we know that the Lisbon girls aren't angels—they're just girls. And primarily through nondiegetic sound, the film stresses their constructedness, how they've been distorted through the eyes of our collective male narrator.

NOTES

1. Robert Stam, "Beyond Fidelity: The Dialogics of Adaptation," in *Film Adaptation*, ed. James Naremore (New Brunswick, N.J.: Rutgers University Press, 2000), 56.

2. One of my underlying aims in this essay is to show how critical work on adaptation might be enriched by a more attentive focus on sound as an adaptive element. In addition to the authors I cite here writing about sound and music, one might also fruitfully consult Phil Powrie and Robynn Stilwell, eds., *Changing Tunes: The Use of Pre-Existing Music in Film* (Aldershot: Ashgate, 2006); Annette Davison, *Hollywood Theory, Non-Hollywood Practice: Cinema Soundtracks in the 1980s and 1990s* (Aldershot: Ashgate, 2004); Paulin Reay, *Music in Film: Soundtracks and Synergy* (London: Wallflower, 2004); Ian Inglis, ed., *Popular Music and Film* (London: Wallflower, 2003); Pamela Robertson Wojcik and Arthur Knight, eds., *Soundtrack Available: Essays on Film and Popular Music* (Durham: Duke University Press, 2001). Linda Hutcheon, I should note, writes in compelling ways about sound and music as elements at the adapter's disposal in her recent book *A Theory of Adaptation* (New York: Routledge, 2006). See in particular her second chapter, "What? (Forms)," 33–78.

3. As Robynn J. Stilwell has instructively noted, the distinction between diegetic and nondiegetic sound is by no means simple, and many films exploit the ambiguity, the "fantastical gap" as she puts it, between them. See Stilwell, "The Fantastical Gap between Diegetic and Nondiegetic," in *Beyond the Soundtrack: Representing Music in Cinema*, ed. Daniel Goldmark, Lawrence Kramer, and Richard Leppert (Berkeley and Los Angeles: University of California Press, 2007), 184–204. Coppola's *The Virgin Suicides* for the most part sharply distinguishes diegetic and nondiegetic sound, but this is done primarily to declare a "fantastical gap" between the Lisbon girls and the male characters hoping to reach and understand them.

4. Jeffrey Eugenides, *The Virgin Suicides* (New York: Warner Books, 1993), 3. Further references will be cited by page number parenthetically in the text.

5. Claudia Gorbman, *Unheard Melodies* (London: BFI Publishing, 1987), 11.

6. Gorbman, *Unheard Melodies*, 12.

7. Gorbman, *Unheard Melodies*, 15–16.

8. Jeff Smith, "Movie Music as Moving Music," in *Passionate Views: Film, Cognition, and Emotion*, ed. Carl Plantinga and Greg M. Smith (Baltimore: Johns Hopkins University Press, 1999), 167.

9. Stilwell observes that nondiegetic music "tend[s] toward subjectivity" and empathic identification with a particular character in the diegesis. Stilwell, "Fantastical Gap," 190–91. In the case of *The Virgin Suicides*, Air's music is indeed in a subjective register as it overlays images of Lux, but it is subjectively keyed to the male characters and the collective male narrator, and due to their own fantasies, any such identification with Lux is prevented.

10. Jerrold Levinson, "Film Music and Narrative Agency," in *Film Theory and Criticism: Introductory Readings*, 6th ed., ed. Leo Braudy and Marshall Cohen (Oxford: Oxford University Press, 2004), 483.

11. Rick Altman, "An Interview with Rick Altman," *The Velvet Light Trap* 51 (2003): 69.

12. Gorbman, *Unheard Melodies*, 20.

Trainspotting (Boyle, 1996)

7

Universalizing a Nation and the Adaptation of *Trainspotting*

Shelagh Patterson

Danny Boyle's 1996 adaptation of Irvine Welsh's novel *Trainspotting* depoliticizes and universalizes the novel's narrative about life at the end of the twentieth century in Scotland. The aesthetic and market-driven choices of this adaptation have political ramifications. The exploration of such decisions is the central theme in this essay. Through close readings of scenes from the novel and scenes from the film, I argue that while it is a good adaptation for its purpose—using the novel's milieu and grit to make a hit film—it is not as strong or subtle as a work of art. Films are necessarily compromised by a more demanding commercial imperative, which, at times, is productive. The adaptation of *Trainspotting* uses the structure of the feature film to destabilize narrative time and uses highly stylized visuals and sounds to enhance its surrealist possibilities. However, even while *Trainspotting* pushes the formal limits of a ninety-minute feature film, the politics of such a form overshadows the politics of the novel and the politics of the adaptation.

Welsh's novel provides a layered portrait of Scotland through focusing on a group of characters that grew up in Leith, a neighborhood in Edinburgh. Welsh experiments with form and uses a narrating voice from multiple perspectives to articulate an understanding of Scotland that addresses racism, misogyny, religious tensions, class tensions, colonization, classism, family, crime, violence, and addiction. The film changes the focus from an investigation into Scottish culture to a general critique of consumer culture.

Figment Films, a production company consisting of John Hodge, screenwriter; Andrew Macdonald, producer; and Danny Boyle, director, decided to adapt the novel's episodic sprawl of a narrative that travels through the perspective of most of the main characters into a ninety-minute film that focuses on just one character. They had thought about adapting the novel in a style more similar to Robert Altman's episodic three-hour *Short Cuts*

(1993), but just by the length of the film, its audience reach would have been smaller.[1] The adaptation of *Trainspotting* achieved the goals set by its production team. They wanted to adapt the brilliantly Scottish novel by Welsh into a film that would have an international appeal. Because of the box office success of *Shallow Grave,* their first film together, Channel Four funded a production budget of £1.7 million, and Polygram agreed to release and market *Trainspotting* with a £850,000 budget.[2] With such economic backing, the team knew that they could create another box office success and chose to adapt the novel accordingly.

The production also decided to universalize the Scottish characters so that the narrative of the film would reflect back to issues of youth (friendship, drugs, sex, consumerism, and employment) rather than the questions of what it means to be Scottish that the novel investigates.[3] They wanted to capture in film the dynamic energy of Welsh's use of language and be faithful to the novel's ambiguous depiction of heroin addiction without alienating an audience unfamiliar with the complicated, nuanced perspectives of Scottishness found in the novel.[4]

By choosing to focus on the elements of the novel that the rich texture of film can capture through the layering of image and sound, Figment Films performed an expert job adapting the novel into a mainstream film. The film was a huge success within Britain and also internationally. However, in this essay, I will ultimately return to my questions about the usefulness of judging an adaptation from a political perspective, for *Trainspotting* becomes a particularly interesting case since the novel provides a sustained critique of nationalism, and the film ends up as fuel for nationalist sentiments on which Britain's "New Labor Party" capitalized. *Trainspotting* the film became part of the "Cool Britannia" movement in the mid-1990s that helped pave the way for Tony Blair's New Labor platform. At the time of Blair's election, the link between *Trainspotting* and the Labor Party may have seemed positive.[5] A decade later, as Britain's culture increasingly resembles the corporate landscape and consumer culture of the United States, it is easy to see that just as the Clinton administration paved the way for the aggressive policies of Bush II, so the Cool Britannia movement paved the way for the destructive alliance between Britain and the United States.

It is difficult to pinpoint the exact dates of events in both the novel and film. The film's treatment of time is complex even though the production adapted the novel's episodic structure into a tighter linear narrative with a focus on a single character, Renton. However, while the film has a single narrative arc, unlike the more complex structure of the novel, the film destabilizes the experience of a linear narrative through repetition and montage. In the novel, spanning the 1980s into the '90s, each chapter follows the next in sequential time (with several exceptions), though the amount of time between each episode is questionable. The number of years that the film covers feels distinctly shorter than the time span of the novel, perhaps because of the speed and energy of the film (in addition to the fact that none of the characters age). However, the soundtrack is used to designate time passing. As Martin Stollery explains, "There is a shift from older to more recent music on the soundtrack as *Trainspotting*'s narrative unfolds. This contributes to the impression that the historical period covered by the narrative is from the 1980s to the early 1990s."[6] The costumes, however, are an amalgam of '80s and '90s styles and serve to destabilize time, as does the repetition of scenes. The vague timelessness in the novel and the film both contribute to recreating the drug state for the audience.

The film opens with Renton (Ewan McGregor) and Spud (Ewen Bremner) being chased by cops through the streets of Edinburgh. Within thirty seconds, Renton rolls over the hood of a stopped car, gets up, puts his hands on the hood, looks through the windshield straight into the camera, and laughs; the word "Renton" appears in white text next to him. The scene then shifts to an interior and Renton slowly falling backwards. After eight seconds, the scene again changes, this time to a football pitch. During the next minute, the other main characters are introduced with the same white text and a freeze frame of the action on the field. Renton is hit on the head with a football and starts falling backwards. The film cuts back to the interior scene and weaves the two different scenes of Renton falling to the ground. This is now one minute and forty seconds into the film, and there is as yet no narrative. The opening montage sequence lasts for a total of six minutes, continuing to weave scenes with Renton's voiceover explaining the attractions and drawbacks of heroin addiction with real-time dialogue that support his theories (the attractions include the intense pleasure; the drawbacks include listening to lectures by self-righteous non-heroin-addicted friends) all to the soundtrack of Iggy Pop's "Lust for Life." As the song ends, Renton lifts himself off the floor and declares that he is "off the scag." The scene then switches to a black-and-white screen, the sound of a train horn, and text that reads "Trainspotting."

The narrative continues in a linear fashion with Renton quitting heroin, then starting back, and forty minutes into a film that we think has been progressing forward, Renton and Spud again are being chased down Princes Street, and Renton again rolls over the hood of the same car as it screeches to a halt. The second time, the shot of Renton running is cut with shots of the person driving the car—a middle-aged man, balding, slightly overweight, with both hands gripping the wheel, and wearing his seatbelt, a blue anorak over a teal fleece, and a wide-eyed look of shock, disgust, concern, and fear.

The last scene of the film repeats the opening scene a third time. However, the geographical space is obviously different; instead of Edinburgh, it takes place on the streets of London. And, because of the linear fashion in which the scenes in the second part of the film have progressed, it feels like it is also in a temporally different space. The voiceover that opens the film, listing the elements of a consumer life, is repeated. This looping narrative works on a metaphorical level as a comment on the addict who keeps returning to the habit. Although *Trainspotting* is a mainstream feature film with a main character and a linear narrative, the repetition within the film continually serves to destabilize the sense of linear time, which serves to help create the drug experience for the viewer while also commenting on the repetitive and cyclical nature of addiction.

In order to create a successful narrative-driven film, characters from the novel had to be cut. Overall, the production team did an excellent job choosing who would stay and how to keep the best scenes even if they had to transfer them to different character. For example, in the novel, the character Matty dies of AIDS. Matty's character is cut from the film, but aspects of his character (including his funeral) are transferred onto the character of Tommy (Kevin McKidd). Where Hodge, Macdonald, and Boyle fall short of the mark is in the way they adapt the female characters in the novel to the screen.

Macdonald and Boyle rationalize the lack of strong female characters in the film based on the understanding that "it is a book about a bunch of guys, and it ends up being a film about a bunch of guys."[7] It is true that the first chapters of the novel are not focused on the female characters, but the third chapter, "Growing Up in Public," is a third-person narration that is tied to the perspective of a female character. Macdonald and Boyle read the novel's chapters dedicated to female perspectives as weak and poorly written, but I completely disagree. Throughout the novel, there is a sustained investigation of Scottish misogyny from the perspective of both female and male characters. Welsh's standpoint as a male allows him to articulate aspects of misogyny that may be more difficult for female writers to access. This is most evident in the scene in which Renton plays a joke on his girlfriend Kelly.

The scene I am referring to is a short chapter of a page and a half titled "The Elusive Mr. Hunt." It is written in the third person and narrates a story in which Kelly is bartending in a pub full of men, including her boyfriend Renton and his friends. Sick Boy calls the pub asks for Mark Hunt, and Kelly shouts to the bar "MARK HUNT...ANYBODY SEEN MARK HUNT?" It takes her a moment of reflecting on the laughter and one guy's comment, "Naw, but ah'd like tae" before she realizes that "Mark Hunt" sounds the same as "ma cunt." Welsh then empathically describes her reaction: "While it's all a laugh to them, she feels humiliated. She feels bad about feeling bad, about not being able to take a joke." Welsh communicates that it is not being made fun of that makes her so angry (she threw a pitcher of water on Renton and his friends), but that she also feels guilt about not being able to find funny what she knows was meant as a joke. Welsh doubly validates Kelly's emotional response through switching the narrative focus from Kelly to Renton. But first he gives Kelly's further understanding of the situation: "it's not just the joke that bothers her, but the men in the bar's reaction to it. Behind the bar, she feels like a caged animal in a zoo who has done something amusing. She watches their faces, distorted into a red, gaping, gloating commonality. The joke is on the woman again, she thinks, the silly wee lassie behind the bar."[8] In this quotation, the men's laughter is portrayed as grotesque, and Welsh's use of the word "commonality" signals the mob mentality that Renton elaborates, "It's not funny laughter. This is lynch mob laughter. How was I tae know, he thinks. How the fuck was ah tae know?" (279). In an incredibly short space, Welsh portrays the cruelty of what are deemed harmless male jokes that arise from ignorance of the vulnerability of a female surrounded by a group of misogynistic men. The reader's sympathy lies with Kelly, and Renton's question with which the chapter closes—"how the fuck was ah tae know?"—leaves space for the reader to answer and reflect on Renton's own treatment of women. Certainly, he is not like Begbie who beats and cheats on his pregnant girlfriend, but Renton is a guy who does seduce his brother's pregnant fiancée at his brother's funeral, and then feels annoyance that she is looking for something more than just one sexual encounter in his parent's bathroom (219–22).

Rather than trying to adapt the more complex character of Kelly, the production trio decides to adapt an incidental character that only appears in one chapter in the novel, "The First Shag in Ages," to be Renton's love interest. The novel's Dianne—a precocious fourteen-year-old who bores Renton with her juvenile complaints against her friends and parents—becomes the film's Diane (Kelly Macdonald). As in the novel, Renton meets Diane at a club and takes a taxi home with her; they have sex; he sleeps on the couch; in the morning, Renton realizes that her flatmates are actually her parents, and that Diane is still in school.

Along with the loss of an "n," Diane also loses most of her immaturity. In the film, she operates as an articulate mentor who inspires Renton to move to London and get a job. While Renton is in London, she writes him letters about his friends who are still in Scotland. Renton's refrain for Diane, a schoolgirl in maroon uniform with yellow trim, is "she was right" and "Diane was right," which gives her a more significant emphasis in the film than the novel. The production team expresses regret that many of her scenes had to be cut, including the scene in which she dumps Renton. They rationalize it by blaming the source material (i.e., the novel). However, if we compare the opening of the film to the opening of the novel, it is obvious that the central female roles have become peripheral.

In the opening montage, the first female characters that we see are watching the male characters play football from behind a fence; none of them are given names. This is a clue that females are mere spectators in this film, passive rather than active. As the scene moves to Mother Superior's flat, Ali (Susan Vidler) is the next female that we see. She is given the important lines of explaining the pleasure of heroin: "That beats any meat injection…that beats any fuckin cock in the world." These lines are taken directly from the opening of the novel. In the film, these lines do not get any direct response; instead, they are used to establish the truth of Renton's voiceover, which at that moment is explaining that heroin is better than any orgasm. In the novel, these lines serve to arouse Renton. The reader's attention is moved from Ali's subjective experience to Renton's response. Any reader who may have become aroused by Ali's statement is left in the film to identify only with Renton's desire, as he touches his genitals through his trousers and then comments, "Touchin masel like that makes me feel queasy though" (9). This transfer focuses the attention firmly on Renton and serves to undercut the distinctiveness of Ali. In the film, Ali remains the sexualized object as the camera focuses on Sick Boy (Jonny Lee Miller), who looks at her with lustful anticipation. As the montage weaves scenes of Renton being lectured about his heroin use, the film focuses on the males. There are female characters in these scenes, but they remain voiceless, their presence indicating their existence as an accessory to the film. The opening montage works to establish the females in the film as objects not subjects. A feminist reading of the adaptation would certainly criticize the film for choosing to flesh out the character of Diane instead of adapting the already-complex character of Kelly for the screen.[9] But I wonder if it is fair to do so? For the film to include the novel's investigation of misogyny would put too much pressure on the form of a narrative-driven feature film that focuses on one character. The themes that the film develops are addiction, consumerism, youth, and male friendships. The goal was to produce an international box office success. As the producers say, the aspects of the novel that were cut leave enough material to make several more adaptations of the novel.[10] The adaptation of Dianne to Diane is an adaptation of a precocious child to a knowing-but-less-complex character who is fodder for illicit male fantasy while also advancing the plot.

If the youth drug culture ousts the critique of Scottish nationalism and misogyny in the novel, the film does a superb job of presenting the draw of heroin use. The production crew reproduces the sensual experiences associated with being high through exploiting film's ability to layer visuals and sound. The film plays up the surrealist aspects of the novel and creates stylized visuals instead of the more realistic portrayal of Edinburgh that is found in the novel.

Kave Quinn, the film's production designer, created a highly stylized set presenting rich visuals that transform the bleak reality of drug dens into aesthetically satisfying sets that are presented from the drug-altered perspective of the characters. Figures are presented against textured backgrounds. The set of Mother Superior's flat, where most of the heroin injection occurs, has long hallways and rooms leading off at interesting angles so that the camera can roam through, inviting the audience to share the intimate perspective of someone who is actually a part of the space.

Quinn's work develops the surrealism of the film. In the novel, Welsh very rarely describes interiors, and when he does, it is with minimal detail, an impressionistic stroke to set the tone: "Spud and Renton were sitting in a pub in the Royal Mile. The pub aimed at an American theme-bar effect, but not too accurately; it was a madhouse of assorted bric-a-brac" (62). Welsh could go on to describe the bric-a-brac, layering the images to work on a metaphorical level, but instead he creates density through narrating the thoughts of the characters rather than through visual imagery.

This enhancement of surrealism is evident when comparing the now-famous toilet scene in the novel to the way the film produces it. In the novel, the scene takes place in the chapter titled "The First Day of the Edinburgh Festival." After Renton has put opium suppositories in his anus, he starts defecating on himself and heads to a pub to use the toilet, which is described as "a seatless bowl fill ay broon water, toilet paper and lumps ay floating shite" (24). After emptying his bowels, Renton realizes that he has lost the suppositories and starts fishing inside the toilet bowl for them:

Ah fall off the pan, ma knees splashing oantae the pishy flair. My jeans crumple tae the deck and greedily absorb the urine, but ah hardly notice. Ah roll up ma shirt sleeve and hesitate only briefly, glancing at ma scabby and occasionally weeping track marks, before plunging ma hands and forearms intae the brown water. [He finds one.] . . . Locating the other takes several long dredges through the mess. . . . Ah gag once, but get my white nugget ay gold. . . . The feel ay water disgusts us even mair than the shite. Ma brown-stained arm reminds us ay the classic t-shirt tan. The line goes right up past ma elbow as ah hud tae go right aroond the bend. (26)

The images that this passage creates are realistic: the urine soaking into Renton's jeans as he kneels on the floor, the vulnerability of his arm from excessive needle injections, and then his arm covered in feces, which leads the reader to meditate on the grim reality of Renton's addiction.

This scene in the film is titled "The Worst Toilet in Scotland" and opens with a held shot of some windows of a housing-scheme building. The shot is composed to cut out the ground and the sky, which makes the building appear like a two-dimensional backdrop. The building is not in good condition, but in the sunshine, the different colored curtains almost seem vibrant. The music used in the previous scene was from the opera *Carmen,* and the last chords sound as this scene opens. Renton, at the bottom of the frame, walks from the far left to the right, momentarily bending over in pain before exiting the shot in a bent-over sprint while the voiceover explains, "Heroin makes you constipated; the heroin from my last hit is fading away and the suppositories have yet to melt. I'm no longer constipated." Already, the scene is more aesthetically pleasing, with the focus on urban beauty compared to the "wet sludge in ma keks" that the novel notes (24).

The film continues to heighten the aesthetic quality of the scene when Renton closes the door to the bathroom and the camera stays focused on the graying white door with a crooked sign that reads "Toilet" and then the phrases "the worst" and "in Scotland" appear in bright white text that bookends the sign. The buzz of flickering florescent bulbs sounds as the film cuts to the dark interior of the bathroom. The gravity of Renton's predicament is undercut by the playful use of magically appearing text and the sound of electricity reminiscent of B-movie sound effects. This is the first scene in the movie that does not set the action to music, and the film capitalizes on the background silence to foreground the buzzing of a fly and the grunts of Renton defecating into the toilet bowl. As the scene moves into realism, it becomes quite disgusting as we see Renton kneel beside the toilet and gag as he sticks both arms in the glop. But then the comic music from the previous scene starts up again. To the orchestral strings of *Carmen,* Renton completely enters the toilet bowl. Again the scene switches, and Renton swims through dark blue water to a soundtrack of symphonic rock until he finds his suppositories. This through-the-looking-glass moment serves to distance the audience from the grim reality of the scene. The soundtrack highlights the humor of the situation. A wet, but not dirty, Renton emerges from the toilet bowl. The next scene cuts to him splashing through the front door of his apartment.

The transition from the bathroom to his apartment in the novel is not as simple as a cut. A feces-covered and urine-drenched Renton walks past the "pish-queue gang," including one guy who makes "threatening remarks" (27). Outside, Renton waits for two buses before he can muster the energy to board one. The film uses its soundtrack and color to translate the realism of a repugnant scene into a surreal and magical experience. This transformation echoes the sentiments concerning heroin use in the opening montage of the film; it is an injection that transforms a life full of worries into pure pleasure.

One of the structural similarities between the novel and film is that the kernel event occurs in the final chapter. After a large drug deal in London, Renton chooses to betray his friends and steal the money that they were supposed to split between them. Both the novel and film end with an explanation of why

Renton chose to steal the money. Through comparing the novel's treatment of this scene to the film's, we can begin to see how the film switches the focus away from Scotland.

The last chapter in the novel, "Station to Station," is the only chapter in the section titled "Exit." Both these titles highlight geographical movement. "Station to Station" is a third-person narration and shows the immediate build-up to Renton's decision to betray his friends. Renton and his friends travel down to London to perform a drug deal, and when Renton is left alone with the money, he decides to steal it. The novel closes with Renton on a ferry to Holland trying to rationalize his guilt toward each of his friends. The final paragraph explains Renton's feelings towards Begbie:

> Ironically, it was Begbie who was the key. Ripping off your mates was the highest
> offence in his book, and he would demand the severest penalty. Renton had
> used Begbie, used him to burn his boats completely and utterly. It was Begbie
> who ensured he could never return. He had done what he wanted to do. He
> could now never go back to Leith, to Edinburgh, even to Scotland, ever again.
> There, he could not be anything other than he was. Now, free from all, for good,
> he could be what he wanted to be. He'd stand or fall alone. This thought both
> terrified and excited him as he contemplated life in Amsterdam. (344)

In this paragraph, Begbie is a gatekeeper to Scotland. By betraying Begbie, Renton effectively exiles himself from the oppressive limits of life in Scotland. This is not the first time in the novel that Renton links Begbie and Scotland. Renton portrays Begbie as representing Scottish failure during a silent rant in which Scotland is described as "a country of failures," "the scum of the earth," "the most wretched servile, miserable, pathetic trash that was ever shat intae creation." This characterization of Scotland is bookended by "Ah hate cunts like that. Cunts like Begbie" and "Ah hate the Scots" (78). Renton's betrayal of Begbie is a betrayal of Scotland, and for Renton, it is this betrayal that will give him the chance to be free.

The title of the last scene in the film, "The Truth is I'm a Bad Person," ignores the themes of location. Here the focus is on character. Renton steals the bag from the room while his friends sleep. There is no voiceover as the film cuts from the dark hotel interior to Renton exiting the hotel's main door for the sunlit London streets. As with many scenes in the film, the soundtrack is used to maintain continuity as a balance to the dramatic cuts. Renton's voiceover then explains his motivations:

> So why did I do it? I could offer a million answers, all false. The truth is that
> I'm a bad person. But, that's going to change. I'm going to change. This is the
> last of that sort of thing. I'm cleaning up and I'm moving on, going straight and
> choosing life. I'm looking forward to it already. I'm going to be just like you. The

job. The family. The fucking big television. The washing machine. The car. The compact disc and electrical tin opener. Good health. Low cholesterol. Dental insurance. Mortgage. Starter home. Leisure wear. Luggage. Three-piece suit. DIY. Game Shows. Junk food. Children. Walks in the park. 9 to 5. Good at golf. Washing the car. Choice of sweaters. Family Christmas. Index pension. Tax exemption. Clearing gutters. Getting by. Looking ahead. The day you die.

The last words of the film, unlike the novel, do not mention Scotland. Instead it focuses on where Renton is heading—the consumer lifestyle of an unidentified "you." Renton confidently defines the lifestyle in sentences that only contain objects—a stark difference from the uncertainty of the novel's last paragraph's slower rhythm of complete sentences and repetition of words.

As in the novel, the choice to steal the money exiles Renton, but the exile is not a result of needing to sever himself from a national culture, but rather to sever his ties to a criminal or "bad" lifestyle. The film's ending is certainly ambiguous and cannot be read as valuing the consumer life over the drug life; rather, the film serves to the blur the existential line between the two by putting the normally marginalized drug culture at the center. This blurring is echoed in the film's last shot of Renton as he walks so close to the camera his face blurs.

As I explored before, this closing scene rhymes with an earlier series of scenes in the film. The first time that Renton looks directly into the camera is during the opening sequence. Renton is being chased through the streets of Edinburgh and flips over the hood of a car braking to a stop. He stands back up, leans both hands on the car, looks straight into the camera, and laughs. The film repeats this scene but transposes it outside of its Scottish context into the streets of London. The driver of the car represents the unidentified "you" in Renton's closing voiceover—the "you" with which the film blurs Renton and the youth drug culture.

What are the implications of adapting a novel that critiques elements of a specific country into a film that has universal appeal? The choice of the form placed limits on the adaptation, preventing the film from investigating the political aspects of the novel. Instead, it presents a stylized portrayal of drug culture and captures the energy of youth.

One could argue that the novel also contributes to the Labor Party's shift to the right, but only because the film then adapted itself onto the novel. The covers of current editions of the novel show photographs of the movie characters, and the title is in the same font and colors of the movie posters. The novel is now packaged as part of the *Trainspotting* brand that sells the movie, T-shirts, posters, soundtracks, and the novel. On its own with its portrayal of a racist, misogynist, and violent British culture, Welsh's novel could never have fed a movement of popular, depoliticized (i.e., consumer) nationalism that helped create the space for Britain's party of the Left to move into the center.[11]

Notes

1. "The Making of *Trainspotting*," *Trainspotting*, special ed. DVD, directed by Danny Boyle (Burbank, Calif.: Buena Vista Home Entertainment, Inc., 2002).

2. Martin Stollery, *Trainspotting: Directed by Danny Boyle* (London: York Press, 2001), 49–50.

3. This issue of erasing national identities in pursuit of a global market is endemic in films of the 1990s. For example, Sophia A. McClennan discusses the way in which 1992's *Like Water for Chocolate* "reduces Mexican identity to easily consumable products empty of history and struggle." McClennan, "Commodifying Latin America in NAFTA-era Film: The World According to Miramax: Chocolate, Poetry and Neo-liberal Aesthetics," in *American Visual Cultures,* ed. David Holloway and John Beck (London: Continuum Press, 2005), 244.

4. "Interviews," *Trainspotting*, special ed. DVD.

5. See, for example, Derek Paget, "Speaking Out: The Transformation of Trainspotting," in *Adaptations: From Text to Screen, Screen to Text*, ed. Deborah Cartmell and Imelda Whelehan (New York: Routledge, 1999) 128–40.

6. Stollery, *Trainspotting*, 36.

7. Danny Boyle, John Hodge, Andrew MacDonald, and Ewan MacGregor, "Feature Commentary," *Trainspotting*, special ed. DVD.

8. Irvine Welsh, *Trainspotting* (Great Britain: Martin Secker & Warburg Ltd., 1993), 279. Hereafter cited by page number in text.

9. It seems that women characters, especially those who pose feminist issues, continually create problems for filmmakers in ways that adaptation makes vivid. Esther Sonnet, in writing about the film *Bunny Lake is Missing* (1965), adapted from Evelyn Piper's novel of the same name (1957), explores the way in which a popular novel gets re-appropriated for feminism and divested of any feminist meaning in its filmic form precisely through avoiding the "challenge she presents" (as Sonnet quotes Dalton Trumbo, one of the screenwriters on the project, describing the single-mother protagonist Blanche Lake) and shifting the narrative focus to new characters created for the film. Sonnet, "Evelyn Piper's *Bunny Lake Is Missing* (1957): Adaptation, Feminism, and the Politics of the 'Progressive Text,'" *Adaptation* 2, no. 1 (2009): 77.

10. Danny Boyle et al., "Feature Commentary," *Trainspotting*, special ed. DVD.

11. See Murray Smith, *Trainspotting* (London: BFI Publishing, 2002) and Jennifer M. Jeffers, "Cool Britannia for Sale: *Trainspotting* and *Bridget Jones's Diary*," in *Britain Colonized: Hollywood's Appropriation of British Literature* (New York: Palgrave Macmillan, 2006).

Ghost World (Zwigoff, 2001)

8

GETTING AWAY WITH HOMAGE

The Alternative Universes of Ghost World

Jonathan Loucks

Film adaptation is a hard thing for me to talk about. When it comes to the music world, I understand what constitutes an unsuccessful song adaptation—the idea that a simple note-for-note cover of a tune is uninspired and useless. Thus, the best song remakes are really new songs in and of themselves. If a literal note-for-note cover can be ascribed as merely a redo, then an adaptation (née remake) of a song would take the spirit/intent/ *je ne sais quoi* of the original tune and reconfigure it in a way that makes it *new/better*. Take Johnny Cash's version of "Hurt" by Nine Inch Nails on his album *American IV: The Man Comes Around*. Originally a Generation X treatise on alienation and self-loathing, Cash strips the song down to its brass tacks, thereby creating an entirely new, folk-ish version of suffering for the septuagenarian set.

What about the cinema? Consider Director Terry Zwigoff's 2001 production of *Ghost World*, adapted from the Daniel Clowes's 1996 graphic novel of the same name. Two rather disparate mediums, authors, and narratives, yet two highly successful texts, at least in terms of professional critical reception. So what makes a filmic adaptation successful? Fidelity to the original text? Faithful narrative sequencing? Spot-on casting? Critical kowtowing?

For all intents and purposes, *Ghost World* is not an adaptation, despite the facts that it bears the same name as the source material, that the author of the novel co-wrote the screenplay, and that it was marketed as such. *Ghost World* the film *resembles* the novel—same two primary characters, same anonymous suburban setting—but that's where the two part ways.

Why adaptation? I mean, literally, why the word *adapt*? Think of biology: Darwin, Mendel, evolution, *The Origin of Species*. The notion that species evolve via adaptation is misguided. Biological adaptation is not a one-to-one correlation. If you cut off my arm, my son won't be born missing a limb. Seen in this light, adaptation isn't quite the conduit to better living we tend to imagine. It's more of a quantum leap—Species A doesn't beget Species B. In fact, the two of them never even met. Thus, if we translate this concept into aesthetic terms, how can *Ghost World* the film really be an adaptation of *Ghost World* the graphic novel? If it isn't, why is it still so good? And if it's not an adaptation, then what is it?

YOU SAY TOMATO

When is something considered "adaptation" as opposed to "influenced by" or "based on"? While there certainly are legal/trademark-related definitions for these categories, one obvious indicator is titling. If the film and the source material have an identical title (e.g., *Romeo and Juliet*), then it seems to make sense that an audience can expect more in terms of narrative fidelity. What's interesting, then, is the fact that Zwigoff's *Ghost World* maintains very little adherence to the plot of the Daniel Clowes graphic novel despite its eponymy. In fact, while certain characters in the film are composites of characters from the novel, and occasionally moments of dialogue hint at larger storylines in the source material, essentially the film takes the two leading ladies out of the graphic novel and creates an entirely new world for them. The question is why? Clowes explains:

> The comic was a bunch of interrelated short stories about teenage girls, Enid and Rebecca, the first summer after they got out of high school. They are not quite sure what they're doing, and they are changing day by day. *Ghost World* had eight interrelated short stories that form a short cartoon novel. It sold close to 100,000 copies, which is amazing, considering it was done by a tiny publisher. Terry Zwigoff is a fan of my work. He had just finished *Crumb* and was looking to do a fictional film. My understanding is that he was being sent scripts from agents and hated all of them. So he kept going back to my comics and decided he wanted to do something closer to what I do in my comics. He came to me and we tried to turn it into a film. That was daunting, because the comic is very episodic, yet filming every panel would only yield about a 45-minute film. So we threw away everything in the comic except the two characters and the time—the summer after high school. We reinterpreted the entire thing and came up with something we were very happy with.[1]

Like many filmic adaptations, changes in the script were made due to the temporal limits of film. While this usually means the narrative must be compressed to fit a ninety-minute timeline, Zwigoff and Clowes found themselves struggling to flesh out the content in order to have a feature-length film.

As a graphic novel, *Ghost World*'s structure is unconstrained, consisting of eight vignettes very loosely connected via locale (most likely a Los Angeles suburb), characters (Enid and Rebecca), and Daniel Clowes's singular illustration style (including his consistent use of two-color [blue and black] inking). Thus, while sometimes it's difficult to ascertain the linearity of Clowes's plot, it's quite clear that we're operating within the same world.

Can the same be said about the film? Bright, colorful, and much more obviously set in Los Angeles (it's one thing to read about strip malls and 72-degree days; it's another to slip into that world visually for 111 minutes), the film unfolds as a series of sequential weeks, a snapshot of a time as opposed to the novel's depiction of a life(style).

GREAT EXPECTATIONS

How many times have you read a novel, then seen the film, and were frustrated or disappointed because the main character had red hair and you always imagined her as a blonde? Or you pictured the fictional town of the story as being gritty and working class whereas the director chose to make it rural and sleepy? What's interesting about graphic-novel-to-film adaptation is that, for the most part, the characters, wardrobe, and mise-en-scène are visually determined for us in the source material—we know, for instance, that Enid has short black hair, thick glasses, and a punk-rock aesthetic; that Rebecca is flaxen and more classically beautiful. We've seen panels and panels of illustrations in which they are exactly this.

This, I believe, is a major deviation from traditional adaptation in that a novel (or the text of a stage play) ultimately exists in the mind of the reader. Sure, we may have detailed descriptions of characters, locales, and the like, but I'd argue that a reader of a novel relies much more on her imagination than a reader of a graphic novel. Because of this, fidelity discourse on *Ghost World* is both restricted and enhanced because one can literally compare and contrast the two mediums' imagery. Thus, the *casting* of the film takes on another level of authenticity in that the actors must not only match the characters' temperaments, but faithfully embody their physiques. When asked about matters of casting and dealing with "inane suggestions from prospective production companies," Clowes and Zwigoff responded:

> Clowes: Oh yeah, sure. We were with almost every studio at some point and they all had their casting ideas—it was just whoever was the actress of the moment for the lead. "We see Jennifer Love Hewitt as Enid." And I'm thinking, "Well, that's sort of the opposite of Enid. That's who Enid should not be, basically." And it went from there to Alicia Silverstone to Claire Danes. There are very few actresses who have any sort of oddness to them or texture that was appropriate for this film. They also had these crazy ideas like Nathan Lane as Seymour. And I'm thinking, "Well, how about Dom DeLuise while you're at it?"

> Zwigoff: Yeah, at various times they were pushing Sarah Michelle Geller, Melissa Joan Hart. Everyone on the list they gave us was wrong for the part. A character like Enid should be a little bit of an outsider, and I don't quite see Jennifer Love Hewitt in a role like that. She should be in a Gap ad. It was pretty ridiculous. I mean, there's a reason we chose Scarlett [Johansson] and Thora [Birch]. There's something about both of them that's a little eccentric. The subtle, idiosyncratic way they deliver their lines was just perfect.[2]

Sure, it can be argued that in traditional novels the characters are often explicitly described. We know that Lestat from Anne Rice's *Interview with the Vampire* is a "tall, fair-skinned man with a mass of blond hair and a graceful, almost feline quality to his movements."[3] Yet it doesn't bother me as much when Tom Cruise is cast as the vampire—I can forgo my mental image of a tall, thin man because film is such a powerful imagistic medium in terms of absorption and perception. Are a few sentences describing a character at the beginning of a novel more accurate, more true, than a two-hour film showing us what this character looks like? In other words, because of the illustrations, if the character of Enid were played by Uma Thurman, I believe that every fan of the graphic novel would be much more likely to cursorily dismiss the film.[4]

CH-CH-CH-CHANGES

Almost all good films have their source in a particular individual's life—it may not be *about* the author, but it is most likely *of* him. *Ghost World* the film is no different. Without a doubt, the most significant divergence from the graphic novel is the character of Seymour. Virtually nonexistent in the source material (I suppose an argument can be made that the character Bob

Skeetes leads to Seymour, though the two are quite different), Seymour is an extremely important character in the film. From his anachronistic love of jazz, blues, and ragtime to his perennial status as a social outcast, Seymour represents everything the graphic novel is desperately trying to communicate: that growing up is something to be suspicious of, not desired; that failures are the most interesting members of society; and that "not fitting in" is actually a social norm. So where did the character of Seymour come from?

> Interviewer: The film differs from the comic book in a number of ways. How did you decide what to change and what to preserve?
>
> Terry Zwigoff: It was a very natural process; it wasn't intellectual at all. If I connected with something, then I included it in the script. If I didn't, I tried to shy away from it and lose it. And I added characters to the script. I added the Seymour character who's basically me. At first, I added him because I wanted an excuse to have a soundtrack of old music, which is what I collect: '20s blues, jazz, and country music. A lot of the stuff you see in his room is actually just dragged down from my house.[5]

But *why* did the character of Seymour come about? Simply to infuse the script with long-forgotten music? Or was it the manifestation of Zwigoff's out-of-control ego? In an interview, Clowes mentions that "Steve Buscemi was our first and only choice for that character. He was the perfect choice and was fantastic in the role."[6] In regards to fidelity of casting, this was a wise, wise decision. Buscemi is a perfect fit for the part—nebbish, homely, and utterly unremarkable, he so accurately portrays the not-so-lovable loser who Enid needs to befriend in her attempt to better understand her life and herself.

Buscemi does quite accurately resemble Zwigoff. While this might seemingly be an obsessive-compulsive attention to detail, it is nevertheless important in a world where directors are as famous, and as publicly present, as actors. Especially when a director states, for the record, that these fictional characters aren't so fictional after all—they are of the real world, just not of *Ghost World*. It's no understatement to say that such an addition to the narrative challenges any argument for the film as an adaptation.

THE RISE AND FALL AND RISE AGAIN OF THE AUTHOR

Let me switch gears for a moment and talk about authorship. Who, specifically, is the author of a film? The screenwriter? Director? Producer? Lead actor? All of the above? In "The Revenge of the Author," Colin MacCabe writes:

> Even a very cheap feature film involves thirty to forty people working together over a period of six months, and the mass of copyright law and trade union practice which has grown up around film has largely as its goal the ever more precise specification of "creativity," the delineation of areas (design, lighting, make-up, costume) where an individual or individuals can be named in relation to a particular element of the final artifact.[7]

The notion of a sole author loses out in these factory-like conditions of production. Or does it? MacCabe goes on to say that "the most general concern of the cast and crew of a film, not to mention the producer, is that the director know what film he is making, that there be an author on the set."[8] But what about accountability? Someone has to be in charge, and therefore culpable. And why even care about accountability at all? Because adaptation theory is obsessed with it.

You can't call a work of art your own if it's a line-by-line adaptation of another text. Isn't that plagiarism? When I write a poem that's influenced by another poet, I'm basically required to call it an imitation or refer to it as being "after" so-and-so author. It's not about technicalities or breaking the law; it's a matter of respect. Fair enough.

In his essay, MacCabe also points out that "if we look back to the Renaissance, we find that the etymologically prior meanings of the word 'author' stress the notion of both cause and authority."[9] Interesting. So who is the authority when it comes to *Ghost World*? First, let's begin by discussing the identity of *Ghost World*—what is it about?

One way to talk about a film's identity is to start with genre. We know what a western is (*Unforgiven* [Eastwood, 1992]), we know what a romantic comedy is (anything starring Meg Ryan). Both texts of *Ghost World* do fit snugly into the coming-of-age genre—two adolescent girls, weeks out of high school, struggle to find jobs, obtain an apartment, outgrow their families, and search for love. Yet they also fit the criteria for what Jeffery Sconce calls the American "smart film," particularly the themes of "interpersonal alienation within the white middle class (usually focused on the family) and alienation within contemporary consumer culture."[10]

Is there such a genre as the comic-book film? As evidence we might consider the spate of graphic novels that have recently been adapted for the screen: *Sin City* (Miller, Rodriguez, 2005), *A History of Violence* (Cronenberg, 2005), *300* (Snyder, 2007), and *Watchmen* (Synder, 2009) among others. If there is such a genre in the United States, something comparable to Japan's cinematic versions of Manga, how would you define it?[11] Must a film be animated to be considered of this genre? Must the target audience consist of prepubescent boys? What about Neil Jordan's *The Butcher Boy* (1997)? It opens with comic-book imagery and incorporates comics as a motif throughout the film (as does the novel from which it is adapted). Is it a comic-book film? Hardly. And perhaps.

As a genre, graphic novels are best defined as book-length narratives featuring comic art; these texts are geared toward a different audience than traditional comics, namely older, more sophisticated teens who—in very real ways—resemble Enid and Rebecca. Sarcastic, hip, ironic, jaded, intelligent people for whom music and art are far more important than venture capitalism.

So is it fair to say that *Ghost World* is a coming-of-age graphic-novel film? If so, then who is the authority of the subject matter? Who better understands this world, Zwigoff or Clowes? It must be noted here that Terry Zwigoff directed *Crumb* (1994), a documentary about one of the first graphic novelists, R. Crumb, and is well versed in that world:

Interviewer: How did you first come across the *Ghost World* story?

Terry Zwigoff: I always had comics lying around my home because Robert Crumb would stay at my house when he came to town. He'd bring over a pile of comics from this comic-book distributor about a mile away from my house called Last Gasp Publishing, where my wife used to work. I read them all. The only ones I liked were Crumb's, Dan Clowes' stuff, and a few others. I thought "Ghost World" was very strong, but I didn't find it as funny as Dan's other stuff. I didn't think it would make a good movie, but my wife kept telling me it would. So I got Dan's phone number, went to meet him in Berkeley, and we hit it off right away. I found him to be very smart and very funny. We talked about different ideas and we eventually came to *Ghost World,* which seemed the most adaptable.[12]

For the record, Terry Zwigoff directed the film and co-wrote the screenplay. Daniel Clowes wrote the graphic novel and co-wrote the screenplay. Here's how it all began:

Interviewer: How did the movie of *Ghost World* get made?

Clowes: It's the first time either of us had written a script, so it was trial by fire with learning along the way and many revisions…Terry [Zwigoff] and

I became such good friends that he wanted me involved throughout pre-production and shooting. He let me supervise anything related to the two main characters, including sets and costumes. That's an amazing gift to a writer, especially a first-time writer. I was on set for every shot of the 35-day shoot in Culver City and L.A.

Interviewer: What was your and Terry's main objective in writing *Ghost World*?

Clowes: The main objective was to get these two characters from the comic to be true when they reached the screen. We really didn't want them to become clichés. We were trying to make something more than a teen comedy. We wanted it to have a broad range of emotions. This is a personal film that the two of us felt strongly about while we were working on it.[13]

Quite a fascinating collaboration. Equal, respectful, and above and beyond your stereotypical director/screenwriting relationship. Notice that Clowes says they were trying to avoid cliché, to make "something more than a teen comedy." For me, this is where the film is most successful; it is much more than a typical teen comedy, but in ways that are different than the graphic novel.

While the case could be made that Zwigoff's involvement in the graphic-novel subculture makes him as much of an authority on the genre as Clowes, I'm compelled to think that ultimately Clowes has a better handle not only on this medium, but on his characters. Thus, while it is certainly a ratio (60/40?), Clowes is the primary author of the film. And if Clowes is the primary author of the film, how can he adapt his own work? He can't.

ALIENATION NATION

Much of *Ghost World* centers around the main characters' associations (and Rebecca's eventual disassociation) with the marginalized: geeks, freaks, losers, loners. Setting their narratives in the '90s, both Clowes and Zwigoff communicate this marginalization via the identification of Enid and Rebecca with a punk rock/alternative subculture.

Both versions of *Ghost World* use music to communicate teen angst and middle-aged ennui, specifically Enid and Rebecca's punk-rock association and the dixie/blues/jazz leanings of Seymour. Initially these genres operate as signifiers: Enid listens to the Ramones while dyeing her hair and dressing, for the day, as a vintage punker.[14] Rebecca flirts with a boy in a band called Alien Autopsy[15] after Enid bashes her for once dating someone who likes reggae.[16]

Contrast this with Seymour's musical preferences. A significant scene that exists only in the film occurs at Seymour's shindig. Shortly after befriending her, Seymour invites Enid (and by default Rebecca) to a party at his house. Remember, these are two young, cool women. Unfortunately, the party turns out to be a record collector's wet dream—a dozen balding, middle-aged men in slacks and sweater vests adamantly debating the value of vintage vinyl. Suffice it to say that while Enid finds it almost charming, Rebecca is clearly alienated by the gaps in age and ethos. This alienation is further emphasized when a youngish lecher (played brilliantly and ironically by indie rock comedian David Cross) hits on the girls moments after stating his favorite axiom: "You can't hit a homerun without swinging the bat."

This party, these people, and their music clearly represent everything about adulthood that Enid and Rebecca neither want nor really understand: settling, loneliness, desperation, frustration. Another example of this motif is the neo-1950s diner the women frequently visit within both texts. While positioned as an authentic *Happy Days* kind of eatery, the diner plays contemporary hip hop, whereas in the graphic novel, golden oldies (e.g., The Righteous Brothers) are the diner's musique du jour.

This is an important distinction, and one that addresses the use of non-narrative forms of adaptation—in particular, how music operates within a film. When Enid colors her hair while listening to the Ramones, this is communicated via a visual image in the graphic novel—we *see* an album with RAMONES lettered across the front. However, in the film, we *hear* the song during the scene—the frenetic guitars and affected vox complement Enid's attitude and frustration far better than any image, making film a more successful medium for communicating overt (teen) identity.[17]

Incidental noise functions in this same manner. For instance, the sound of traffic and city buses hurtling by the characters as they saunter down the sidewalk not only draws attention to their metropolitan existence (white noise, all around them), but also draws attention to the fact that these girls are car-less in a society where that's almost sacrilege. Whether it's by choice or fate, walking in L.A. is the ultimate form of being a social outcast. And while this is never explicitly communicated, non-narrative sound ensures that Enid and Rebecca (and the viewer) are well aware of this.

In addition to using music and non-narrative sound, films can show desire in a way that novels can't—and I mean literally show. While the case can be made that erotic fiction is commercially successful because one's imagination is stimulated, at the end of the day nude imagery is simply more powerful than words on a page. But this philosophy doesn't really apply to graphic novels. Their use of illustration allows for images and words to work in concert, creating very powerful sex scenes. At the same time, it's hard not to feel uncomfortable when looking at naked *cartoons,* especially ones as realistic as those found in Clowes's *Ghost World.*

Rated R, presumably for language, *Ghost World* the film is not for children. However, the graphic novel, with its emphasis on sex and sexuality, is far more adult. Containing moments of nudity, casual sex, strong lesbian undertones, and masturbation, its panels are far more shocking than anything found in the film. Why? On one hand, it can be argued that a rendering of a topless female teenager is less offensive than the real thing. It's just a drawing, right? On the other hand, for readers who are more familiar with newspaper comics, a graphic novel's incorporation of sex, nudity, and vulgarity can be quite shocking. Is this why Zwigoff chose to eliminate this material from the film? Probably not.

My theory is that while nudity in comic art is shocking for the above reasons, depicting teenagers masturbating, discussing homosexual feelings, and having explicit sex in a mainstream film is rather risky in the age of neo-puritan moral values. However, that argument (how much is too much?) can be applied to many choices a filmmaker faces. And obviously some films incorporate teen nudity and explicit sexual content; just not this one. Why?

To answer that, we must return to my larger question of whether or not this is an adaptation. Sexuality operates within the graphic novel because it is a series of vignettes about teenage existence. This includes sex or the lack thereof. But the film is more about Enid's fading relationship with her best friend and her blossoming friendship with an older man as she struggles to enter (or not enter) the real world. Furthermore, the sexual content in the graphic novel revolves exclusively around Enid's relationship with Josh, a neighborhood boy about whom she fantasizes, struggles to court, finally beds, and eventually loses. Thus, the sexual content of the novel concerns two peers—two teenagers—and is therefore (a) archetypal and (b) acceptable.

In the film, the character of Josh is significantly truncated. Instead we focus on Seymour, a man almost three times Enid's age. Their relationship is primarily platonic; much of the narrative consists of her helping him find a girlfriend. What's interesting, though, is how nervous I felt about this relationship from the get-go. Although she recently graduated from high school and is presumably eighteen years old, Enid functions very much as a young girl. She lives at home with her dad, has no income of her own, no automobile, and so on. Thus, maintaining a highly sexualized version of Enid for the film would bring up too many moral issues[18] in the context of her relationship with Seymour, issues that weren't evident in the novel due to Josh's age. But more important, the absence of frequent explicit sexuality is ultimately a result of the significant narrative deviations—it's a different work of art and therefore calls for less-graphic content.

GETTING AWAY WITH HOMAGE

If the film *Ghost World* is not an adaptation, why is it still so good? And, perhaps more importantly, how do you get around the fact that, while it is a new piece of art itself, the film would not exist if it weren't for the graphic novel. Let's tackle the term *homage*. Etymologically, homage has its roots in the Middle English noun *homme,* meaning "man." Essentially, the origin of the word comes from a ceremony by which a vassal acknowledges himself to his lord. From there we get the contemporary meaning of paying respects or honoring someone.

In film theory, adaptation is rarely likened to this act of respect or admiration. However, critical reception based on fidelity is essentially centered around this construct—how faithful (i.e., respectful) is the film to the original text? Terry Zwigoff's *Ghost World* is faithful to Clowes's text in spirit. The tone, primary characters, setting, and overall themes are the same. But in many ways it's more of a paean to the original than a correlation. In other words, an homage.

"Accentuate the negative"—that's the film's tagline. Clearly a clever Gen X "*You're Unique!*" ironic gesture, these three words can apply to both the cinema (film being a series of negatives), as well as my argument that Zwigoff's *Ghost World* is successful because it's *not* faithful to the source material: in short, the idea that what is added to a film, or what is left out of a novel, ultimately makes the movie *more* successful.

NOTES

1. "Interview with Terry Zwigoff and Daniel Clowes," http://www.wga.org/pr/awards/2002/clowes-zwigoff.html.

2. Rex Doane, "A Conversation with Terry Zwigoff and Daniel Clowes," *Salon*, July 27, 2001, http://archive.salon.com/people/conv/2001/07/27/zwigoff_clowes/print.html.

3. Ann Rice, *Interview with the Vampire* (New York: Ballantine Books, 1976), 13.

4. While I am making claims specific to the graphic-novel-to-film adaptation, matters of casting and performance are crucial to any discussion of adaptation, as some scholars have taken note. See, for instance, Thomas Leitch's discussion of the various performances of Sherlock Holmes in his chapter, "The Hero with a Hundred Faces," in *Film Adaptation and its Discontents: From* Gone with the Wind *to* The Passion of the Christ (Baltimore: Johns Hopkins University Press, 2007), 207–35.

5. Daniel Steinhart, "Interview: Comic Book Confidential," *indieWIRE*, http://www.indiewire.com/people/int_Zwigoff_Terry_010720.html.

6. "Interview."

7. Colin MacCabe, "The Revenge of the Author," in *The Eloquence of the Vulgar* (London: British Film Institute, 1999), 37–38.

8. MacCabe, "Revenge," 33.

9. MacCabe, "Revenge," 34.

10. Jeffrey Sconce, "Irony, Nihilism and the New American 'Smart' Film," *Screen* 43 (Winter 2002): 349–69.

11. Despite the recent boom in adaptation studies, the graphic-novel-to-film adaptation has not received much critical attention, even as it has become a Hollywood staple. Linda Hutcheon is one of the few to address this cultural form, but her remarks are not sustained beyond a few passing observations. She does, however, note a specific attribute that's lost in the translation of *Ghost World* to the screen, one she claims that fans of the graphic novel strongly associated with the attitudes of Enid and Rebecca: "the drained-out blue-green tint of the comics' pages." Hutcheon, *A Theory of Adaptation* (New York: Routledge, 2006), 43.

12. Steinhart, "Interview."

13. "Interview."

14. Daniel Clowes, *Ghost World* (Seattle: Fantagraphics Books, 1993), 21.

15. Clowes, *Ghost World*, 26.

16. It goes without saying that, in this context, reggae represents all that is hippie, which is the nemesis of all that is punk. Thus, Enid's dismissal of Rebecca's crush is more of a cultural value judgment than a statement about that particular boy. Although you can't argue about taste.

17. I suppose this discrepancy may be intentional. While relatively mainstream, punk is still positioned as countercultural. Thus, the slight nod to the Ramones in the novel (you have to be looking for it) operates as a kind of secret handshake, whereas in the film it's impossible to miss the song, even if you have no idea who's singing it, which is essentially a matter of (assumed) audience.

18. It's important to note there is a brief, highly edited, implied love scene between the two near the end of the film that is devoid of nudity and still quite uncomfortable. It can be argued that this scene, and its execution, exist to communicate to the viewer that any more sexual content in the film would be unnecessary and inappropriate.

Lawrence of Arabia (Lean, 1962)

9

INDEXING AN ICON

T. E. Lawrence's Seven Pillars of Wisdom *and David Lean's*
Lawrence of Arabia

Alison Patterson

> I had one craving all my life—for the power of self-expression in
> some imaginative form—but had been too diffuse ever to acquire a
> technique. At last accident, with perverted humor, in casting me as a
> man of action had given me place in the Arab Revolt, a theme ready
> and epic to a direct eye and hand, thus offering me an outlet in litera-
> ture, the technique-less art.
> Whereupon I became excited only over mechanism.
>
> —T. E. Lawrence, *Seven Pillars of Wisdom*

In his seminal adaptation studies text *Novels into Film,* George Bluestone presents what Kamilla Elliott describes as his "famous maxim" that
"between the percept of the visual image and the concept of the mental
image lies the root difference between the two media."[1] Elliott argues that
Bluestone's notion has been extended incorrectly to suggest that there is
an unbridgeable divide between literary and filmic modes of representation. Elliott rightly notes that some of the drama of adaptation—the
"metamorphosis" of a text from word to screen image—lies in the very
tension between the word and the image. Thus, while adaptation studies
often imply or assert that the written word is somehow the *idea* while the
technically achieved image is the word made flesh, we might challenge
this notion by considering more complex interchanges between word and
image, book and film.

Although not an adaptation in the strictest sense,[2] David Lean's *Lawrence of Arabia* (1962) is an interesting case study of a *practice* of adaptation, taking as one of its primary sources T. E. Lawrence's *Seven Pillars of*

Wisdom.[3] The pairing of Lawrence's text with Lean's gives us an opportunity for working out Bluestone's remarks and Elliot's careful reconsiderations by providing a context for exploring the tensions between representation in word and image (whether still or moving).

As I examine the relationship of Lean's film to the written text and images of *Seven Pillars of Wisdom,* my principal concern will be for the dynamic between literary and cinematic bodies and human subjects. I am not concerned here so much with the film's historical authenticity and its attention (or inattention) to fact. I will, however, discuss how the film both relies on and negates what is known (and knowable) about Lawrence, particularly in the ways in which Lawrence presents himself.

While conventional notions of the relationship between book and film suggest that a film is, or can be, the "embodiment" of a written text, Lawrence's text and Lean's film complicate this. Lawrence's text offers a complex interchange between representations of bodies and representations of ideas, textual materiality and material being. This complexity is clearest in Lawrence's 1926 subscriber's abridgement, complete with author-commissioned and author-selected images. Lean's film moves from depictions of a concrete historical (if enigmatic) body to the abstraction of bodies from their materiality and back. Produced less than forty years later, *Lawrence of Arabia* yields new problems and possibilities for Lawrence's project, exemplified in the differences between the book's and the film's modes of figuring the human body and the human subject.

> It's very simple, sir. I'm looking for a hero.
>
> —Jackson Bentley (Arthur Kennedy)

Richard Aldington's much-contested 1955 "biographic enquiry" into the life of T. E. Lawrence begins famously with a letter to poet, essayist, and provocateur Alister Kershaw, who had urged Aldington to undertake the task: "You will remember how startled I was when you suggested that I should gratify your admiration for a hero by writing a life of Lawrence of Arabia."[4] Aldington claims an inability to gratify such a request: he has completed his enquiry, but he has been unable (and unwilling, though this he does not reveal) to produce an unequivocal hero. Aldington's letter is only part apology. He signals his awareness that his text—a critique of a national figure raised to the stature of myth in a short time, as well as a critique of a national project of mythmaking with respect to the East—shall itself meet with criticism. For his part, Aldington suggests that he has discovered a complicated man with a host of psychological complexes. Aldington thus engages in now-commonplace readings of Lawrence: the man as myth (fraud, even) and the man as enigma.

Aldington suggests that the Lawrence legend is a product of Lawrence's manufacture, and in this he is not incorrect:

> The legend of Lawrence has been built up by nearly all those writers who have taken Lawrence as their subjects, whether for a full-scale biography or for a three-page reminiscence. The edifice shows a fairly solid front to the uncritical reader but once it is examined it is shown to be an inverted pyramid at the base of which stands Lawrence himself on whom the legend rests.[5]

Critique came easily for Aldington, but "the truth about the man was harder to come by, as no one crack in the edifice revealed the whole truth."[6] Aldington's text—infamous for its abridgment of Lawrence's biography—indicates the Lawrence scholar's first problem: separating the man as idea of the national hero from the historical man. Aldington fails, however, to consider the second and, I would argue, more important problem, particularly with respect to any notion of the "fidelity" of Lean's film to Lawrence's life or literature: how to consider Lawrence's own construction of himself in and out of his texts as an aesthetic project and not simply, as Aldington does, as a campaign of self- or public deception.[7]

Lawrence biographies, including those by Aldington (1955) and biographer-psychiatrist John Mack (1976), and more recent works by Kaja Silverman (1992) and David Mengay (1994), have connected the fragmentary nature of Lawrence's text and his embellishments to Lawrence's angst over his own illegitimacy, his hybrid British national identity, and his reported sadomasochism and homosexuality.[8] Yet an interest in psychological analysis should not preclude criticism of *Seven Pillars* on literary terms and examination of the film's "fidelity" to Lawrence's work in formal terms. Strict emphases on Orientalism, sexual difference, and illegitimacy risk cutting off complex readings of the relationship between the text's form and content. I would argue that the form of *Seven Pillars* is intentionally indeterminate,[9] and that Lean takes up this indeterminacy.

Lean's film is composed of spoken words, sweeping orchestration, and masterful moving images of human bodies in an expansive desert, and Lawrence's own text is composed of 250,000 words, plates of commissioned portraits, and vorticist images. Both texts are multi-modal. Elliott argues that author-illustrated texts such as William Makepeace Thackeray's *Vanity Fair* complicate traditional adaptation studies notions of the exchange between images in words and images in illustration. Elliott focuses on "inter-art analogies," presumed and commonplace relationships between visual images and verbal imagery. Like other authors of literary source texts, Lawrence offers filmmakers more than a scenario, a biography, or a history; unlike others, however, he offers a multi-modal aesthetic and ontological project. Lean helps us shift the debate from the adaptation of content to the adaptation of form and content.

> For some men, nothing is written unless they write it themselves.
>
> —Sherif Ali (Omar Sharif)

By any account, Lean's text is not a conventional adaptation. Blacklisted American screenwriter Michael Wilson's first draft of the screenplay includes events from *Seven Pillars* along with characters and incidents of his own invention. Lean's second screenwriter, playwright and former history instructor Robert Bolt (contracted after Wilson's departure over "ideological differences" with the film's director and producer, Sam Spiegel), describes *Seven Pillars* as his "prime, almost [his] only source."[10] However, Wilson and Bolt are both likely to have consulted *T. E. Lawrence by His Friends,* and it is clear that Bolt consulted Wilson's earlier script: the structure of Bolt's screenplay closely follows the structure of Wilson's.[11] Wilson defends his position as legal author of the text: "Most of my inventions have been retained in the shooting script...By invention I mean incidents, situations and events which are not to be found in *Seven Pillars of Wisdom* or any other work about Lawrence."[12] In the debate over screenwriting credit for the film (a share of which was granted recently and only posthumously to Wilson), both Wilson and Bolt privilege *Seven Pillars* as their source text. Neither writer appeals to an authentic Lawrence: the search for an authentic Lawrence seems a much less interesting and much less productive project.

Defending against criticism that he had maligned the epic's hero, Bolt argues:

> A man's account of his deeds is already at one remove from the deeds themselves. A second man's evaluation of that account is at another remove again. His dramatization of that evaluation is at a further remove still.[13]

Bolt situates his own writing within *its* historical context and indicates the fundamental problem of all representations: signification can never close the gap between that which is represented and the representation of it. In his own defense, Bolt suggests that any notion of fidelity to a text, an event, or a subject is a naïve one. This may be truer in Lawrence's case than in nearly any other: by Lawrence's own account, his project is less history or autobiography than it is an attempt at a modernist epic, with all the narrative and generic instability such a designation suggests.[14] This includes the episodic nature of the narrative and the co-presence of competing modes of storytelling, along with self-allegorization balanced by self-critique and self-parody.

In a letter to D. G. Hogarth, Lawrence suggests that he carried Malory's *Le Morte d'Arthur*, the *Oxford Book of English Verse*, and Aristophanes's *Peace* on campaign. Rather than adopting or eliminating the allegorical mode, Lawrence takes his own romanticizing tendencies and his own perceptions as his objects of record and interrogation. Charles Grosvenor writes that Lawrence intended his work to be an "English fourth" to *The Brothers Kara-mazov*, *Thus Spake Zarathustra*, and *Moby Dick*.[15] In his letters, however, Lawrence indicates the challenge posed by the epic as demonstrated by his failed attempt to translate the *Odyssey*. Accordingly in *Seven Pillars*, Lawrence writes, "The epic mode was alien to me, as to my generation. Memory gave me no clue to the heroic, so that I could not feel such men as [Howeitat leader] Auda in myself. He seemed fantastic as the hills of Rumm, old as Mallory."[16] The epic mode was not so much alien to Lawrence as he was alienated from it, committed equally to the material form of the book and to literature as both Idea and Ideal. Lawrence suggests that the epic-hero subject-position is inaccessible to him, and equally so the epic-writing one. Thus, while many Lawrence scholars (for example, Mack and Silverman) suggest that Lawrence's sexual Otherness determines his psyche, which in turn determines the form and the content of his text, it seems to me that this is the less compelling reading, and not the interpretation to pursue in order to consider Lean's own reading of the text. In the introduction to his text, Lawrence writes:

> In these pages the history is not of the Arab movement, but of me in it. It is a narrative of daily life, mean happenings, little people. Here there are no lessons for the world, no disclosures to shock people. It is filled with trivial things, partly that no one mistake for history the bones from which someday a man may make history, and partially for the pleasure it gave me to recall the fellowship of the revolt.[17]

As early as the introduction, Lawrence locates the "me" of which he writes on the side of the body, the bodily, the quotidian. By doing so, Lawrence does not deny the scope and significance of the epic mode but puts such scope in tension with the banal. I would argue that this is the central tension in the text to which Lean's film is faithful—Lean takes up Lawrence's own questions of textual and historical materiality, and of immanence and transcendence. This is a challenge to be sure. Yet perhaps Lean was best suited to portraying these complexities: his *Lawrence* is situated between *Bridge on the River Kwai* (1957) and *Doctor Zhivago* (1965), both adaptations, and both films in which the problems of history and history-telling are tied to bodies, to landscapes, and to nation.[18]

You have a body like other men.

—Sherif Ali (Omar Sharif)

Kaja Silverman suggests that in *Seven Pillars,* Lawrence undergoes a change of psychic identity with a change of clothes. To some degree, the film *Lawrence* bears this out. Lawrence writes of the transformative moment in which he first adopts Arab dress,

> Suddenly, Feisal asked me if I would wear Arab clothes like his own while in the camp. I should find it better for my own part, since it was a comfortable dress in which to live Arab-fashion as we must do. Besides, the tribesmen would then understand how to take me.[19]

This is the inaugural moment of a trope, the significance of which Lawrence makes explicit. In *Seven Pillars,* the robes are Prince Feisal's wedding robes, given and worn so that Feisal's men might know to take Lawrence as both leader and led. The clothes become a signifier of both sameness and difference:

> It was notoriety to be the only cleanshaven one, and I doubled it by wearing always the suspect pure silk, of the whitest (at least outside), with a gold and crimson Meccan head-rope and gold dagger. By so dressing I staked a claim which Feisal's public consideration of me confirmed.[20]

In Lean's film, on the other hand, Lawrence dons the robes of Sherif Ali Ibn el Karesh (Omar Sharif), a composite character based only in part on the historical Harith chief Sherif Ali Ibn el Hussein. Lawrence's robes lose their marital—and hence explicitly subordinating—significance and come to signify almost exclusively his difference from the "masses" of the Arab army and his mis-fit with his British peers in Cairo. His willingness to don these robes and to perform this difference accords with Silverman's position on the role of the robes in the written text (and for Lawrence's historical person). She asserts that taking on the dress and customs of the Arabs with whom Lawrence traveled and fought evinces an imperialist "will to power."[21]

Yet I would argue that his Arab dress, in both Lawrence's text and Lean's, and its challenges to gender and nationality, functions as a *critique* of Western imperialist subjectivity. If "being Arab"—a costumed person of an externally constituted people, constructed largely in the time and through the effort at unification of Lawrence's campaign—is a matter of dress and cultural code, then perhaps, Lawrence argues, Britishness is a matter of custom and costume as well.[22] The film, though, suggests that Lawrence-ness (if not Britishness) is an identity performed through complex, culturally codified behavior and psychological singularity. It suggests that Lawrence-ness is a matter of costume and gesture. As with all historical films and biopics, the actor Peter O'Toole's very body refers to the body of the historical Lawrence while guaranteeing the "actual" Lawrence's absence.[23] By contrast, in the written and illustrated text, we may have both Lawrence the author and the figure, or we may have neither.

In Lawrence's text, Prince Feisal raises even greater questions about immanence and transcendence, man and idea, than his own sartorial transformation. He constitutes a central problem for Lawrence's text and subsequently for Lean's. Through Lawrence's Feisal, we see that men for Lawrence are inescapably corporeal, singular, and historical, but that this immanence is always in tension with a kind of transcendence (though not of the spiritual-eternal nature but rather of the philosophical or aesthetic). In "The Last Preaching," Lawrence observes Feisal's almost-physical transformation from the man into the Idea. Lawrence writes of his appraisal of Feisal at the end of the campaign:

> Of course it was a picture-man, not flesh and blood but nevertheless true, for his individuality had yielded its third dimension to the idea, had surrendered the world's wealth and artifices. Feisal was hidden in his tent, veiled to remain our leader: while in reality he was nationality's best servant, its tool, not its owner. Yet in the twilight nothing seemed more noble.[24]

In his words—in his description of Feisal as veiled, as yielding his "third dimension"—Lawrence images a kind of disappearing act or a disembodiment. Lawrence's text insists on the veil here not only as a limitation of our vision but also as a critique of the abstraction of material bodies from their historicity.[25] Here, in disappointment, Lawrence describes a Feisal veiled to appear to his people as the abstract Ideal which they served, all the while knowing this Ideal would ultimately serve the very concrete Western European political ideal of the partitioning of the Middle East into French and British spheres of influence.[26]

This "veiling" is a partial-disappearing act that Lawrence's written language can perform, but which Lean's film does not. If the very act of adaptation to the cinema is an act of "embodiment," in this case it is decidedly to Feisal's disadvantage. This is not merely a result of the casting of English actor and film icon Alec Guinness as the Arab prince. In Lean's film, we lose the potential for Feisal to approach an ideal because Lean's (and Guinness's) Feisal is ever the politician, and the film's concluding negotiations prove him to be the Western-modeled bureaucrat. What's more, he is materialized in cinematic space and time in ways that prevent Lawrence's depiction of Feisal as symbol—arguably one part of the automatic difference between written language and the indexicality of film—and this closes off to us Lawrence's own vexing of the status of historical people. In Lawrence's text, Feisal moves between the man and the idea; he operates as a signifier of the Idea and the Possible but never embodies either. Lawrence's depiction of Feisal as an icon indicates the tension between material being and the capacity to *represent*. Kamilla Elliott reminds us of Christian Metz's argument that "[t]he cinema is the 'phenomenological' art *par excellence*," that the "signifier is coextensive with the whole of the significate, the spectacle is its own signification, thus short-circuiting the sign itself."[27] This is not to reinstate the percept/concept divide, but to suggest rather our need to interrogate such a division. In this case, it seems that Lawrence chooses to contrast images with imagery in order to leave ontological and epistemological questions open, while Lean's film does not or cannot.

> …in the naked desert, under the indifferent heaven.…
>
> —T. E. Lawrence

Of the desert and its vastness, Lawrence writes at the start of *Seven Pillars*:

> For years we lived anyhow with one another in the naked desert, under the indifferent heaven. By day the hot sun fermented us; and we were dizzied by the beating wind. At night we were sustained by dew, and shamed into pettiness by the innumerable silences of stars.[28]

The desert's expanse and the sky's infinity are contrasted with the daily marches and camel rides, the color and texture of fabric, bloodied and bloodying hands, and what Lawrence in the end describes as the liquescence of dead and decaying bodies—"fluid" and "jellying" in trenches.[29] Yet despite a materiality of the body conveyed by such language choices, Lawrence rejects graphic body images in favor of metaphor and absurdist graphic illustration.

In Lawrence's text, tensions between body and landscape are worked out in choices of what to image in words and what to depict in images. Scenarios are realized in vorticist and various modernist images, and the desert is shown sparingly. Even in language, the desert's scope is largely unexpressed: Troy Boone has suggested that perhaps in Lawrence's text there are no literary equivalents to long shots, only close-ups and medium close-ups.[30] Yet what matters for Lawrence is that in the juxtaposition of the two modes of representation—writing and imaging—both prove wanting in terms of the construction and revelation of subjects and subjectivities as words and images veil and unveil Lawrence's cast of characters in literal and figurative senses.

> …my impotence of vision showed me my shape best in painted pictures.
>
> —T. E. Lawrence

To accompany his text, Lawrence selected drawn portraits and comic and vorticist images, reproduced under the art direction of Eric Kennington.[31] That Lawrence positioned the images he and Kennington selected at the back of the text in each copy of the subscriber's edition suggests to Gregory Graalfs that Lawrence was displeased by the contrast between the Victorianism of his text and the modern style of the portraits.[32] Charles Grosvenor writes that Lawrence had communicated to Bruce Rogers that "[t]o combine representational images (above all in colour) with the formality of type seemed to me an impossible achievement."[33] Yet Grosvenor justifies the positioning of the portraits always in the appendix to the dramatic elements of the text:

> If the book may be regarded, as Lawrence himself did, as "partly theatre" it is natural to expect a curtain call for the performers at drama's end. This is what the Appendix provides, as well as a complement to Lawrence's "summary descriptions" of his performers.[34]

Neither Grosvenor nor Graalfs's assessment of the significance of the portraiture to *Seven Pillars* is entirely satisfying.

Of his decision to employ portrait artists, Lawrence himself writes, "It seemed to me that every portrait drawing of a stranger-sitter partook somewhat of the judgment of God. If I could get the named people of this book drawn, it would be their appeal to a higher court against my summary descriptions."[35] It is most significant that the human process of adapting the subjects to two-dimensional images "partook somewhat" of the highest authority and worked against Lawrence's own "summary descriptions," in much the same way that Lawrence suggests that he was best known to himself as he was "overheard and overseen" by others. Lawrence suggests in 1921 that "words, especially an amateur's words, are unsatisfactory to describe persons. It seemed to us that it would be balanced somewhat by an expert view, from another angle: and so Kennington went out to correct my men."[36] This indicates that Lawrence was interested not in evidence, which photography might provide, but in alternate interpretations as correction.

The portrait images are interesting for their ability to signify without representing. Grosvenor writes, "Eric Kennington's independent modernity is preserved in his brilliant series of pastel portraits."[37] Lawrence, too, was aware of this emergent modernity. One of the most striking observations he makes of the images concerns their demonstration of the relationship of the particular to the general.[38] Lawrence admits to practical reasons for such generalizations (Kennington did not speak the language and hence had no access to the psychology of the characters he studied, and of necessity he had been abandoned by Lawrence, his would-be guide). Lawrence counts among the virtues of the Kennington portraits that "some are quite typical" and that "often Kennington has reached behind the particular, and made them also types." For Lawrence this dual capacity is most important:

> However it is, in this study and in that you can see not only So and So, son of So and So, but a representation of all the Ageyl, who ever rode out from Baghdad, or all of the freedmen of the palm-oases of Nejd. In his Sherifs and in his Sheiks you see the spirit of the race of sherifs, or of the class of sheiks sitting within these men's clothes, inhabiting their features, giving a broader significance to their shapes.[39]

This assessment of the images surely supports readings of Lawrence's text and Lawrence himself, as man and figure, as Orientalist, even as this typifying capacity of the images applies for Lawrence to the images of the British figures as well—but it also reveals something about his conception of modes of representation in his moment.

Yet he de-emphasizes this rationale by insisting on the psychological accuracy of the portraits: "I saw first one and then another of the men whom I had known, and at once learned to know them better."[40] For Lawrence, it is this last quality that permits us to observe these works individually as works of art and which makes them so significant to both the writer and the reader/viewer of the text.

In either case, whether figural or psychological, Lawrence's portrait images cannot be described as narrative, in that they fix their subjects, decontextualize them, and abstract them. They recall André Bazin's notion that the filming of an object is equivalent to the subtraction of dimension and the addition of duration. No longer historically situated subjects, the portrait-sitters become timeless. The portraits thus simultaneously fix subjectivity and efface it. Here we must recall that Lawrence later wrote, "while I like decorated books, I do not like illustrated books."[41] If this is so, nothing subtends the image—not even the historical person who sat for each portrait.

Yet Bazin's notion is indirectly applicable to Lawrence's project, revealing tensions between iconic and indexical images.[42] Lawrence has not selected photographic images, despite his own documented capabilities as a photographer and despite the photographic images of the campaign in Arabia available to him. This is also despite Lowell Thomas's film *With Allenby in Palestine and Lawrence in Arabia* (1919), and Lawrence's contemporary Gertrude Bell's selection of photographic images for her own text, *The Desert and the Sown* (1907). While Bell's text is ethnographic in mode, offering to her readers a particular kind of knowledge and knowability of the East, Lawrence's image selection suggests the complexities of knowing and representations of being known. Lawrence elects to represent the text's subjects in words and in artistic images while he chooses to leave the mythical status and proportions of the desert to words. Perhaps, then, the first adaptation of Lawrence's text is his own set of accompanying images.

In Lean's film, the values indicated by this first "adaptation" are necessarily reversed. The camera literalizes and concretizes human bodies in their glory and grotesquery. Bolt argues that this is inescapable: "'Others' lives became toys to break and throw away' is a statement, but a poeticized statement: it is all metaphor. To put it on the screen you have to uncover what it means in terms of concrete action...take a picture of that, and show it; the comforting blanket of metaphor has gone."[43] For Bolt, the cinematic image—or that of an essentially realist cinema—is not capable of the kind of metaphor possible in words.

If *Seven Pillars* either fails to capture or knowingly subverts expectations by limiting the expression of an endless desert, the film *Lawrence* indulges in them. Images of the openness of the desert landscape, endless as the sea to which the film's characters and Freddie Young's cinematography compare it, contrast with the sense of enclosure (almost claustrophobic) of the later British scenes. Our first view of the desert appears as a painting, until the sun rises with the orchestration; so, too, does our second view but for the movement in the far distance of two small figures, barely more than black dots on the pastel horizon. Throughout the film, still and mobile frames capture a desert both real and unreal. Bolt suggests that the purpose of the film *Lawrence* is, with the unparalleled possibilities in cinematic technologies, to *show* both the historical figures and the desert that is their setting—particularly, in this case, in Cinemascope. Bolt writes, "in a deeper sense than that of the plot, the background to the story is the Desert. Words cannot trap that landscape. The camera almost can, and did. It is the essence of the saga."[44]

Yet what Lean's film does maintain from Lawrence's text/image divide is the problem of the proportion of human figure to desert landscape that the text and illustrations construct. In a famous example, Freddie Young ingeniously employs a 450 mm lens from a thousand feet away to produce the mirage shot of Sherif Ali "'materializing out of the heat waves,' capturing and compressing the rising vibrations."[45] In a less well-remembered but particularly provocative sequence, a thin band of bare desert ground shares the screen only with an endless, "indifferent" sky. The scope and the depth of the shot are ambiguous until a foot breaks the frame in medium close-up. Immediately we are aware that although we know the character Gasim struggles alone in the endless desert, we are not seeing the endlessness of the desert itself but only one low-angle shot of it. Lean thus adapts Lawrence's description of the "sand haze," and in one moment our sense of, or expectation for, cinema's optical mastery of space is inverted. The desert is endless. Our own vision—even cinematic vision, even Cinemascopic vision—is *not*. Taking

these technologies together, words and illustrations for Lawrence and Cinemascope for Lean, author and filmmaker seem equally engaged with the
problems and possibilities of vision: seeing, showing, and knowing.

> As faithful…as a drama can be to a document.
>
> —Screenwriter Robert Bolt

Bolt ends his "Apologia," at heart a defense of his interpretation of Lawrence
against charges of infidelity, thusly: "I do claim that [*Lawrence*] is a reason-
ably faithful dramatization drawn from his own account. As faithful, that is,
as drama can be to a document."[46]
     In his essay "For an Impure Cinema," Bazin writes:

> One might suggest that in the realm of language and style cinematic creation
> is in direct ratio to fidelity. For the same reasons that render a word-by-word
> translation worthless and a too free translation a matter for condemnation, a
> good adaptation should result in a restoration of the letter and the spirit.[47]

Bazin's suggestion never seems to lose pertinence, and in Lawrence's case we
must always ask about the letter and letters/images. To this set of concerns
we must add that more important than a "faithful" adaptation of a text to the
screen is a film text's ability to perform or produce interesting, viable, and
useful readings of the preceding text. Perhaps this is why an unfaithful text
may *seem* faithful, why a faithful text may be uninteresting, and why an adaptation that is *not quite* an adaptation may revitalize a source text in another
valence. Finally, perhaps this is what Lean gives to Lawrence: another technology for the pursuit of questions of immanence and transcendence, myth
and matter, in a particular historical moment.

NOTES

A version of this paper was first published as "Imaging Subjects and Imagining Bodies: T. E. Lawrence's *Seven Pillars of Wisdom* and David Lean's *Lawrence of Arabia*," in
In/Fidelity, ed. David L. Kranz and Nancy C. Mellerski (Newcastle: Cambridge Scholars Publishing, 2008), 138–54. I am indebted to Troy Boone for his generous response
to my earlier reading of *Seven Pillars of Wisdom*, to Colin MacCabe for his response to
the initial version of this essay, and to Marcia Landy.

1. Kamilla Elliott, *Rethinking the Novel/Film Debate* (New York: Cambridge University
   Press, 2003), 221.
2. Although Jason Ingram shows no hesitation in using the term in his article "Con-
   flicted Possession: A Pentadic Assessment of T. E. Lawrence's Desert Narrative," *K.B.*

Journal 4, no. 1 (Fall 2007): http://www.kbjournal.org/ingram. Indeed, recent work in adaptation studies have dramatically opened up what we consider an adaptation from the more conventionally held idea that it is the translation of a novel into a film. However, if we take Linda Hutcheon's fundamental premise from *A Theory of Adaptation* (New York: Routledge, 2005) that an adaptation must be understood as such by its audience, *Lawrence of Arabia* as adaptation becomes, again, complicated.

3. Quotations from the text are from *Seven Pillars of Wisdom: A Triumph* (New York: Anchor-Random, 1991), while descriptions of images and illustrations refer to *Seven Pillars of Wisdom: A Triumph*, Subscriber's Abridgment (London: text and decorations, Manning Pike with H.J. Hodgson; plates, Charles Whittingham and Griggs; binding, McLeish, 1926. New York Public Library, Arents Rare Books Collection, first owned by Charlotte Shaw. Viewed by special permission.)

4. Richard Aldington, *Lawrence of Arabia: A Biographical Enquiry* (Chicago: Henry Regnery Co., 1995), 11.

5. Aldington, *Lawrence of Arabia*, 13.

6. Aldington, *Lawrence of Arabia*, 13.

7. For recent studies that address this dilemma, see William Mooney, "Memoir and the Limits of Adaptation," in *The Film/Literature Reader: Issues of Adaptation*, ed. James Michael Welsh and Peter Lev (Lanham, Md.: Scarecrow Press, 2007), 285–96; and Alessandra Raengo, "A Necessary Signifier: The Adaptation of Robinson's Body-Image in 'The Jackie Robinson Story,'" *Adaptation* 1, no. 2 (2008): 79–105.

8. John E. Mack, *A Prince of Our Disorder: The Life of T. E. Lawrence* (Boston: Little, Brown, 1976); Kaja Silverman, *Male Subjectivity at the Margins* (New York: Routledge, 1992); David Mengay, "Arabian Rites: T. E. Lawrence's *Seven Pillars of Wisdom* and the Erotics of Empire," *Genre* 27 (1994): 395–416.

9. While any proper consideration of Lawrence's text should take into account Edward Said's formidable *Orientalism*, 25th anniv. ed. (New York: Vintage-Random, 2003), especially Said's concern that Lawrence in his text, politics, and practices is not only an Orientalist but *the Orientalist par excellence*, I will not engage with such matters here. Without rejecting Said's reading of Lawrence, Kaja Silverman indicates in *Male Subjectivity at the Margins* that "Said's formulation forecloses upon Lawrence's homosexuality as well as the hyperbolic permeability of his psyche" (299). I would argue that Silverman's own reading and others dependent on it foreclose on issues I wish to take up here.

10. Robert Bolt, "Apologia," *Cineaste* 21, no. 4 (1995): 33.

11. Joel Hodson, "Who Wrote *Lawrence of Arabia*?" *Cineaste* 20, no. 4 (1994): 17.

12. Hodson, "Who Wrote *Lawrence of Arabia*?" 14.

13. Before this, Bolt writes, "By the time Shakespeare wrote [*Richard III*] Richard had no surviving friends or relatives. Even if they had they might have been disarmed by Shakespeare's verse. No such inhibition operates in my case and some of T. E. Lawrence's surviving friends have expressed indignation at my account. I am not indifferent to their reaction and feel now that it was perhaps a mistake to attempt

to dramatize such very recent history even though the hero has almost forfeited his historical actuality and become a figure in contemporary mythology" (33).

14. For one literary-critical consideration of *Seven Pillars'* generic instability, see William Halloran's dissertation, "Titan, Tome and Triumph: T. E. Lawrence's *Seven Pillars of Wisdom* as Modernist Spectacle" (PhD diss., University of California at Los Angeles, 2001).

15. Charles Grosvenor, "The Subscriber's *Seven Pillars of Wisdom*: The Visual Aspect," in *The T.E. Lawrence Puzzle*, ed. Stephen Tabachnick (Athens: University of Georgia Press, 1984), 159.

16. Lawrence, *Seven Pillars*, 549.

17. Lawrence, *Seven Pillars*, 24.

18. See Christine Geraghty's chapter, "Revising the Western: Movement and Description in *Last of the Mohicans* and *Brokeback Mountain*" for an extended discussion on the place of landscape in adaptation. Geraghty, *Now a Major Motion Picture* (Lanham, Md.: Rowman & Littlefield, 2007), 135–66.

19. Geraghty, *Now a Major Motion Picture*, 126.

20. Geraghty, *Now a Major Motion Picture*, 547.

21. In *Male Subjectivity at the Margins*, Silverman writes, "In seeking to imitate the Arabs to the point where they might be prompted to imitate him back, the Lawrence of *Seven Pillars* both inverts and doubles the classical colonial paradigm" so that the adopting of Arab customs and manners demonstrates a "will to power" (312), though she makes clear Lawrence's "discomfort with conventional notions of 'Empire'" (307). Silverman's analysis enables ways of reading Lawrence and *Seven Pillars* other than through a simple lens of colonialism, but her emphasis on sexuality and sublimation cut off other considerations of the construction of the text.

22. Lawrence's subsequent text, *The Mint*, written between 1922 and 1928, first published in 1955, suggests that this is so.

23. For an extended discussion of this question of embodiment, see Sarah J. Heidt, "'Ça, c'est moi': *The Diving Bell and the Butterfly* as Autobiographical Multitext," *Adaptation* 2, no. 2 (2009): 125–48. Heidt explores the ways in which this question is made visible in both filmic and written texts.

24. Lawrence, *Seven Pillars*, 547.

25. Early in this same text, he writes of the Arabs: "They were incorrigibly children of the idea, feckless and colour-blind, to whom body and spirit were forever and inevitably opposed. Their mind was strange and dark, full of depressions and exaltations, lacking in rule, but with more of ardor and more fertile in belief than any other in the world" (42).

26. France's François Georges-Picot and Britain's Mark Sykes oversaw this partitioning of the Middle East into French and British areas of direct control and territories of influence, hence negating Lawrence's promises to his Arab counterparts of an independent Arabia.

27. Elliott, *Rethinking the Novel/Film Debate*, 218.

28. Lawrence, *Seven Pillars*, 29.

29. Lawrence, *Seven Pillars*, 657.

30. Personal communication, 2006.

31. The extent to which Kennington directed, and Lawrence did not, is debatable and often debated in the critical literature.

32. Gregory Graalfs, "Lawrence of Arabia, Designer and Printer," *Print* 50 (1996): 56.

33. Grosvenor, "Subscriber's *Seven Pillars*," 165.

34. Grosvenor, "Subscriber's *Seven Pillars*," 166.

35. Lawrence, *Seven Pillars*, 15.

36. T. E. Lawrence, *Note on Kennington's Arab Portraits* (London: Ernest, Brown & Phillips, the Leicester Galleries, 1927), 15.

37. Grosvenor, "Subscriber's *Seven Pillars*," 177. The author ultimately considers the design of Lawrence's book an interesting failure, in which "multiplicity seems to have replaced complexity as Lawrence looked at a visual problem in literary terms" (180). My own impression of the physical book is that it is precisely in this multiplicity that we see nascent modernity and a passing Victorianism.

38. Or is it a contrivance? It is impossible to know whether this consideration preceded, and hence guided, the production of the images.

39. Lawrence, *Note on Kennington's Arab Portraits*, 16.

40. Lawrence, *Note on Kennington's Arab Portraits*, 16.

41. Lawrence, from a letter to Bruce Rogers, quoted in Grosvenor, 161.

42. Here I mean to indicate the semiotic difference between representations of topological similarity and representations that imply the prior existence of that which is represented, as the difference between a sketch and a photograph.

43. Bolt, "Apologia," 34.

44. Bolt, "Apologia," 34.

45. Gary Crowdus, "Just Make it Marvelous, Freddie: Interview with Freddie Young," *Cineaste* 21, no. 3 (1995): 19.

46. Bolt, "Apologia," 34.

47. André Bazin, "For an Impure Cinema [In Defense of Mixed Cinema]," in *What is Cinema?* vol. 1, trans. Hugh Gray (Berkeley and Los Angeles: University of California Press, 1971), 67.

The Shining (Kubrick, 1980)

10

SHADES OF HORROR

Fidelity and Genre in Stanley Kubrick's The Shining

Jarrell D. Wright

Initial critical reactions to Stanley Kubrick's 1980 film adaptation of *The Shining*, the bestselling 1977 novel by Stephen King, were almost uniformly hostile. A striking pattern emerges from a survey of these reviews, in which critics repeatedly cited two major problems with *The Shining*. First, reviewers often complained that Kubrick's adaptation departed too radically from the novel. According to one critic, "The truly amazing question is why a director of Kubrick's stature would spend his time and effort on a novel he changes so much it's barely recognizable, taking away whatever originality it possessed while emphasizing its banality."[1] Second, there was a consensus that the film failed to satisfy the expectations attending its status as Kubrick's entry into the horror film genre—it was not scary. One reviewer asked, "Did Stanley Kubrick really say that [it] would be the scariest horror movie of all time? He shouldn't have."[2]

Although my assessment of *The Shining* is quite different—indeed, I argue that Kubrick's substantial alterations to the structure and details of King's narrative are essential to the unorthodox, yet no less frightening, horror film he created—the purpose of this essay is not to take issue with these early reviews. Rather, this essay will offer an analysis of *The Shining* that explores in the context of adaptation theory more generally the two concerns that animated those reviews: fidelity and genre.

The question of fidelity has vexed film theory for so long that to some scholars it has become "tiresome."[3] Yet for many observers, it remains "at the center of the adaptive problem,"[4] and—as the response to Kubrick's *The Shining* (and uncounted other film adaptations before and since then) attests—many film critics and general audiences continue to believe André Bazin's maxim that a "good adaptation should result in a restoration of the letter and spirit" of the original work.[5] As a consequence, no general theory of adaptation—to the extent that one is even possible—can be considered complete unless it accounts for the stubbornly persistent notion that an adaptation's fidelity to its source text is, at a minimum, relevant to criticism of the filmic text.

Using *The Shining* as a test case, this essay suggests that an analysis of the differences between a film and its source might offer a useful starting point for a critique of the film by illuminating the question of what the filmmaker sought to accomplish by adapting a particular work, a necessary first step in ascertaining whether or not the adaptation is successful.

However, to frame the issue in these terms is to make two assumptions that go against the grain of current scholarship in film studies. First, it constitutes an appeal to "evaluation as a critical project," a concern that "except in the area of adaptation study" has come to be perceived as quaintly old-fashioned.[6] Although I cannot hope to demonstrate that the evaluative endeavor is at the cutting edge of critical theory, I do expect that this essay will illustrate how the kind of fidelity analysis I propose can contribute to the supposedly more sophisticated task of "asking how [a film] works," and to an understanding of how the question of fidelity does not necessarily amount to "an appeal to anteriority" or to "a valorization of literature as such in the face of the insurgent challenge of cinema studies."[7] Second, my project also assumes the validity, if not the primacy, of auteur theory as a way of understanding adaptations or other filmic texts. Although a defense of auteur theory is beyond the scope of this essay, my assumption that this approach to film studies is valuable requires at least an explanatory aside.

Whatever shortcomings auteur theory may have as a general enterprise, it is certainly a useful tool for understanding the films of Stanley Kubrick. Perhaps more than any other contemporary director, Kubrick possessed and exercised plenary authority over his projects:

> He prefers to prepare a project, collect material for it over a period of months, even years, pore over books and magazines with the systematic curiosity of an autodidact, monitor the seating capacity and average takings of cinemas in each foreign capital or the design and deployment of posters or even the distance between seats and screen at press shows, not to mention the size of newspaper ads and the rates of currency exchange. He also has the subtitles of every foreign version of his films completely re-translated into English to make certain that nothing crucial has been omitted, supervises all dubbed versions, and checked out the quality of the seven hundred prints of *The Shining* which were released the same day in the United States.[8]

Kubrick also enjoyed the coveted right to final cut, which he was able to exercise in the case of *The Shining,* only screening the film to studio executives a mere ten days before its release.[9] And Kubrick himself—who wrote or co-wrote all of his feature films except for *Fear and Desire* (1953) and *Spartacus* (1960)—saw his task as a director to be nothing "more or less than a continuation of the writing. I think that is precisely what directing should be."[10]

Kubrick, however, is an unusual case. One of the weaknesses of auteur theory is that it not only "privileges the contributions of directors over the contributions of other creative artists in the production of a film, but it also privileges some directors over others"—specifically directors like Kubrick who are considered to be auteurs.[11] But at least one scholar and film producer has suggested that some form of auteur theory can legitimately play a broader role in film studies: "The experience of production relations within a film makes clear how one can award an authorial primacy to the director without adopting any of the idealist presuppositions about origin or homogeneity which seem to arise unbidden in one's path."[12] The auteurist bias embodied in this essay, therefore, need not be seen as an impediment to the validity or wider applicability of the fidelity analysis I advocate. Instead, my choice of an auteur's film to elucidate that analysis is a methodological tool, simplifying the presentation of a technique that, in principle, can be employed in critical work on films that do not lend themselves as readily to auteurist approaches.[13]

In contrast to the issue of fidelity, considerations of genre sporadically arise in adaptation studies.[14] Genre tends to become a concern only in analyses of particular films that are themselves deemed to be genre pieces. What makes such an oversight remarkable is the fact that adaptation theory and genre theory share so many points of congruence. Most notably, genres can be analyzed as aesthetic forms that are assembled from the gradual accretion of a diachronic series of adaptations. Likewise, both genre theory and adaptation theory interrogate the Romantic notion of authorship as an individualistic endeavor and the status of texts as hermetically independent entities. And a resource for adaptation theory that has yet to be explored adequately arises from the metaphorical relationship between "adaptation" in the filmic or literary sense and "adaptation" as a concept of the natural sciences, a relationship that parallels the connection between the ideas of genre and genera.[15]

Because of these commonalities, and the emerging consensus that adaptation criticism is too heavily invested in the primacy of the source text, this essay proposes, with *The Shining* as an example, that adaptation theory can benefit from considering a film in relation to the history of generic conventions within which both the film and its source text are situated. In other words, a film participates in—and should therefore be conceptualized as part of—a *sequence* of adaptations of which the "original" text, in turn, constitutes a segment.[16]

My reading of Kubrick's *The Shining* both frames and unites these two general strands of argument. In the first section of this essay, I contend that the fidelity analysis I propose as a component of adaptation criticism, when applied to *The Shining*, casts doubt upon the most common interpretation of the film: that Kubrick's adaptation is an indictment of violence on a historical scale, with particular reference to European colonial practices in America. Instead, the film's most significant departures from the novel suggest that Kubrick's primary concern is the source of evil, which Kubrick locates within the ambit of human reality rather than the domain of the supernatural. In the second section, through the lens of genre theory, I examine Kubrick's shift toward realism and away from the marvelous elements of the Stephen King novel. Treating the King and Kubrick iterations of *The Shining* as instances of the Gothic, I explain Kubrick's modulation of the narrative in terms of the tensions within that genre between rationalistic and nonrationalistic discourses. Both aspects of my argument in this regard are offered as models that other scholars might adopt, or adapt, in taking adaptation criticism in a different direction.

RECONSIDERING FIDELITY

Critical perspectives on the proper role of fidelity in adaptation theory have varied from enshrining the source text as the ideal that a film must emulate to the other extreme of according it no importance at all. Bluestone—who posits the linguistic medium of source text as so fundamentally different from the visual medium of film as to render the two virtually incommensurable—argues that some degree of infidelity is "*inevitable* the moment one abandons the linguistic for the visual medium," and therefore that fidelity analysis is, if not irrelevant, then at least uninteresting.[17] In this respect, he anticipates more recent critics like Thomas Leitch and Robert Stam who offer more virulent arguments against fidelity analysis.[18] At the opposite pole, where Bazin argued that an adaptation should reproduce "the letter and spirit" of the original, more moderate claims in favor of fidelity considerations have recently emerged. James Griffith, for one, suggests that "fidelity to effects rather than details" can be an appropriate element in criticism of an adaptation.[19]

What renders all of these perspectives inadequate is the assumption that to a greater or lesser extent undergirds each of them—the idea that transferring a narrative from one medium to another necessitates transforming the narrative in a manner coded as infidelity. Bluestone, of course, makes this assumption explicit in his analysis of adaptation,[20] but it implicitly informs Leitch's claim that fidelity "is unattainable... and theoretically possible only in a trivial sense. Like translations to a new language, adaptations will always reveal their sources' superiority because whatever their faults, the source texts will always be better at being themselves."[21] Similarly, Griffith's dismissal of an adaptation's fidelity to the details of its source narrative relies upon a model of mimesis inspired by Samuel Taylor Coleridge's distinction between imitations and copies: "deductively abstract critics who emphasize the medium agree with Coleridge that the written work need not taste like an apple, but they insist that the film adaptation taste like ink."[22] Even Bazin, by mentioning the possibility that a film can remain faithful to the spirit of the original work, tacitly admits that fidelity to its letter is problematic.

But the notion that adapting a written work for the cinema requires change is true only in the most reductive sense and false in every other. The closest a film could come to being a perfectly faithful adaptation of a novel would be for it to display the novel's scrolling text on the screen in the manner of closing credits—or perhaps to frame the opened novel from a reader's-eye view with a hand occasionally appearing to turn the pages—but even then the film would not, in Griffith's words, taste like ink. While on one level this suggestion is absurd, it serves on another to highlight the fact that what we would deem as a practical matter to be the "perfectly faithful," or even slavish, adaptation is far from a chimera. Such films are produced routinely; critics usually hate them. When Stephen King produced a six-hour television-miniseries version of *The Shining* based on the screenplay that Kubrick had rejected twenty years earlier,[23] "the result [was] what you might call a literal interpretation of *The Shining*, as dramatically attenuated and thin on emotional substance as most of King's books."[24]

One consequence of the inaccurate view that narrative transformation is an inevitable product of adapting a written work to the screen has been film criticism that all too readily explains away such changes as the necessary result of the adaptation process. Greg Jenkins, for example, states that his main objective in studying Kubrick's adaptations is to examine how and why Kubrick alters characters, narrative structures, and other elements of his sources. Yet Jenkins's analysis of *The Shining* most often attributes major departures from King's novel to the requirements of the medium of cinema, particularly the financial pressures to limit running time and the resulting phenomenon of narrative compression.[25]

For instance, the interview scene in the film shows Jack Torrance (Jack Nicholson) and the Overlook's manager, Stuart Ullman (Barry Nelson), agreeably if awkwardly participating in an unremarkable ritual of the

business world. King's novel, on the other hand, depicts an overtly antago-
nistic relationship between the characters: "I don't believe you care much for
me, Mr. Torrance," says Ullman. "I don't care. Certainly your feelings toward
me play no part in my own belief that you are not right for the job."[26] According to Jenkins, this change reflects Kubrick's need to streamline the story by
de-emphasizing Jack's history of alcoholism—the reason Ullman is reluctant
to hire him and, ironically, the reason Jack gets the job anyway (an old drink-
ing buddy sits on the Overlook's board of directors); "Ullman's affability need
not be explained—but his hostility would be."[27] A similar technical concern
figures into Jenkins's analysis of the scene between Dick Hallorann (Scat-
man Crothers) and Danny Torrance (Danny Lloyd), in which the concept
of "shining" is first introduced. In the film, Danny is reticent about the powers he shares with Hallorann; most of his close-ups in the scene show him
silently staring at Hallorann, and he only speaks a few lines of dialogue. In
the novel, however, Danny is immediately responsive to Hallorann's inquiries
and talkative throughout the scene, which consumes eleven pages consisting
mostly of close dialogue (80–90). Jenkins's primary explanation for this difference is the limited ability of a child actor to memorize lines, although he
adds that this "minimalist give-and-take" also builds suspense.[28]

Jenkins is by no means alone in offering a fairly narrow range of explanations for the changes Kubrick made to King's novel. Charlene Bunnell has
noted that, although Kubrick's film "does not quite do the novel justice in
terms of character development and suspense, it does capture the theme and
atmosphere of the original and provide some effective cinematic touches."[29]
And Michael J. Collins explains that Kubrick "distills the events and characters of King's novel and augments them with skill—Kubrick transforms
the characters, events, and settings of the novel into elements better suited
to film."[30] Perhaps more important, none of these critics is wrong to invoke
cinematic exigencies as explanations for Kubrick's alteration of King's narrative. It is beyond cavil that a story originally presented in a textual medium
must accommodate itself to the demands of cinema in the process of adaptation, and that filmmakers sometimes make changes for precisely the reasons
that Jenkins, Bunnell, and Collins identify. Rather, the problem with these
accounts is that they have so little explanatory power—the fact that narrative
compression is necessary does not illuminate the question of why a filmmaker chooses to compress one aspect of the story rather than another.

Although it would therefore be naïve to imagine that every novelistic
vision can be transferred feasibly to the screen, and therefore to eschew
entirely the divergent strengths of text and cinema as potential reasons for
changes evident in a film adaptation, there are at least two reasons why we
ought to be wary of relying upon that explanation. First, film is a much more
potent and flexible medium than this rationale tends to imply.[31] Second, this

theory of change fails to account for the most common differences between film and source text: small-scale omissions and interpolations that are not mandated by the cinematic context.

The first point can be illustrated by critical responses to one of the most visually striking features of Kubrick's *The Shining*—the Overlook's hedge maze. Conventional wisdom holds that Kubrick must have opted for the labyrinth because the menagerie of topiary animals featured in King's novel would have been "an insoluble special-effects problem."[32] Yet the maze itself has been called "one of the most intriguing creations in the history of motion pictures" and "one of the most pernicious sets ever to work on"; constructed of pine boughs stapled to plywood forms, the maze had to be assembled twice (once for exterior shots in the United States and again for studio work in England), but was so large and intricate that crew members frequently became lost inside.[33] Given these logistical difficulties, Kubrick probably could have created King's hedge animals without appreciably greater effort or expense. This is particularly true in light of the fact that, with the exception of one scene, fidelity to the novel did not even require the menagerie to be animated. The animals only needed to appear in different positions and locations in a series of subjective point-of-view shots, gradually becoming more lifelike, assuming more predatory poses, and moving inexorably closer to the lens. Because one can easily imagine how such an effect might look when rendered in Kubrick's distinctive mise-en-scène—I am thinking specifically of Kubrick's tachistoscopic jump-cuts to a stark tableau of the slaughtered Grady girls in *The Shining*, and to David Bowman's silent screams as he crosses through the stargate in *2001: A Space Odyssey* (1968)—one must ask why Kubrick elected the hedge maze instead.

In this connection, we should also reconsider the purpose of the hedge maze in Kubrick's film. The maze and King's animals are usually equated in scholarly commentary on *The Shining*, but from the standpoint of narrative function they have nothing in common but the fact that they are both made of hedges. In the novel, the animals figure in three episodes (among the most frightening King has ever penned) that have no equivalents in Kubrick's film: they menace Jack, closing in on him, by seeming to move while his back is turned (205–12); they chase Danny to the Overlook's front porch, only evidencing their progress when Danny looks over his shoulder to find them closer, yet motionless (286–94); and, their movements finally perceptible, they intercept Hallorann upon his arrival at the Overlook (408–9, 415–19). As far as narrative function is concerned, Kubrick's maze plays the same role as the Overlook's boiler in King's novel—the former is responsible for Jack's death by hypothermia; the latter kills Jack, and destroys the Overlook, when it explodes in the novel's finale (436–37). Accordingly, we must not only ask why the topiary scenes are omitted, but also why Kubrick kills Jack with ice rather than fire and why he allows the Overlook to survive at all, questions that are not easily answered by reference to the mandates of the film medium alone.

The second point—that relatively small narrative changes are not explainable by the transposition of a story from one medium to another—can be illustrated by a set of minor interpolations Kubrick made in his version of *The Shining*. During the closing-day tour of the Overlook, Ullman explains to Jack and Wendy (Shelley Duvall) that the hotel "is supposed to be located on an Indian burial ground, and I believe they actually had to repel a few Indian attacks as they were building it." The film also incorporates a wealth of Native American imagery: set decorations, costumes, and even aspects of the plot evoke the motif—Danny's escape from his father by retracing his footsteps in the snow has been described as "an old Indian trick."[34] These details are absent from King's novel, which only references Native Americans in passing; Danny thinks about the subtle, barely perceptible changes he has noticed in his parents since they arrived at the Overlook, and is reminded of a puzzle-picture in which images of Indians have been hidden: "if you strained and squinted, you could see some of them" (196). Nothing about the medium of cinema compelled Kubrick to add these minor nuances, but they were obviously significant to him. His co-screenwriter, Diane Johnson, has explained that the Indian burial ground idea was Kubrick's and that he did a great deal of research on Native American history and customs while working on the screenplay.[35] Without some other or more complete theory of narrative change in adaptation, however, these interpolations appear to be gratuitous.

In light of these examples and the problems they illustrate, I contend that the differences between a film adaptation and its source text should be understood whenever credible as the filmmaker's conscious and purposive choices rather than as matters of necessity foisted upon the filmmaker by the cinematic medium. Let me be clear: this not to say that there are two discrete categories of change and that the critic must assign each instance of infidelity to one group or the other. Rather, it is to acknowledge that while the transposition of a narrative from a textual medium to the cinema might be able to explain the fact that the narrative has changed, the characteristics of cinema as a medium cannot explain why *particular* changes are made instead of others. Even if we assume, for example, the impossibility of capturing King's topiary animals or Overlook inferno on film, that fact would not explain why Kubrick replaced these aspects of King's novel with a hedge maze rather than with one of the numberless other possible substitutes that were available to him. Similarly, the fact that Kubrick had to concretize the Overlook in order to put *The Shining* on screen does not explain why his hotel sets featured Native American designs. A filmmaker who is confronted by a cinematic imperative that makes adhering to the source text problematic must choose an alternative based upon an overall vision for the film, and the critic's task is to develop a reading of the film that provides a coherent explanation for as many of those choices as possible.

Bill Blakemore calls details like the Indian-burial-ground reference in *The Shining* "confirmers" and, for him, the sum total of Kubrick's changes to the novel confirms that the film "is explicitly about the genocide of the American Indians. Every frame, word, and sound of it."[36] Brian McFarlane examines the parts of a novel that a filmmaker discards in making an adaptation, as well as what elements the filmmaker adds that were not present in the novel, in order to analyze how the adaptation "enunciates" the narrative functions originally performed by the novel.[37] In a similar vein, I suggest that fidelity should be considered as an index of the filmmaker's vision for the adaptation, a set of cues that supplies a guide for how to read the film. Of course, this approach to fidelity does not amount to a valorization of the source text. Instead, it reflects Bluestone's insight that "the film-maker merely treats the novel as raw material and ultimately creates his own unique structure . . . What he adapts is a kind of paraphrase of the novel."[38]

When this model of criticism is applied to *The Shining*, it becomes apparent that the most common reading of the film is, at best, incomplete. The overwhelming majority of critics who have discussed *The Shining* tend to concur with Blakemore—the film is a meditation on historical evils, particularly racism, and how they echo down to the present.[39] Many of Kubrick's departures from King's novel tend to confirm this hypothesis, most notably the final shot showing Jack Torrance in a photograph from an Independence Day celebration at the Overlook in the 1920s. But this reading is inconsistent with the fact that Kubrick jettisoned a plethora of material from the novel that would have resonated with this theme:

> If Kubrick is to be remonstrated for his rendition of *The Shining*, it must be for his unwillingness to recreate any texture of the historical evil that informs King's novel, and to which the latter devotes enough attention so that the individual pasts of his protagonists merge into the collective pasts of the Overlook.[40]

Two examples should suffice to establish this point. A major narrative strand in the novel involves a scrapbook that Jack finds in the hotel basement. Reading newspaper clippings about the sensational and often-disturbing events that have regularly occurred at the Overlook, Jack is fascinated, even seduced, by the hotel's story, and the scrapbook is essential to his transformation into a thrall of the hotel: "It seemed that before today he had never really understood the breadth of his responsibility to the Overlook. It was almost like having a responsibility to history" (161). Although Kubrick gives us a teasing glimpse of the scrapbook next to Jack's typewriter in one brief shot in a single scene, he never takes advantage of it to reinforce his supposed theme of historical evil.

Another major episode in the novel is Jack's discovery of a wasp's nest, which becomes an occasion for Jack to recall encounters with evil in his own personal history: a drunken fit of temper in which he breaks Danny's arm, his dismissal from a teaching post when he loses his temper and nearly beats a student to death, and his brushes with a physically and emotionally abusive father. Jack even calls the nest "a workable symbol for what he had been through" (109). Kubrick, however, de-emphasizes Jack's past and eliminates the wasp's nest from the narrative entirely, despite the fact that it evokes the idea of an evil that refuses to remain buried in history—after being poisoned with a bug bomb, the wasps mysteriously regenerate and sting Danny.

As Stephen King explains in his account of the genesis of *The Shining*: "The past *is* a ghost which haunts our present lives constantly," and the Overlook, as a variation on the haunted-house theme, is a "symbol of unexpiated sin."[41] If Kubrick's vision of *The Shining* were informed by the notion of historical evil, then why did he omit significant elements of the novel that were palpably relevant to that vision? The kind of fidelity analysis I have proposed in this section suggests that Kubrick was doing something different. It therefore becomes necessary to offer a more complete reading of the film, one that resolves the discrepancies between Kubrick's adaptive choices and prior interpretations of his film, and one that explains the major departures from King's source text.

The fact that the various political interpretations of the film do not mesh with Kubrick's own stated philosophy offers one hypothesis:

> When Rousseau transferred the concept of original sin from man to society, he was responsible for a lot of misguided social thinking which followed. I don't think that man is what he is because of an imperfectly structured society, but rather that society is imperfectly structured because of the nature of man.[42]

My argument, developed in the next section, is that Kubrick's concern in *The Shining* is to shift the source of evil out of the supernatural realm—where it is primarily sited in King's novel—and into the human heart.

This reading of the film subsumes the historical interpretation without superseding it. Kubrick was always fascinated by human beings' inhumanity to each other—*Dr. Strangelove, or How I Learned to Stop Worrying and Love the Bomb* (1964), *A Clockwork Orange* (1971), and *Full Metal Jacket* (1987) are particularly emphatic articulations of the theme—and the idea of genocide is too strongly evident in the subtext of *The Shining* to be ignored. Yet this is merely an aspect of the film's larger message. Moreover, my reading takes into account the fact that Kubrick's entire career was marked by an intense interest in genre, including attempts to redefine genres and experiments with generic conventions. As I contend in the next section, Kubrick's treatment of evil in *The Shining* is inextricably intertwined with history after all—the history of a genre, the Gothic.

CONSIDERING GENRE

The most frequently noted difference between Kubrick's adaptation and King's source text is the manner in which Jack is portrayed. In the novel, Jack is a fundamentally good person—a loving husband and father, an effective teacher, a gifted writer—who nonetheless is tormented by weaknesses like his temper and his alcoholism, weaknesses that the supernatural forces of the Overlook exploit. King goes to great lengths to foster sympathy for Jack. Even after Jack has nearly succeeded in strangling Wendy to death, King has her explain to Danny: "Listen to me…It wasn't your daddy trying to hurt me…The hotel has gotten into him, Danny. *The Overlook has gotten into your daddy.* Do you understand me?…It's not your daddy talking, remember. It's the hotel" (375, 380). And at the height of Jack's homicidal rampage, Danny is able to break through to what still remains of his father: "You're not my daddy," he says, as Jack is poised to strike him with a roque mallet. "You're a mask…Just a false face. The only reason the hotel needs to use you is that you aren't as dead as the others" (429–30). "Doc," Jack responds, "Run away. Quick. And remember how much I love you" (431).

In the film, however, Kubrick offers a characterization of Jack that is much less complex: "There appears to be no serious attempt at tracing the psychological regression involved in Torrance's breakdown and in its later stages it seems to possess little psychological subtlety."[43] Certainly by the end of the film, in which Jack Nicholson adopts a hunchbacked posture and an Igor-like gait that telegraph his character's utter wickedness, there is no hint that Jack is a sympathetic figure or that a kernel of goodness still resides within him—if one ever had. Indeed, many critics have complained that Jack Nicholson's portrayal of the character makes him appear psychotic from the moment he first appears on screen. But this impression has little to do with Nicholson's performance or with Kubrick's script or direction. Rather, Kubrick conveys this sense in a non-narrative fashion simply by casting Jack Nicholson in the role. Particularly in light of the fact that the character and the well-known actor share the same first name, it is difficult for an audience to avoid superimposing its perception of Nicholson and his previous film roles upon his performance as Jack Torrance. Yet the result is that the film version of Jack conveys a markedly different impression than does the Stephen King original.

Less commonly remarked upon, but no less significant, is the fact that the Overlook never physically harms any of the characters in the film. This departure from King's novel is most apparent in the way Kubrick renders the scenes involving Danny and Room 237. King's novel is unambiguous. Hallorann warns Danny to stay out of the room; Danny's "dreadful kind of curiosity" (172) prompts him to steal the hotel's passkey, but he resists the temptation to use it; on a second attempt, however, Danny gains the courage to enter the room, where he finds a "woman in the tub [who] had been dead for a long time...The years-damp, bloated, fish-smelling hands closed softly around his throat and he was turned implacably around to stare into that dead and purple face" (219–20). Kubrick, on the other hand, never reveals what happens to Danny after he goes into the room—a ball rolls into the frame as he plays with toy cars, he follows its path expecting to find his mother, and he walks through the already-opened door from which the room key still dangles. In fact, Kubrick strongly hints that Jack was the attacker, and even when Jack goes into the room to investigate, "we ourselves have difficulty in determining which vision is actuality and which is fantasy."[44]

Finally, whereas King takes pains to offer the reader evidence that the supernatural is a bona fide presence at the Overlook, Kubrick leaves open the possibility of a rational explanation until virtually the end of the film. King's novel includes an episode—after Jack has fallen under the influence of the Overlook, and Wendy and Danny have begun to suspect that they are in danger—in which the hotel's elevator begins operating on its own. Although Jack insists that it merely has a short circuit, Wendy hears voices in her mind talking about a party, "*Goodnight...goodnight...yes, it was lovely...no, I really can't stay for the unmasking*" (301). Jack stops the elevator between floors, pries the door open, and assures her that it is empty. But Wendy pulls him away, and looks inside:

> "What about this, Jack? Is this a short circuit?" She threw something and suddenly the hall was full of drifting confetti, red and white and blue and yellow. "Is *this?*" A green party streamer, faded to a pale pastel color with age.
> "And *this?*"
> She tossed it out and it came to rest on the blue-black jungle carpet, a black silk cat's-eye mask, dusted with sequins at the temples.
> "*Does that look like a short circuit to you, Jack?*" she screamed at him. (303)

One could hardly ask for more confirmation that the supernatural realm has penetrated into normal reality. By contrast, as Jonathan Romney notes, "the film does a lot to discount its more conventional horrors."[45] Every scene in which Jack witnesses a "ghost" features a prominently placed mirror—in the case of Lloyd's manifestation, directly in front of Jack—which suggests that "Jack is conversing with himself."[46] Kubrick only establishes that Jack's visions have a genuine, physical existence when he absolutely must, after Jack promises that he will "correct" his wife and son and we hear the bolt slide open outside the pantry where Wendy has imprisoned him.

What all three of these major differences between Kubrick's film and King's novel have in common is a radical shift in the narrative's locus of efficacy, a shift away from the supernatural as a potent force. In the novel, the spirit of the Overlook must work tenaciously and manifest itself physically in order to turn Jack against his family. In the film, as Kubrick has said, "Jack comes to the hotel psychologically prepared to do its murderous bidding. He doesn't have very much further to go for his anger and frustration to become completely uncontrollable."[47] Significantly, Kubrick identifies anger and frustration as affirmative causes of Jack's violence, not as character flaws that give the external influence of the Overlook a way to manipulate him. Jack is predisposed to lash out against his family; isolation, claustrophobia, and stress do the work of pushing him toward homicide. Supernatural forces in the film become less palpably real than in the novel, serving merely to decorate or metaphorically to amplify the primary horrors that Kubrick wants to depict, horrors with fundamentally human causes. The ghost of Delbert Grady can unlock a door, but only a person of flesh and blood can break through one with an axe. Because the Overlook is not the source of evil in the film, it need not be destroyed at the film's conclusion—and particularly not by fire, which has traditionally been associated with the purgation of supernatural evil.

This aspect of the film—Kubrick's use of horror-movie conventions to tell a story of human evil—accounts for the common critical view that "*The Shining* is less a horror film than a meticulous, enthralling academic imitation of one."[48] Kubrick consistently miscues the audience, priming viewers to expect the kind of story that he never delivers. Danny's croaking, vaguely sinister vocalizations for his imaginary friend Tony imply a plot focused on demonic possession. References to the Donner party, and to "a little boy who lives in [Danny's] mouth" and hides in his stomach, presage a cannibalistic end for the Torrance family. Because "the Disturbed Indian Burial Ground is such a Usual Suspect in horror narratives that it is almost a generic archetype itself,"[49] Kubrick's apparently superfluous interpolation prompts another distinct type of expectation. And when Kubrick arrives at frightening points in the narrative that might be handled with greater suspense, "the building of tension is often deliberately short-circuited."[50] We see Jack spying on Wendy's discovery of his manuscript well before he interrupts with the chilling question, "Do you like it?" Kubrick allows us to "see or hear nearly every vivid heft, descent, and blow of the axe" when Jack chops through the bathroom door,[51] even though the camera must execute a violently rapid pan in order for Kubrick to do so. The point is to emphasize that evil itself is not a surprise, a sudden, unexpected intrusion from an invisible domain, but a product of a very material and even, at times, mundane humanity.

By modulating King's narrative and positioning evil in the rational world, Kubrick situates his adaptation of *The Shining* within a continuing generic dialogue that has defined the Gothic tradition since it emerged in the eighteenth century. The dichotomy between rational and nonrational discourses—"the tension between the desire to arouse belief and the need for verification"—is a constant feature of supernatural fiction.[52] Most famously, Tzvetan Todorov has identified these two tendencies within "the literary Gothic" as "the supernatural explained (the 'uncanny') [and] the supernatural accepted (the 'marvelous')."[53] Todorov's "fantastic," of course, "occupies the duration of [the] uncertainty" between the two extremes.[54]

Even the first Gothic novelists, perhaps uneasy with the otherworldly themes with which the form was often preoccupied, were "concerned with maintaining an external plausibility."[55] Indeed, one critic has gone so far as to call realism "the sine qua non of the ghostly tale," which "stands or falls on its power to convince the reader that the *feeling of the supernatural* corresponds to some element in reality."[56] The effort to blend or reconcile these two antithetical strains of the Gothic has been an animating force for the genre since the beginning, during its evolution through Romanticism and the Victorian era, and into the ghost-story or horror-story forms that it assumed in the twentieth century.[57]

The fact that the Gothic exists along a continuum defined by these polarities might explain why Kubrick was interested in *The Shining*, which has been described as an instance of the genre. Kubrick was fascinated by the eighteenth century because it "saw the conjunction of reason and passion," "the two poles of Kubrick's universe."[58] Not coincidentally, those are also the pillars of the Gothic tradition, an eighteenth-century phenomenon. And it is probably not coincidental either that Diane Johnson, whom Kubrick selected to cowrite the screenplay, is a professor of literature whose specialty is the Gothic novel. As a consequence, it is possible to understand *The Shining* as an adaptation not—or not merely—of Stephen King's novel, but as an adaptation of themes that King was also developing in the source text.

Although King's version of *The Shining* is located close to the marvelous end of Todorov's Gothic spectrum, it involves a complex interaction between reality and the supernatural. The tradition of realism, or the uncanny, is present in the characters' attempts to explain Danny's shining and the tumultuous events at the Overlook: Jack explains that "if precognitive trances are possible, they're probably functions of the subconscious mind" (266), and the wasp attack is attributed to a defective bug bomb—"Had to have been. How else can you explain this?" (136). Fantastic elements are also evident, most obviously in the episodes with the topiary animals: Jack is *almost* convinced that his encounter was a "hallucination" or "some kind of breakdown" (224), and he consoles Danny by pointing out that there are no hedge-animal footprints in the snow leading up to the front porch (296). These uncanny and fantastic elements of the novel, along with the predominating marvelous components, dynamically reflect and reinforce each other. The paranormal evils of the Overlook act as a catalyst upon the dormant tensions that the Torrance family brings to it, yet those troubled familial relationships and Danny's psychic talents also fuel the hotel's malevolent power. The Overlook's refusal to allow its evil legacy to remain buried in the past is a metaphor for Jack's inability to suppress the violent potential that lurks within and haunts him, yet Jack's personal demons also represent the psychic pressures building within the hotel and rendered concrete in its "often patched" boiler—"You'll want to keep your press up to no more than fifty, maybe sixty.... She creeps" (18–20).

Kubrick, on the other hand, disentangles the two strands that are so tightly woven together in King's novel while moving decisively toward the uncanny side of the Gothic continuum, ending somewhere close to its fantastic center. Throughout most of the film, Kubrick maintains a fine balance between rational and supernatural without forcing the audience into a choice between them. This might explain why Kubrick disposed of the overtly fantastic hedge-animal episodes—the brute physicality of the animals would have more urgently pressed viewers to choose sides in the rational/nonrational dialectic than would Danny's intangible visions or the ambiguously rendered events in Room 237. The reverberating sound of the bolt being pulled back when Jack is released from the pantry punctuates this segment of the film, shifting it into the marvelous mode before the eerie epilogue—rife with ambiguities—returns it to a fantastic balance-point.

The demands of the fantastic mode upon a filmmaker would have presented an almost-irresistible temptation to Kubrick, offering another possible reason why he might have decided to adapt *The Shining*. The fantastic "constitutes the shock between what is real and what is imaginary," and it "can only originate from a background of strongly defined 'realism.' For there to exist an opposition between the real and the imaginary, and conceivably a frisson between the two, the framework of reality must be scrupulously respected."[59] Kubrick's unique mise-en-scène, what one critic has termed his "realist/surrealist style,"[60] lends itself perfectly to this effect. The cold lighting, the geometric sets and camera movements, the deliberate pacing, and the remote starkness of atmosphere—recognizable marks of a Kubrick film—in *The Shining* accentuate the reality and materiality of the story, almost wounding us with a sense of hardness and solidity and making the irruptions of violence all the more terrifying. Richard Jameson's assertion that "*The Shining* is a horror movie only in the sense that all of Kubrick's mature work has been horror movies," is therefore absolutely correct.[61]

Finally, Kubrick's manipulation of these themes can be seen as part of what has been called the "process of secularization of literature."[62] The Gothic novel was transformed in the nineteenth century, when fiction "increasingly began to suggest that the chaos and disruption previously located mainly in such external forces as vampire or monster... was actually produced within the mind of the human subject."[63] A similar phenomenon was part of the evolution of the horror film in the late twentieth century, when Alfred Hitchcock's *Psycho* (1960) "put the horror in the here and now."[64] As a result, Kubrick has not merely adapted a novel; he has contributed to the adaptation of a genre. While Kubrick's *The Shining* remains in the field of the Gothic, it modulates King's narrative so aggressively that it trespasses upon recognized boundaries within that genre. So is *The Shining* an adaptation, or something else? As I asserted at the beginning of this essay, a genre can be considered as the diachronic accumulation of traces left by a series of adaptations. That is, the process of adaptation is one in which those boundaries are deformed, expanded, and even defined. In this view, Kubrick's *The Shining* is an adaptation precisely because it squarely confronts, and remakes, generic imperatives.

Notes

1. Jim Harwood, "*The Shining*: But Not Bright," review of *The Shining*, directed by Stanley Kubrick, *Variety*, May 28, 1980, 14. Similar evaluations of the film include: Dennis Bingham, "The Displaced Auteur: A Reception History of *The Shining*," in *Perspectives on Stanley Kubrick*, ed. Mario Falsetto (New York: Simon and Schuster Macmillan, G. K. Hall, 1996), 290 ("The reviews which were angry and negative tended to be bothered by... Kubrick's tendency to drop plot and character details out of the novels he adapts"); Noël Carroll, "The Future of Allusion: Hollywood in the Seventies (and Beyond)," *October* 20 (1982): 61 (Kubrick "jettisoned Stephen King's carefully built rhythm of tension and replaced a number of King's smoothly timed shocks... with an abyss of languor").

2. Richard T. Jameson, "Kubrick's *Shining*," in *Perspectives*, ed. Falsetto, 243. Jameson concludes his review by describing *The Shining* as "a horror movie that isn't a horror

movie, that the audience has to get into and finish" (252). Similar evaluations of the film include: John Brown, "The Impossible Object: Reflections on *The Shining*," in *Cinema and Fiction: New Modes of Adapting, 1950–1990*, ed. John Orr and Colin Nicholson (Edinburgh: Edinburgh University Press, 1992), 117 ("*The Shining* is a kind of critical parody of the [horror film] genre, which deliberately exposes and undercuts all the stock motifs of the genre while keeping within its general domain and maintaining a straight face"); Morris Dickstein, "The Aesthetics of Fright," in *Planks of Reason: Essays on the Horror Film*, ed. Barry Keith Grant (Metuchen, N.J.: Scarecrow Press, 1984), 65 (Kubrick "appears to have forgotten that the main point of a horror film is to frighten us").

3. Dudley Andrew, *Concepts in Film Theory* (Oxford: Oxford University Press, 1984), 100.

4. Greg Jenkins, *Stanley Kubrick and the Art of Adaptation: Three Novels, Three Films* (Jefferson, N.C.: McFarland, 1997), 6.

5. André Bazin, "In Defense of Mixed Cinema," in *What Is Cinema?* vol. 1, trans. Hugh Gray (Berkeley and Los Angeles: University of California Press, 1967), 67.

6. Thomas Leitch, "Twelve Fallacies in Contemporary Adaptation Theory," *Criticism* 45 (2003): 162.

7. Leitch, "Twelve Fallacies," 162.

8. Michel Ciment, *Kubrick: The Definitive Edition*, trans. Gilbert Adair (New York: Faber and Faber, 2001), 41.

9. Ciment, *Kubrick*, 42.

10. Stanley Kubrick, "Words and Movies," in *Hollywood Directors, 1941–1976*, ed. Richard Koszarski (New York: Oxford University Press, 1977), 308. See also Thomas Allen Nelson, *Kubrick: Inside a Film Artist's Maze*, new and exp. ed. (Bloomington: Indiana University Press, 2000), 8. Nelson discusses Kubrick's "standard practice" of adaptation throughout his career as based on V. I. Pudovkin's 1929 text, *Film Technique*.

11. Michael Patrick Allen and Anne E. Lincoln, "Critical Discourse and the Cultural Consecration of American Films," *Social Forces* 82 (2004): 878.

12. Colin MacCabe, *The Eloquence of the Vulgar: Language, Cinema and the Politics of Culture* (Berkeley and Los Angeles: University of California Press, 1999), 38. But see Leitch, "Twelve Fallacies," 150 (questioning whether, and to what degree, the production of a film adaptation is as collaborative as the production of a film based on an original screenplay).

13. In his discussion of auteurism and adaptation, Thomas Leitch touches briefly on Kubrick and the director's "open warfare" with screenwriters and source-text authors in his attempt to assume complete authorial control. Leitch, "The Adapter as Auteur," in *Adaptation and its Discontents: From* Gone with the Wind *to* The Passion of the Christ (Baltimore: Johns Hopkins University Press, 2007), 236–56.

14. The work of George Bluestone is a notable exception. His skepticism about the usefulness of fidelity as an evaluative criterion for adaptations is explicitly predicated upon

his view that "the end products of novel and film represent different aesthetic genera, as different from each other as ballet is from architecture." Bluestone, *Novels into Film* (Baltimore: Johns Hopkins University Press, 1957), 5. Among the more recent studies of adaptation that address questions of genre at some length is Sarah Cardwell, *Adaptation Revisited: Television and the Classic Novel* (Manchester: Manchester University Press, 2002). Thomas Leitch proposes to consider adaptation, within the contexts of reception and analysis, as a genre unto itself. Leitch, "Adaptation, the Genre," *Adaptation* 1, no. 2 (2008): 106–20.

15. "The concept of genre (or species) is borrowed from the natural sciences." Tzvetan Todorov, *The Fantastic: A Structural Approach to a Literary Genre*, trans. Richard Howard (Ithaca, N.Y.: Cornell University Press, 1975), 5. In literature, however, "evolution operates with an altogether different rhythm: *every* work modifies the sum of possible works, each new example alters the species" (6). In adaptation theory, a nascent awareness of the connections between film and biology is present in the work of Bluestone, who remarked that "mutations are probable the moment one goes from a given set of fluid, but relatively homogenous, conventions to another." *Novels into Film*, 5. For a treatment of literature and literary theory from a biological perspective, see Joseph Carroll, *Evolution and Literary Theory* (Columbia: University of Missouri Press, 1995). Within the context of film adaptation, Spike Jonze's film *Adaptation* (2002) has inspired a few notable attempts to compare cultural and biological models. See Gary R. Bartolotti and Linda Hutcheon, "On the Origin of Adaptations: Rethinking Fidelity Discourse and 'Success'—Biologically," *New Literary History* 38 (2007): 443–58.

16. See Robert Stam, *Literature through Film: Realism, Magic, and the Art of Adaptation* (Malden, Mass.: Blackwell, 2005), 66.

17. Bluestone, *Novels into Film*, 5.

18. Leitch, "Twelve Fallacies," 161. See also Stam, *Literature through Film*, 3–5.

19. James Griffith, *Adaptations as Imitations: Films from Novels* (Newark: University of Delaware Press, 1997), 73.

20. Bluestone, *Novels into Film*, 5.

21. Leitch, "Twelve Fallacies," 161. Stam's similar view relies explicitly on the idea that fidelity is lost from the moment a narrative is transposed from text to screen: "it is questionable whether strict fidelity is even *possible*. An adaptation is *automatically* different and original due to the change of medium." *Literature through Film*, 3–4.

22. Griffith, *Adaptations as Imitations*, 41.

23. Tony Magistrale, *Hollywood's Stephen King* (New York: St. Martin's, Palgrave Macmillan, 2003), 95. In fairness to King's script, it was written as part of his contractual obligation to the studio, and Kubrick, not wanting to be influenced by King's vision for the film, simply did not read it. Jeff Conner, *Stephen King Goes to Hollywood* (New York: New American Library, Plume, 1987), 32. See also Harlan Kennedy, "Kubrick Goes Gothic," *American Film* 5.8 (1980): 50.

24. Robin Dougherty, "Vanity, Thy Name is Stephen King," review of Stephen King's *The Shining*, directed by Mick Garris, *Salon*, April 25, 1997, http://www.salon.com/april97/shining970425.html.

25. Jenkins, *Art of Adaptation*, 77.

26. Stephen King, *The Shining* (New York: Doubleday, 1977), 6. All further citations to *The Shining* will appear as parenthetical references in the text.

27. Jenkins, *Art of Adaptation*, 75–76.

28. Jenkins, *Art of Adaptation*, 81. Likewise, Kubrick's streamlined action has the incidental benefit of making the narrative "elliptical [and] mysterious" (77).

29. Charlene Bunnell, "The Gothic: A Literary Genre's Transition to Film," in *Planks of Reason*, ed. Grant, 92.

30. Michael J. Collins, "Culture in the Hall of Mirrors: Film and Fiction and Fiction and Film," in *A Dark Night's Dreaming: Contemporary American Horror Fiction*, ed. Tony Magistrale and Michael A. Morrison (Columbia: University of South Carolina Press, 1996), 119.

31. Leitch, "Twelve Fallacies," 150–53. It is curious that Leitch resists "the essentialist view that novels and films are suited to fundamentally different tasks," yet concludes elsewhere in the article that "re-creating specific textual details or the effect of the whole" is impossible (151, 161).

32. Jameson, "Kubrick's *Shining*," 245. See also Jenkins, *Art of Adaptation*, 94 (Kubrick deemed "the unwieldy hedge animals" to be "dispensable"); and Nelson, *Kubrick*, 199 ("in an era before Computer Graphic Imaging," such effects would have been impossible).

33. Garrett Brown, "The Steadicam and *The Shining*," *American Cinematographer* 61 (1980): 785–90.

34. Bill Blakemore, "Kubrick's Shining Secret: Film's Hidden Horror Is the Murder of the Indian," *Washington Post*, Sunday Show section, July 12, 1987.

35. Ciment, *Kubrick*, 294–95.

36. Blakemore, "Kubrick's Shining Secret."

37. Bluestone, *Novels into Film*, 20.

38. Bluestone, *Novels into Film*, vii, 62. In the words of a Stephen King critic, "the best approach to Kubrick's *The Shining* is to divorce it from connections with Stephen King—not because Kubrick failed to do justice to King's narrative, but simply because it has ceased to be King's." Michael R. Collings, *The Films of Stephen King* (Mercer Island, Wash.: Starmont House, 1986), 62. Of course, separating the Kubrick and King iterations of *The Shining* is the very opposite of what I am suggesting, but my purpose in arguing that the two should be considered together is to identify exactly *how* the narrative has become Kubrick's rather than King's.

39. David A. Cook writes: "*The Shining* is less about ghosts and demonic possession than it is about the murderous system of economic exploitation which has sustained this country since, like the Overlook Hotel, it was built upon an Indian burial ground."

Cook, "American Horror: *The Shining*," *Literature Film Quarterly* 12 (1984): 2. As Frederic Jameson puts it, "The Jack Nicholson of *The Shining* is possessed neither by evil as such nor by the 'devil' or some analogous occult force, but rather simply by History." Jameson, *Signatures of the Visible* (New York: Routledge, 1990), 90.

40. Tony Magistrale, *Landscape of Fear: Stephen King's American Gothic* (Bowling Green, Ohio: Bowling Green State University Press, 1988), 70.

41. Stephen King, *Danse Macabre* (New York: Berkley Books, 1983), 265.

42. Kubrick, interview by Ciment in *Kubrick*, 163.

43. P. L. Titterington, "Kubrick and *The Shining*," *Sight and Sound* 50.2 (1981): 117.

44. William Paul, *Laughing, Screaming: Modern Hollywood Horror and Comedy* (New York: Columbia University Press, 1994), 349. See also Jameson, "Kubrick's *Shining*," 249; and Randy Rasmussen, *Stanley Kubrick: Seven Films Analyzed* (Jefferson, N.C.: McFarland, 2001), 265–66.

45. Jonathan Romney, "Resident Phantoms," *Sight and Sound* 9.9 (1999): 11.

46. Rasmussen, *Seven Films*, 263.

47. Kubrick, interview with Ciment in *Kubrick*, 194.

48. Dickstein, "Aesthetics of Fright," 65.

49. Darryl Jones, *Horror: A Thematic History in Fiction and Film* (London: Arnold, 2002), 145.

50. Titterington, "Kubrick and *The Shining*," 117.

51. Greg Smith, " 'Real Horrorshow': The Juxtaposition of Subtext, Satire, and Audience Implication in Stanley Kubrick's *The Shining*," *Literature Film Quarterly* 25 (1997): 304.

52. Glen Cavaliero, *The Supernatural and English Fiction* (Oxford: Oxford University Press, 1995), 23. See also Bunnell, "Gothic," 8; Margaret L. Carter, *Specter or Delusion? The Supernatural in Gothic Fiction* (Ann Arbor, Mich.: UMI Research Press, 1987), 2; and S. L. Varnado, *Haunted Presence: The Numinous in Gothic Fiction* (Tuscaloosa: University of Alabama Press, 1987), 121.

53. Todorov, *Fantastic*, 41–42.

54. Todorov, *Fantastic*, 25.

55. Cavaliero, *Supernatural*, 23. See also Robert F. Geary, *The Supernatural in Gothic Fiction: Horror, Belief, and Literary Change* (Lewiston, N.Y.: Mellen, 1992), i; and George E. Haggerty, *Gothic Fiction / Gothic Form* (University Park: Pennsylvania State University Press, 1989), 3.

56. Varnado, *Haunted Presence*, 5.

57. For a study of the Gothic in some its recent cinematic manifestations, see Lisa Hopkins, *Screening the Gothic* (Austin: University of Texas Press, 2005). See also Kamilla Elliott, "Gothic—Film—Parody," *Adaptation* 1, no. 1 (2008): 24–43.

58. Ciment, *Kubrick*, 66.

59. Ciment, *Kubrick*, 125.

60. Nelson, *Kubrick*, 199.

61. Jameson, "Kubrick's *Shining*," 245.

62. Geary, *Supernatural*, 11.

63. David Punter and Glennis Byron, *The Gothic* (Oxford: Blackwell, 2004), 25.

64. Stephen Prince, "Introduction: The Dark Genre and Its Paradoxes," in *The Horror Film*, ed. Stephen Prince (New Brunswick, N.J.: Rutgers University Press, 2004), 4. See also Peter Hutchings, *The Horror Film* (Harlow, Engl.: Pearson Education, Longman, 2004); and Punter and Byron, *Gothic*, 68.

Histoire(s) du cinéma (Godard, 1988–98), chapter 1B

11

CONTEMPT REVISITED

Godard at the Margins of Adaptation

Rick Warner

In his interviews and multimedia essays, Jean-Luc Godard has often referred to the written word as his "number one enemy." But he has done so with remarkable ambivalence, not quite ready to throw out "the text" on the one hand or to confine himself to the audio-visual on the other. He has said that "texts are death, images are life," but "both are needed."[1] Indeed, he has experimented with literary forms—such as book-length commentaries[2] and "phrases," as he calls them, that poetically transcribe spoken lines from his films[3]—as a means of offsetting his image practice. If this literary output has occurred mainly in his later stages, it continues from an impulse that surfaced much earlier, both in his *Cahiers du cinéma* criticism of the 1950s and in his New Wave features of the 1960s. Famously, he claimed to have written reviews as though he were already making films, and to make films as though he were still writing on a blank page.[4]

As he shifted between film criticism and filmmaking, Godard tried to "write" in cinematic terms, whether integrating handwritten or typewritten text into the image, or appropriating text from all manner of sources—a device which, as Marie-Claire Ropars argues brilliantly, opens "fracture zones" between levels of signification and permits a "cinescriptural" force to overwhelm both mimetic depiction and narrative progression.[5] Godard's use of writing has served a number of aims over the years, from quotation to anagrammatic wordplay, but it has always marked an intense engagement with image-text relationships.[6] The practice allows Godard to put across "both his love and distrust of words," while "opening up his work to the complex and dialectic interplay between the order of the visible and that of the readerly."[7]

Given his attraction to forms of writing and his insistence on placing cinema among the other arts, one might assume that Godard would gravitate naturally toward adaptation. A glance at his filmography during the

1960s might seem to confirm this assumption, as six of the eight features he made between 1962 and 1966 are credited as adaptations of original material: *Les Carabiniers* (1963) from a Benjamin Joppolo play; *Le Mépris* (1963) from an Alberto Moravia novel; *Bande à part* (1964) from Dolores and Bert Hitchens's novel *Fool's Gold; Pierrot le fou* (1965) from Lionel White's novel *Obsession; Masculin féminin* (1966) from Guy de Maupassant's short stories "Le Signe" and "La Femme de Paul"; and *Made in USA* (1966) from Richard Stark's novel *The Jugger*. However, few of these productions qualify as adaptations in the usual sense, and even fewer faithfully transpose elements of their source texts. As Colin MacCabe has pointed out, only *Le Mépris* offers a "genuine reworking" of its source, whereas the other examples regard their sources mainly as pretexts for formal experiments.[8] Godard thus remains averse to adaptation as it is commonly practiced, but from time to time he does suggest alternative methods, such as filming the pages of a novel while a character reads them aloud, or filming actors while they audition for roles *in* an adaptation (see *Grandeur et décadence d'un petit commerce de cinéma* [1986]).[9]

Godard's own views notwithstanding, I want to suggest that he is actually among the most prolific "adapters" in cinema, and that adaptation plays a critical role in his still-evolving practice as a multimedia montage artist. More specifically, I want to examine how his work in film and video brings together the notions of adaptation, translation, and quotation without simple analogy or equivalence. The crucial work in this regard is *Le Mépris* (*Contempt*), an adapted film which in many ways hinges on these three related concepts and which Godard continues to quote visually, verbally, and musically at key moments in his late video projects, most notably in *Histoire(s) du cinéma* (1988–98). As we'll see, Godard effectively re-adapts *Contempt* to suit new conditions as his work progresses. Responding to this practice calls for a broader understanding of adaptation than is customary in film criticism, but one which attends to a fuller range of its cultural and aesthetic possibilities. By placing the French-Swiss director at the junction of these three transcriptive modes, I hope to shed light on his equivocal attitude toward "the text" and to offer some possible ways of addressing adaptation in a multimedia context.[10]

THE TASK OF THE MISTRANSLATOR

Contempt bears a complicated relation to Godard's experience as a *Cahiers* critic and New Wave filmmaker. As has become legend, Godard, François Truffaut, Jacques Rivette, and their fellow auteurists writing for *Cahiers* in the 1950s revered Hollywood on account of its stable system of genres and its directors like Howard Hawks, Nicholas Ray, and Fritz Lang who, despite working in the world's most labor-intensive production environment, developed their own mise-en-scènes. *Contempt* laments the passing of this Hollywood as Godard had known it, from its casting of Lang as an aging director called "Lang" to its metacritical treatment of the international coproduction. Moreover, in that the film features a superstar (Brigitte Bardot) and adapts a bestselling novel (*Il disprezzo*) written by a respected author (Moravia), it ostensibly resembles the "tradition of quality" that the *Cahiers* group found so detestable. In Truffaut's famous polemical essay of 1954, "A Certain Tendency of the French Cinema," adaptation looms large in the attack on retrograde practices in postwar French filmmaking. Yet Truffaut's quarrel is less with adaptation itself than with its undue focus on the "scenarist" instead of the director. He reproaches the "quality" screenwriters Jean Aurenche and Pierre Bost for misconstruing their source texts, for slipping in extraneous political commentary, and for failing to take advantage of cinema's unique aesthetic possibilities. For Truffaut, only a veritable "man of the cinema" can adapt and transform literature acceptably.[11]

The *Cahiers* critics and eventual New Wavists were equally inclined to celebrate adaptations that stylistically embellish lowbrow sources, a tendency that stemmed from their support of American B-films. Godard's own *Pierrot le fou* and *Made in USA* (and for that matter Truffaut's *Tirez sur le pianiste* [1960]), fall squarely within this category, whereas *Contempt* is more difficult to situate. Despite Moravia's reputation as a novelist and the accomplished psychological realism of *Il disprezzo*, Godard dismissed the book as a *roman de gare*—a cheap paperback one might read aboard a train—"full of classical, old-fashioned sentiments in spite of the modernity of the situations. But it is with this kind of novel that one can often make the best films."[12] He claims to have "stuck to the main theme" while making few changes, although he insists that "something filmed is automatically different than something written, and therefore original."[13] Relative to Godard's other adaptations, *Contempt* does seem rather orthodox, but otherwise it radically transforms its source text, recasting Moravia's melodrama as an exploration of the cinematic state of things in 1963.

Moravia's *Il disprezzo* (translated into English as *A Ghost at Noon*), like Godard's *Contempt,* has to do with a contentious adaptation of Homer's *The Odyssey.* Its less-than-reliable narrator and protagonist, Ricardo Molteni (Paul in the film), a playwright turned screenwriter, recounts and tries to make sense of the events that led to the unraveling of both his marriage and his involvement in the production. He sets out to prove to himself and the reader that his wife, Emilia (Camille in the film), who has died in a freakish auto accident while embarking on a relationship with *The Odyssey*'s producer, is to blame for their breakup inasmuch as "she judged me and in consequence ceased to love me."[14] But Ricardo gradually comes to see that his retelling of *The Odyssey* and his recounting of his personal life are intimately bound up, and that his textual and personal representations of Odysseus (to his wife's Penelope) fall miserably short of the idealism and simplicity of the Homeric original. On the point of "reasoned insanity" by the novel's end, and unable to accept his story's ambiguities, he finds himself alone on a boat, talking to Emilia's ghost.

Given that Ricardo's first-person narration is the novel's most distinctive feature, *Contempt* might have used a reflective voiceover, framed its narrative with scenes of the protagonist writing his tale, and flashed back and forth throughout. But Godard proceeds in a fashion that immediately discards textual notions of fidelity and directs our attention to the technological disparities between cinematic and literary production. In the opening shot at Rome's deserted Cinecittà, a camera operated by Raoul Coutard tracks alongside a young woman as she studies a script and approaches from the background, tailed by three crew members, one holding a boom microphone, one pulling cable, and the other pushing the Mitchell apparatus along a dolly track. As the figures enter the foreground, and as George Delerue's score plays on the audio track, a male voiceover announces the film's credits, starting with, "It's from a novel by Alberto Moravia." Coutard soon occupies the entire frame, then turns his lens toward the extra-diegetic camera and thus the spectator. The voiceover cites a passage attributed to André Bazin, "The cinema substitutes for our gaze a world more in harmony with our desires," then tells us that "*Contempt* is a story (*histoire*) of that world."[15] From the very beginning Godard assures us that his film will be "automatically different" from its source novel, and he anticipates Lang's defense of his own cinematic rendering of *The Odyssey*: "In the script it's written, and on the screen it's pictures... motion picture, it's called."[16]

In keeping with the prologue, Godard iterates throughout the primacy of sound and image over text, maximizing the potential of widescreen framing, color composition, camera movement, shot duration, and montage, often putting sound and image in conflict to foreground cinema's multiple registers. Yet his assault on the text is characteristically ambivalent: at times he uses books dismissively as props for non-literary functions, while at others he shows his characters engaged in meaningful acts of reading, as when Camille (Bardot) recites a passage from Luc Moullet's book on Fritz Lang, or when Paul (Michel Piccoli)—performing an activity that occurs throughout Godard's work—flips through an art book and encounters images within a primarily text-based medium. This interplay of texts and images intensifies in the sequence in which Camille and her new love interest, the boorish American producer Prokosch (Jack Palance), fatally crash his red convertible between two tractor-trailers. Such an event calls out for spectacular treatment, but just before impact, the film cuts to a lateral track across Camille's hand-scribbled farewell letter to Paul. At the moment most typically suited to audio-visual elaboration (and to showing the limits of literature), Godard instead offers an image of cursive writing.

Besides his omission of Moravia's retrospective and introspective narration, Godard's other major changes include a reduction of plot duration. While *Il disprezzo* covers more than a year, Godard condenses the events into two consecutive days, one at Cinecittà and the other on the isle of Capri. He compresses the couple's arguments into a single thirty-minute scene that occurs inside their apartment, and although this section takes up almost a third of the film's running time, it strips their marital conflict to its most basic elements, leading Harun Farocki to consider this sequence "a trailer for a film based on Moravia's *Ghost at Noon*."[17] Godard's self-described "Aristotelian" economy[18]—together with the film's Homeric intertext and its critique of the commercial forces propping up modernity and polluting the contemporary arts—has led several commentators to describe *Contempt* as an embrace of classicism.[19] In terms of film aesthetics, the matter is not so simple. In the extended apartment sequence, Godard channels, without discord, the innovations of Michelangelo Antonioni (the relentless play of frames within frames, the "autonomous mediating gaze" of the camera, the "inquiring detachment" that regards incidental details as elements of suspense[20]), as well as the mise-en-scène of Vincente Minnelli (a delicate, anxious choreography of motion and gesture in domestic space, the cuts relatively sparse and unimposing, the camera mid-range and itinerant, the color pitched to emotional shifts in the CinemaScope frame). Godard made *Contempt* in a time of serious tension between classicist and modernist positions at *Cahiers du cinéma,* led by Eric Rohmer and Jacques Rivette respectively, and the film treads somewhere in the middle, as though to test what a teacher scrawls on the chalkboard (and attributes to T. S. Eliot) in Godard's next feature, *Bande à part*: "classique = moderne."[21]

And yet, Godard is troubled by the decline of the Hollywood studio system as an aesthetic *sensus communis*. As MacCabe explains, Hollywood had offered Godard and his *Cahiers* associates not simply a pantheon of auteurs but a guarantee of "an audience secure in its knowledge of genres and stars, who allowed the artist to demonstrate his art within a popular and established medium."[22] *Contempt* registers anxieties over the loss of this stability, not least because the New Wave figures had begun to face "the problem of the audience in its most direct form—failure at the box office."[23]

While mourning the loss of Hollywoodian classicism, *Contempt* suggests that Hollywood has mutated into an abject commercial force that now occupies European cinema. It's against this backdrop that Godard internationalizes the production of *The Odyssey* (which in Moravia's novel is an all-Italian project, save for its German director, Rheingold). By pitting the German émigré Fritz Lang against a domineering American producer in an Italian-French-American coproduction beset by miscommunication and artistic compromise (conditions that mirror Godard's struggles in the film's making[24]), and by suggestively changing the Greek names and titles in the Homeric source to their Roman counterparts (Ulysses, Minerva, and Neptune in place of Odysseus, Athena, and Poseidon), *Contempt* doesn't embrace classicism so much as it stages its irrecoverability. Through the figure of Lang, the classicist aesthetic paradigms of ancient Greece and Old Hollywood are shown to be equally out of reach.

This set of concerns motivates Godard's invention of the character of Francesca (Giorgia Moll), a multilingual translator for whom there is no equivalent in *Il disprezzo*. His casting of Moll, the actress we see reading a script in the film's prologue, fits neatly into the industrial context sketched above. Moll had gained recognition for her roles in Italian peplum epics—a popular genre which helped to sustain the Italian film industry during the 1950s and 1960s (and which Godard mimics in the rushes for Lang's film of *The Odyssey*—perhaps because two of *Contempt*'s producers, Joseph Levine and Carlo Ponti, had made forays into the genre).[25] Moll had caught Godard's attention because of her performance in Joseph Mankiewicz's 1958 adaptation of Graham Greene's *The Quiet American,* a film in which, as Godard put it, each character "speaks his own language."[26]

The significance of Francesca goes well beyond matters of casting. We can be sure that Godard saw her role as crucial to the film's overall design, since he withdrew his name from Carlo Ponti's alternate version, which dubbed all the dialogue in Italian, removed the subtitles, and replaced Francesca's translations with trivial remarks. Some critics have speculated that Godard introduced the quadri-lingual translator as a means to guard against dubbing and to ensure subtitling. It's worth noting on this score that in the late 1950s, Roberto Rossellini—whose films, especially *Viaggio in Italia* (1954), provide a key reference point for *Contempt*—launched an influential attack in *Cahiers du cinéma* on dubbing for broader, non-regional distribution, calling this practice a "mad idea" that robbed the film of its authenticity, minimized cultural distinctions, and thereby "assured failure."[27] Godard obliquely relates Rossellini—and perhaps his stance on dubbing—to Francesca by giving her a surname from a Rossellini film, "Vanini" from *Vanina Vanini* (1961), the poster for which appears on the back-lot wall at Cinecittà. While embedded in the usual Godardian fashion, this reference would seem to imbue the translator with a creative license not unlike that of a filmmaker. After all, Francesca not only enables the cross-lingual discussion among the German director, French screenwriter, and American producer, she also participates, as a fourth authorial agent by contributing and reshaping ideas through her own translations.

Her translations frequently enlarge on, obscure, or recontextualize the "original" statements. For instance, when Prokosch first appears at Cinecittà and gripes about the replacement of movie houses by supermarkets, Francesca translates to Paul, "C'est la fin du cinéma" ("It's the end of cinema"), thus rendering a commercial complaint an artistic lament, and one which looks ahead to Godard's closing titles for *Week-end* (1967): "End of story. End of cinema." This moment is important to note, as it marks one of Godard's earliest articulations of an idea that has assumed an increasingly prominent role in his work: the death of cinema. In his series *Histoire(s) du cinéma*, Godard hinges cinema's demise on three separate moments: (1) the ill-timed and mismanaged arrival of sound in the late 1920s, which stunted the growth of silent cinema, or rather replaced it with the artistically inferior talkie; (2) the failure of cinema to sufficiently confront and document the atrocities of World War II, namely the Nazi death camps; and (3) the commercial and aesthetic "occupation" of cinema and its modes of reception by television.[28] Stemming from our reading of *Contempt*, we might add a fourth "death": the failure to combine the resources and stability of Hollywood with the sensibility of the New Wave. As Godard stated in a 1962 *Cahiers* interview, "When we were at last able to make films, we could no longer make the kinds of films which had made us want to make films. The dream of the Nouvelle Vague—which will never come about—is to make *Spartacus* in Hollywood on a ten million dollar budget."[29] If Godard exaggerates this point, it is only to emphasize the importance of *the popular* in his conception of cinema and its possibilities.

Prokosch's original statement persists in translation, but in a radically altered form. In this way, Francesca's method of translating accords with Godard's method of adapting—*Il disprezzo* endures its transformation to the screen, but in fragments that barely echo the original. Most of her inventive translations come at the expense of the monolingual Prokosch, whereas she more accurately reproduces the comments of Lang and Paul, two fellow Europeans. But without rehashing a clichéd opposition between American wealth and European culture, Godard interweaves the devices of translation and quotation to draw attention to the production's core conflicts. For instance, Lang not only shifts gracefully among German, French, and English (while inspiring Francesca to speak in her own Italian), he also draws on a range of quotations to argue his points and highlight his predicament. With Francesca he cites verses from Hölderlin's "The Poet's Vocation," compliments her French translation, then discusses three different variants of the original German that harbor three distinct meanings. With Paul he quotes Bertolt Brecht's short poem "Hollywood," which concerns selling out to the American film industry, "the market where lies are bought." In contrast, these quotations are lost on Prokosch and not just because of a language barrier. Prokosch similarly recites maxims from a small book he carries in his pocket, but he has neither memorized them nor grasped their relevance. At one point, apparently without knowing it, he rephrases Hermann Goering's infamous motto "Whenever I hear the word culture, I get out my revolver" as "Whenever I hear the word culture, I bring out my checkbook."[30] An unwitting misquotation thus underscores the film's connections between fascism and Hollywood's presence in European markets.[31]

Contempt's most instructive use of translation occurs when Francesca translates comments in advance of their being spoken. She does this more than once, again with Prokosch as the primary target. For instance, when Prokosch describes his take on *The Odyssey* so as to persuade Paul to rewrite the script, Francesca's "Toutes les émotions humaines" precedes Prokosch's "All the real human emotions!" It would be simple to attribute this moment either to Prokosch's mundane predictability or to Godard's well-known hostility toward "chains of causation."[32] But given that it occurs in a film that thematizes problems of adaptation, this reordering of "original" and "translation" clearly has more important implications. The effect isn't merely to challenge the twin concepts of anteriority and seniority,[33] but to subvert and invite reflection on the temporal aspects of translation (and hence of adaptation), which are routinely understood in chronological terms. In other words, though Moravia's novel predates its adaptation, the transcriptive process sets up what Leo Bersani and Ulysse Dutoit describe as a "temporality without priority."[34] Discussing *Contempt,* they suggest intriguingly that "*within the translation,* there is a relation that is neither a betrayal nor an identity nor, finally, a coming after or a coming before." Translation in its Godardian sense enacts "the *opening* of the text to be translated, its removal from a supposed textual finality and its renewal as something still in the process of being made." This process permits us "to see the openness, the always-taking-place, which is the incorporative mode of translation and citation."[35] Put simply, whether we see Godard's adaptive work in terms of adaptation, translation, or quotation, it opens intertextual relationships that, at some level, remain incomplete and subject to further transcription.[36]

RE-ADAPTING *CONTEMPT*

The characters in *Contempt* cite their sources, but Godard often quotes without quotation marks, consciously or not, as many "borrowings" appear to just seep in, their sources forgotten.[37] Somewhere between a Romantic plagiarist,

Eliot's self-sacrificing absorber of tradition, and Barthes's mosaicist, he doesn't quote so much as he appropriates outright. He has often said that he never borrows but steals, riffing on both Picasso and Eliot—the latter of whom in turn quotes John Dryden's description of Ben Jonson: "He invades authors like a monarch; and what would be theft in other poets, is only victory to him."[38] Jacques Rivette once called Godard an "intertextual terrorist,"[39] and Jean-Pierre Gorin has summed up Godard's entire career as an "assault on the notion of intellectual property."[40] Indeed, the French courts have more than once found Godard in violation of copyright laws, leading him to argue publicly for a legal distinction between "quotations" and mere "extracts." In a 1997 interview with Alain Bergala, he maintains that while an "extract" involves the unaltered use of existing property, a "quotation" involves creativity in its own right and should therefore require no fees or duties.[41]

Still, Godard's use of quotations remains open to whatever possibilities might be carried by the "original." Over the past three decades, he has cultivated a videographic style that densely combines sonic and visual fragments taken from a wide array of sources. In this "historical montage," as he calls it, Godard creates new rhythms and new relations while letting the fragments conjure up the wholes of their original contexts.[42] The video mixer allows him to achieve extremely precise superimpositions, among other techniques that have only loose filmic equivalents, such as jagged speed alteration and a strobing effect of iris-ins and iris-outs between two or more overlapping images (though of course some of these techniques take their cues from early cinema conventions). As the layers retain a hard-edged feel, never coalescing into seamless whole, Godard's montage allows for the co-presence of multiple and seemingly disparate histories. Far from the play of surfaces that some have seen as characterizing his early work, Godard quotes in his later stages as a means of reckoning with the past as it intrudes on the present. To return to our earlier point, these quotations are never quite complete: Godard opens the original and brings it into an "always-taking-place." He samples, modulates, re-adapts, not repeating the original as it was but reworking the conditions of possibility attached to it.

For our purposes, the first significant quotation of *Contempt* occurs in *Soft and Hard* (1985), a video essay codirected by Godard and his partner Anne-Marie Miéville. As the two filmmakers talk about their different attitudes toward creative production in the comforts of their own apartment in Rolle, the video continues *Contempt's* unsettled exploration of image-text relationships. Godard, aligning himself with the visual and the cinematic, tells Miéville that what he values in the image is precisely what she seems to find "inaccessible" and "obstructive." He refers to himself as a father of images instead of children and at one point claims he could make a film out of something as meager as a box of matches. As for Miéville, who comes down more firmly on the side of the verbal and the literary, she throws doubt on the image's ability, whether filmic or televisual, to provide any sort of truth, and she implies that Godard's image-based approach would do well to explore the possibilities she locates in the cinema's "voice."[43] In spite of his self-confidence, Godard ultimately entertains the idea that he might be neglecting something crucial in his overemphasis on the image. It would be a stretch to suggest that he adopts a position that sets image and text on equal footing, but his hostility toward the text is significantly softened by the dialogue's end.

Soft and Hard strikingly concludes with a quotation of Contempt that enables Godard and Miéville to reconcile, if for the moment only, some of their differences. In the midst of their discussion regarding television's inability to "project," we see Contempt's opening sequence playing on a television monitor. Then Godard and Miéville's camera—as if to mimic Coutard's pan toward the audience, or Godard's ultimate pan toward an unseen Ithaca— turns from the image to focus on an adjacent white wall, where Godard projects the same sequence. We see the silhouetted arms of Godard and Miéville superimposed on the images. We hear Godard ask, "All those projects to grow, to be enlarged into subjects…Where has it all gone?" And Miéville replies with, "It is hard to say," a statement that carries multiple meanings. Throughout Soft and Hard, the filmmakers have associated the term "soft" with Miéville, femininity, and the verbal, and "hard" with Godard, masculinity, and the visual.[44] "Hard to say" implies both an uncertainty about cinema's future and an alignment of opposing terms. Though the plight of cinema is difficult to address in words, the rapprochement of the verbal and the visual, of "soft" and "hard," might offer a place to begin.[45]

Soft and Hard thus revisits Contempt in a moment shot through with anxieties related to the vitality of cinema and the "fraternity" of image and text, concerns which register with greater emphasis in Histoire(s) du cinéma, Godard's eight-part history of cinema and of the twentieth century as filtered through cinema. One of the ironies of the project is that not much film was used in its making—the clips are taken primarily from VHS cassettes. Versions of the first chapters, which Godard substantially revised, aired on French television in the late 1980s, then the series as a whole was projected theatrically ten years later. In a testament to the confusion regarding its exhibition, Histoire(s) was even displayed in Dan Graham's New Design for Showing Videos at Documenta X in 1997, a glass-based, multi-screen construction which, in its superimpositions, subjected Godard's series to its own critical methods.[46] We might also note that Histoire(s) du cinéma is not a singular object—its title also refers to the VHS tapes (1998) and DVDs (2007) released by Gaumont, to the four art books published in Gallimard's esteemed Blanche Collection (first in 1998, then re-issued in 2006), and to the box set of audio

CDs released by ECM in 1999. Godard says he regrets that *Histoire(s)* was not received as a multimedia work, as an art object dispersed across these different formats. Perhaps overstating his case, he has said that the art books, which consist of reworked stills from the videos and snippets of commentary, are the centerpiece of *Histoire(s)* inasmuch as they place image and text "strictly on equal footing."[47] Of course, in the video "version," Godard keeps the visual and the verbal in tandem, whether quoting literary and philosophical texts to advance his thoughts on cinema, or balancing images with an elaborate system of titles.

Nearly all of the key quotations of *Contempt* occur in 1B: "Une Histoire seule" ("A Solitary [Hi]Story" or "Only One [Hi]Story"), a chapter that continues to sketch out the aims and concerns of the entire series. Shortly after stating that cinema has become part of "the cosmetics industry...the mask industry, which is itself a minor branch of the lies industry," Godard's voiceover reflects on the phrase "poor B.B." uttered by Fritz Lang in *Contempt*, a reference both to Bertolt Brecht and Brigitte Bardot. We see a grainy, black-and-white photo of Brecht and titles declaring, "I make jewels for the poor." We hear the revving engine and screeching tires of *Contempt*'s car wreck, but instead of a track across Camille's letter, we see an irised shot of Camille/Bardot reading the book on Lang in her bathtub, superimposed with a film strip speeding through the bobbins of Godard's editing station. The irised image flashes between photos of the young and old Bardot, ultimately stopping on *Contempt*'s car accident (which is now pasted onto one of the most repeated images in *Histoire(s)*, a single frame from Bergman's *Prison* [1949] of a man and woman seated behind a film projector, absorbed by what they see, and arguably standing in for Godard and Miéville). As such, Godard reinscribes *Contempt* as a work concerned with artistic disappointment (through Lang and Brecht), while exploiting the shot of Prokosch and Camille's crash as a figuration of death and tragedy.

But more significant are the quotations that immediately follow. After a flashing montage of a still of Fritz Lang from his German period and an insert of the nude Bardot in *Contempt*, we see an image of Godard in 1988, lighting a cigar in slow motion in front of his bookshelves. This image is superimposed with the closing moments of *Contempt*, where Lang, his crew, and his assistant (played by Godard) shoot the scene in which Ulysses spots his homeland. A languid cue from *Psycho* (Hitchcock, 1960), Bernard Herrmann's "The City," mixes with the opening bars of Béla Bartók's *Third Piano Concerto* (1945), a melody of strings that calls to mind Delerue's music for *Contempt*. We track in to see the vast emptiness of the Mediterranean, and though we abruptly cut to a scene from *The Magnificent Ambersons* (Welles, 1942), we still hear the young Godard shout, "Silence!" Here again Godard entwines his personal *histoire* with the larger *histoire* of cinema.

As Roland-François Lack remarks of this sequence, "the mere contrast in tone between the phrases muttered in 1988 and the 'silence' shouted in 1963 gives his voice a history, just as what we are watching tells the history of an image, in the superimposition of Godard's face now [in *Histoire(s)*] on his body then [in *Contempt*]."[48]

The closing shot of *Contempt* takes on additional meanings as it enters into the figurative economy of *Histoire(s)* and rhymes with other images of water and shore—a leitmotif in the series and a recurring figure in Godard's other works over the past three decades.[49] Whether it functions as a site suggestive of death and potential renewal as in *King Lear* (1987), a place for solemn reflection as in *JLG/JLG: Autoportrait de décembre* (1995), a stimulus for remarks on memory and resistance as in *Éloge de l'amour* (2001), or a U.S. Marine–patrolled border of "Paradise" as in *Notre musique* (2004), the water's edge has become a prominent and especially charged element in Godard's cinema. Waves pervade much of his late work—sonically as well as visually. In her sensitive description of *Nouvelle Vague* (Godard, 1990), Claire Bartoli, a blind critic, suggests that lapping waves are a central expressive figure in Godard's sound design—its polyphonic surges that build, overlap, disperse, and then resurface anew. As Bartoli puts it, "Little waves in a large sea, unfolding and subsiding: it's the same water, but not the same wave".[50] Her words could well extend to the image track in Godard's late films and videos, the ebbing and flowing in constant variation.

In *Histoire(s)*, imagery of waves often alludes to the New Wave, which Godard specifically engages and revises in chapter 3B: "Une Vague nouvelle" ("A New Wave" or "A Vague Piece of News"). There Godard soberly rethinks the late 1950s, early 1960s artistic school by changing its roster of directors, stressing the *politique* over the *auteurs* ("not the authors, the works") and atoning for its historical amnesia in the wake of World War II.[51] Shorelines and breaking waves and rippling currents abound in the episode, in images sampled from *The River* (Borzage, 1949), *Napoleon* (Gance, 1927), *By the Bluest of Seas* (Barnet, 1936), and *India* (Rossellini, 1958). We see a stunning image reworked from Godard's own *King Lear*, Cordelia in a white robe, lying flat and motionless on a large rock, Don Learo at her side with a rifle, gazing toward the water ("I know when one is dead and when one lives"); in *Histoire(s)*, the image is interwoven with a photograph of Virginia Woolf, the titles "Nouvelle Vague," and a female voice reciting the next-to-last line of Woolf's 1931 novel *The Waves*: "Against you I will fling myself; unvanquished and unyielding, O Death!" At one level, these quotations reinforce Godard's remarks in voiceover that the New Wave filmmakers were mistaken to consider their breakthrough as a beginning instead of a last gasp. Godard gives us a condensed account of this *histoire* midway through the chapter, using one of the most iconic scenes at his disposal. As we hear

Shostakovich's score for *Hamlet* (Kozintsev, 1964)—tense strings and horns for the young prince's last duel—Antoine (Jean-Pierre Léaud) runs along the beach at the end of *Les 400 coups* (Truffaut, 1959). His path to the surf takes him through and across three other images that appear in successive, pulsing superimpositions: the ill-fated couple on the lam in *You Only Live Once* (Lang, 1937), Joan of Arc (Ingrid Bergman) in flames in *Giovanna d'Arco al rogo* (Rossellini, 1955), then Scottie (James Stewart) swimming to retrieve Madeleine (Kim Novak) from the bay in *Vertigo* (Hitchcock, 1958). Breaking up this stream of images are staggered intertitles in national accents—"*égalité...et fraternité...entre la réel...et fiction*"—and then a throbbing alternation between a black-and-white photo of a middle-aged Godard and documentary footage of combat.[52] With two crashing piano chords we return to Antoine on the beach, and Godard revises Truffaut's freeze frame by superimposing a static close-up with a long shot of Antoine turning back from the waves. In this complicated sequence, Godard shows us the New Wave emerging from its intense critical interaction with Neorealism and popular American cinema, with Lang, Rossellini, and Hitchcock figuring here as something like a Holy Trinity; and he reasserts his 1962 claim that "fiction is interesting only if it is validated by a documentary context," which he initially offered as a way of defining the movement.[53] At the same time, the segment works to suggest that the aims of the New Wave, as embodied in the figure of Truffaut's Antoine, were as doomed from the start as Lang's lovers, and that their apparent rescue of French cinema was no more genuine than Scottie's rescue of Judy/Madeleine. Their revolution is subsumed within a larger *histoire* in which French film culture moves from its military occupation by Nazi Germany to its commercial occupation by Hollywood—a trajectory already mapped out in *Contempt*.

Toward the end of 1B in *Histoire(s)*, Godard again quotes *Contempt* in a manner suggestive of cinema's deaths. His voiceover declares: "Not a technology or even an art, an art without a future as immediately the [Lumière] brothers had urbanely warned." We then cut to the screening-room sequence in *Contempt*, where Lang defends his adaptation by telling Prokosch that "motion pictures" automatically depart from their written scripts. In the original film, the "death of cinema" already imbues their quarrel in the form of the Lumière quote that lines the wall beneath the blank screen (in untranslated Italian): "The cinema is an invention without a future." In *Histoire(s)*, Godard highlights this prophecy by superimposing onto *Contempt*'s empty screen a photo of Louis Lumière standing next to his Cinématographe. As Prokosch hurls a film canister like a discus, the words "*erreur tragique*" flash on screen, and Godard states: "Not even a hundred years later we can see that [the Lumières] were right and that if television has achieved Leon Gaumont's dream of bringing spectacles from all over the world into the simplest bedrooms, it was done by shrinking the shepherd's giant sky to Tom Thumb's level."

In a sense, what emerges from Godard's re-adaptation of *Contempt* in his video essays is an elaboration of the signs and warnings already visible in the 1963 film. The aging Godard affirms retrospectively what the young Godard had just begun to realize—that without the popular stability of Old Hollywood, the New Wave could only muster a short-lived aesthetic revolution; that the kind of cinema that had inspired Godard to make films in the first place had slipped into irreversible decline; that an embittered Rossellini was right to announce, as he did at an Italian press conference in 1962, that despite being singularly equipped to "spread ideas," cinema had become part of the problem, the *crisis* facing modern civilization (which for Rossellini was a crisis of public education[54]). Still, it would be too neat to conclude on this note. We shouldn't overlook the irony that each time Godard mourns the death of cinema, his discourse is outstripped by his own formal inventiveness. Even as he revisits *Contempt* to reprise its grim assertions, his manner of quotation tries to open and explore what is still thinkable. And even as *Contempt* leaves us with a downbeat FIN title, its shot of sea and sky, as it echoes and permutes across his body of work, doubles as a site of potential renewal. To miss this regenerative aspect of his late work is to miss how Godard tirelessly adapts existing materials, how he animates an archive of cinematic pasts, a living archive under constant revision.

NOTES

1. Jean-Luc Godard, interview by Serge July, in *Jean-Luc Godard par Jean-Luc Godard, tome 1: 1950–1984*, ed. Alain Bergala (Paris: Cahiers du cinéma, 1998), 416. My translation.

2. Godard, *Introduction à une véritable histoire du cinéma* (Paris: Albatros, 1980).

3. Godard, *JLG/JLG: Phrases* (Paris: Éditions POL, 1996); *For ever Mozart: Phrases* (Paris: Éditions POL, 1996); *Allemagne neuf zéro: Phrases* (Paris: Éditions POL, 1998); *Les enfants jouent à la Russie: Phrases* (Paris: Éditions POL, 1998); *2 × 50 ans de cinéma français: Phrases* (Paris: Éditions POL, 1998); *Éloge de l'amour: Phrases* (Paris: Éditions POL, 2001).

4. Godard, interview by Jean Collet et al., in *Godard on Godard*, ed. Jean Narboni and Tom Milne, trans. Tom Milne (New York: Da Capo, 1972), 171–96.

5. Marie-Claire Ropars, "The Graphic in Filmic Writing: *A bout de souffle*, or the Erratic Alphabet," *Enclitic* 5–6 (1982): 147–61. "Cinescriptural" is an imperfect translation of Ropars's *ciné-écriture*.

6. See Tom Conley, "Language Gone Mad," in *Jean-Luc Godard's Pierrot le fou*, ed. David Wills (Cambridge: Cambridge University Press, 2000), 81–107.

7. Philippe Dubois, "The Written Screen: JLG and Writing as the Accursed Share," in *For Ever Godard*, ed. Michael Temple, James S. Williams, and Michael Witt (London: Black Dog, 2004), 232.

8. Colin MacCabe, *Godard: A Portrait of the Artist at Seventy* (New York: Farrar, Straus and Giroux, 2003), 155. This is not to say that the literary sources have little significance in these films—they often supply the only vestiges of plot.

9. Titles in *Grandeur et décadence* declare "based on an old novel by J.H. Chase." But Godard's made-for-television video about the pre-production of a made-for-television video shows no interest in the James Hadley Chase novel, *The Soft Centre*, that Godard had been commissioned to adapt, beyond playing with atmosphere and plot conventions vaguely suggestive of *Série noire* crime fiction. Jean-Pierre Léaud is cast as a director struggling to cast performers in a work that is to be an adaptation, but the source text is yet to be decided, or committed to, because Léaud's character does not like the pulp crime story he is expected to adapt. In one extended scene, a procession of actors auditioning for a part in the production file one-by-one past a video camera, pausing momentarily to speak line-fragments that are not from Chase's novel but from William Faulkner's short story, "Sepulture South: Gaslight."

10. I should note here at the outset that my concerns depart somewhat from those of other contributors to this volume. While *Contempt* is in some ways Godard's only legitimate adaptation—the script went through four rewrites, a rather un-Godardian process of fine-tuning at the behest of his producers—the end result alters its source in such a way as to make a sustained comparison impossible. If fidelity has a place in Godard's work, it is where he works to establish a broader sense of "fraternity or equality between the image and the text," between the audio-visual and the verbal. Godard, in dialogue with Youssef Ishaghpour, *Cinema: The Archeology of Film and the Memory of a Century*, trans. John Howe (New York: Berg, 2005), 49.

11. François Truffaut, "A Certain Tendency of the French Cinema," in *Movies and Methods*, vol. 1, ed. Bill Nichols (Berkeley and Los Angeles: University of California Press, 1976), 224–37.

12. Godard, *Godard on Godard*, ed. Narboni and Milne, 200.

13. Godard, *Godard on Godard*, ed. Narboni and Milne, 200.

14. Alberto Moravia, *Contempt* (London: Prion, 1999), 1. This more recent translation again changes the title of *Il disprezzo* to *Contempt*, but for the sake of clarity I will refer to Moravia's novel by its Italian title.

15. As Jonathan Rosenbaum points out, it is quite possible that Godard misattributes this quote to Bazin, and that the actual passage comes from one of Michel Mourlet's articles in *Cahiers du cinéma* in 1958: "Since cinema is a gaze which is substituted for our own in order to give us a world that corresponds to our desires, it settles on faces, on radiant or bruised but always beautiful bodies, on this glory or devastation which testifies to the same primordial nobility, on this chosen race that we recognize as our own, the ultimate projection of life towards God." Rosenbaum, "Trailer for Godard's *Histoire(s) du Cinéma*," *Vertigo* 7 (Autumn 1997): 13–20.

16. It is also worth noting that Godard thinks of the screenplay as a blueprint for producers who rely on the document for scheduling and budgetary purposes. This view
appears in the parenthetical note Godard attached to early drafts of the script to
explain the shortage of pages. See Peter Lev, *The Euro-American Cinema* (Austin:
University of Texas Press, 1993), 85. Godard reiterates this notion in *Scénario du
film "Passion"* (1982), where he expresses the desire to "write" a script while creating
the film simultaneously, and where he claims that the first script came about when
producers of a Mack Sennett film wanted to account for payroll.

17. Harun Farocki and Kaja Silvermann, *Speaking about Godard* (New York: New York
University Press, 1998), 46.

18. Godard, *Godard on Godard*, ed. Narboni and Milne, 201.

19. See, for instance, Paul Coates, "*Le Mépris*: Women, Statues, Gods," *Film Criticism* 22,
no. 3 (Spring 1998): 38–52. Coates writes that despite the film's investments in Brecht,
it ultimately assumes a classicist stance in its "un-Romantic" embrace of Lang as a
father figure and its longing for an art form untouched by consumer capitalism.

20. Gilberto Perez, *The Material Ghost: Films and Their Medium* (Baltimore: Johns Hopkins University Press, 1998), 87–91, 367–416.

21. On the film's equivocal relation to classicism, see Marc Cerisuelo, *Le Mépris* (Chatou:
Transparence, 2006); Joe McElhaney, *The Death of Classical Cinema: Hitchcock, Lang,
Minnelli* (Albany: State University of New York Press, 2006), 1–3.

22. MacCabe, *Godard*, 146. See also Colin MacCabe, "On the Eloquence of the Vulgar," in
The Eloquence of the Vulgar: Language, Cinema, and the Politics of Culture (London:
BFI Publishing, 1999), 151–53.

23. MacCabe, *Godard*, 146; see 80–82 for a broader positioning of the *Cahiers* gang in
terms of classicist and modernist outlooks.

24. See Lev, *Euro-American Cinema*, 83–89.

25. For a different take on Lang's rushes that notes the possible influence of Fritz Lang's
lesser known Indian films, as well as of Jean-Daniel Pollet's *Méditerranée* (1963), see
Jonathan Rosenbaum, "Critical Distance: Godard's *Contempt*," in *Essential Cinema:
On the Necessity of Film Canons* (Baltimore: Johns Hopkins University Press, 2004),
182–83.

26. Godard, *Godard on Godard*, ed. Narboni and Milne, 200. For an interesting take on
Moll's role in the film, see Jacques Aumont, "The Fall of the Gods: Jean-Luc Godard's
Le Mépris (1963)," in *French Film: Texts and Contexts*, ed. Susan Hayward and Ginette
Vincendeau (New York: Routledge, 2000), 175.

27. Roberto Rossellini, "Ten Years of Cinema," in *Springtime in Italy: A Reader on Neo-
Realism*, ed. and trans. David Overbey (Hamden, Conn.: Archon Books, 1978), 96,
111–12. For an interesting overview of the subtitling versus dubbing debate, see
Mark Betz, "The Name Above the (Sub)Title: Internationalism, Coproduction, and
Polyglot European Art Cinema," *Camera Obscura* 16, no. 1 (2001): 1–44.

28. See Michael Witt, "The Death(s) of Cinema According to Godard," *Screen* 40, no. 3
(Autumn 1999): 331–46; and Witt, "'Qu'était-ce que le cinéma, Jean-Luc Godard?':

An Analysis of the Cinema(s) at Work in and around Godard's *Histoire(s) du cinéma*," in *France in Focus: Film and National Identity*, ed. Elizabeth Ezra and Sue Harris (New York: Berg, 2000), 23–42.

29. Godard, interview by Collet et al., in *Godard on Godard*, ed. Narboni and Milne, 192.

30. The source of this quote is actually the character of Thiemann in Hanns Johst's 1933 play *Schlageter*: "When I hear the word culture...I release the safety on my Browning."

31. For more on the film's complex relation to fascism, see Robert Stam, *Literature Through Film: Realism, Magic, and The Art of Adaptation* (Malden, Mass.: Blackwell, 2005), 279–99.

32. Peter Wollen, "Godard and Counter Cinema: *Vent d'est*," in *Film Theory and Criticism: Introductory Readings*, 6th ed., ed. Leo Braudy and Marshall Cohen (New York: Oxford University Press, 2004), 525–33.

33. Robert Stam, "Introduction: The Theory and Practice of Adaptation," in *Literature and Film: A Guide to the Theory and Practice of Film Adaptation*, ed. Robert Stam and Alessandra Raengo (Malden, Mass.: Blackwell, 2005), 4.

34. Leo Bersani and Ulysse Dutoit, *Forms of Being: Cinema/Aesthetics/Subjectivity* (London: BFI Publishing, 2004), 64.

35. Bersani and Dutoit, *Forms of Being*, 64–65.

36. For more on the analogous relation of adaptation to translation, see Linda Hutcheon, *A Theory of Adaptation* (New York: Routledge, 2006), 16–17. Hutcheon's description of adaptation is fairly close in spirit to the process-based model I am attributing to Godard: "a derivation that is not derivative—a work that is second without being secondary. It is its own palimpsestic thing" (9).

37. For a fascinating study of quotation that applies to Godard's work and that could valuably inform adaptation studies, see Mikhail Iampolski, *The Memory of Tiresias: Intertextuality and Film*, trans. Harsha Ram (Berkeley and Los Angeles: University of California Press, 1998).

38. John Dryden, *An Essay of Dramatic Poesy* (1668), in *Critical Theory Since Plato*, 3rd ed., ed. Hazard Adams and Leroy Searle (Boston: Thomson Wadsworth, 2005), 272. I refer to this text not only to trace the origins of this celebrated notion of artistic appropriation, but to highlight its political underpinnings. In addition to Dryden's provocative use of the term "monarch," his essay immediately emphasizes the context of the commercial and colonial competition between the warring British and Dutch empires. The implication is that there is something violent and *militaristic* about Jonson's conquest and appropriation of other authors' material.

39. Jacques Rivette, quoted in Jean Narboni, Sylvie Pierre, and Jacques Rivette, "Montage" [*Cahiers du cinéma* March 1969], in *Rivette: Texts and Interviews*, ed. Jonathan Rosenbaum, trans. Amy Gateff and Tom Milne (London: BFI Publishing, 1977), 74–75.

40. Jean-Pierre Gorin, quoted in MacCabe, *Godard*, 123.

41. Godard, quoted in *Jean-Luc Godard par Jean-Luc Godard, tome 2: 1984–1998*, ed. Alain Bergala (Paris: Cahiers du cinéma, 1998), 32–33.

42. Some critics have attacked *Histoire(s) du cinéma* on the grounds that its montage is ultimately disinterested in the content of the quotes and their original contexts. See, for example, Jacques Rancière, *Film Fables*, trans. Emiliano Battista (Oxford: Berg, 2006), 171–88. As I hope to show in this essay, the series is frequently haunted by original contexts—to varying degrees, the force of the original survives and either conflicts or resonates with Godard's own designs. In other words, the logic that motivates Godard's quotation isn't purely one of surface affinity and metaphor.

43. This trope resurfaces in *Histoire(s) du cinéma*, chapter 4A, which begins with a recitation, in a female voice, of Paul Valéry's "Psalm on a Voice" ("In a soft voice and a faint voice saying great things: Important, astonishing, profound, and true things...") and a succession of photographs of women, Miéville among them.

44. This is one of Kaja Silverman's points in "The Dream of the Nineteenth Century," *Camera Obscura* 17, no. 3 (2002): 14. However problematic these gendered terms might seem, it is important to remember that the production company "Sonimage" established by Godard and Miéville in the early seventies was romantically conceived as the montage of her "sound" and his "image"; or together "his/her image."

45. Whereas *Contempt* originally tied the end of a certain kind of cinema to the end of a certain kind of couple—by implication Godard and Anna Karina—here the film as quoted and reworked poses a chance of cinematic renewal and also allows for a reconciliation within a different kind of couple—Godard and Miéville.

46. Trond Lundemo, "The Index and Erasure: Godard's Approach to Film History," in *For Ever Godard*, ed. Temple, Williams, and Witt, 434n4.

47. Godard, quoted in Godard and Ishaghpour, *Cinema*, 45–52.

48. Roland-François Lack, "Sa Voix," in *For Ever Godard*, ed. Temple, Williams, and Witt, 320.

49. "Figurative economy" is a phrase and concept I borrow, somewhat loosely, from the writings of Nicole Brenez. See Brenez, *De la figure en général et du corps en particulier. L'invention figurative au cinéma* (Bruxelles: De Boeck Université, 1998); Brenez, *Abel Ferrara*, trans. Adrian Martin (Chicago: University of Illinois Press, 2007).

50. Claire Bartoli, "Interior View: Jean-Luc Godard's *Nouvelle Vague*," trans. John M. King, included in the booklet to the sound recording Jean-Luc Godard, *Nouvelle Vague* (Munich: ECM Records, 1997), 89.

51. While Godard articulates these ideas in chapter 3B in *Histoire(s)*, he takes them up at length in a dialogue with Alain Bergala in *Jean-Luc Godard par Jean-Luc Godard, tome 2*, ed. Bergala, 24.

52. The documentary footage is difficult to make out given the speed of the montage, but it appears to be of the Algerian War, which adds another important layer to this sequence. While Godard repeats his earlier definition of the New Wave as a new sort of relationship between fiction and documentary, he suggests that the New Wave directors didn't engage sufficiently with the pressing realities and social issues of their own moment. Within the framework of *Histoire(s)*, this failure stands in contrast to the Italian Neorealists, whom Godard addresses in the preceding chapter,

claiming that they "won back a nation's right to look itself in the eye." This, it seems, is why Godard includes a photo of himself taken after the New Wave had dissolved, when he had entered a period of militant filmmaking.

53. Godard, interview by Collet et al., in *Godard on Godard*, ed. Narboni and Milne, 192.

54. Rossellini, quoted in Tag Gallagher, *The Adventures of Roberto Rossellini: His Life and Films* (New York: Da Capo Press, 1998), 554. See also Adriano Aprà, "Rossellini's Historical Encyclopedia," in *Roberto Rossellini: Magician of the Real*, ed. David Forgacs, Sarah Lutton, and Geoffrey Nowell-Smith (London: BFI Publishing, 2000), 126–48. Adrian Martin has suggested that Godard "in his own, eccentric way, renews Rossellini's 'televisual project' and the 'grand plan' to unite art, research, information, science and history, in works from *Je vous salue, Marie* (1985) to the *Historie(s) du cinéma*." Martin, "Always a Window: Tag Gallagher's Rossellini," *Screening the Past* 9 (2000): http://www.latrobe.edu.au/screeningthepast/shorts/reviews/rev0300/ambr9a.htm.

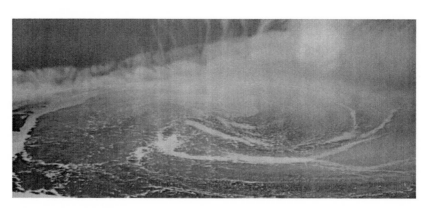

Solaris (Tarkovsky, 1972)

Afterword

Adaptation as a Philosophical Problem

Fredric Jameson

1.

The present collection demonstrates the variety of results that can be achieved by attention to the adaptation of novels in film; and it also suggests the futility of trying to reduce these practices to any fundamental interpretive perspective, as Robert Stam's list of terminological possibilities confirms: "translation, actualization, reading, critique, dialogization, cannibalization, transmutation, transfiguration, incarnation, transmogrification, transcoding, performance, signifying, rewriting, detournement"[1] (to which we might add Dudley Andrew's influential triad: "borrowing, intersecting, transforming"[2]).

But maybe this is to start out in the wrong direction: in fact, despite the multitudinous directions such terms encourage us to explore, they all seem to have one fundamental starting point, namely the denunciation of the notion of fidelity to the original text. Indeed, today, this notion seems to enjoy some of the universal opprobrium showered on notions of the "centered subject" in the old days, and for many of the same reasons. What is to be avoided is then the illusion that there could ever be anything like an organic or referential, undifferentiated unity in what the printed text shares with its moving image. The scarecrow of fidelity is then a reminder to keep faith with some Lacanian gap or rift within this equally split subject which is the object of adaptation studies; it stages a well-nigh Derridean vigilance to the multiple forms difference takes in the object of such studies and insists on fidelity to that difference rather than to this or that ideology of the original.

To a certain extent, of course, this reflects a generational repudiation of the practices of an older film criticism based on versions of the classics, and also the long-standing commercial practice of reissuing the novel after the release of a successful film version. But these results may well be variable: I have to say that I am pleased to find so many young people going back to the originals after the current wave of Jane Austen films, for the most part rather admirable productions.

On the other hand, I find that I am also often annoyed by excessive "fidelity": it is for example disappointing to find, in *Blood Work* (2002)—the first film in what we may call Clint Eastwood's late period—that the scenario often reproduces word for word the dialogue of Michael Connelly's excellent novel (making up for it, to be sure, with a truly monumental "infidelity").

Stroheim's *Greed* (1924), as truncated as it may be, can stand as the paradigm case in this area, for no one coming fresh from Frank Norris's electrifying novel *McTeague* can fail to be frustrated by Stroheim's slavish and literal reproduction of page after page of the novel's detail. Yet who would give up the golden tooth or the final struggle in Death Valley (to be found in both versions)? Indeed, who would give up either film or novel? The better part of valor here might lie in abstaining from studying this particular adaptation at all, in keeping the toxic twins as far from each other as possible.

I hope we are talking about more than preferences or personal taste here, but one probably always begins with those. If, as one of Stam's categories suggests, the film version is to be grasped as a kind of "performance" of the original, then I have to say that in the theater I appreciate the "postmodern" preference for outlandish adaptations, of which the paradigms were (yesterday) Orson Welles's fascist *Julius Caesar* or his all-black *Macbeth* (let alone his Scottish one), or today Peter Sellars's modern staging of classical operas. Indeed, let there be a steady stream of these new versions—the truly sinister Osric of Robin Williams, or the psychotic Fortinbras, in Kenneth Branagh's *Hamlet* (1996)—leading one ultimately on to the question whether there ever were originals in these cases, or only the conventional stage traditions that preceded them. The word "text" obscures the dawning suspicion that Shakespeare's original script (or scenario) is not an original in our sense, nor could it ever be. This is no doubt a distressingly subversive apprehension, which might well lead us on to another one: namely that the older paradigms of fidelity—and the newer Merchant-Ivory versions—do not faithfully reproduce their originals so much as they produce them—in the process turning them into classics (that is to say, by definition "originals" that invite further such adaptations and performances).

One of the distinctive features of film adaptations that seems to me less often taken into consideration is indeed the translation of the character in a book into a recognizable flesh-and-blood star (or at least a familiar character actor). True, the story always was that Margaret Mitchell wrote *Gone with the Wind* with Clark Gable in mind (something she obviously could not have done with Vivien Leigh). But supposing George Raft had remained the protagonist of *Casablanca* (1942); or that Hitchcock had been successful in casting Cary Grant as the lead in *Torn Curtain* (1966)? That these substitutions also bear on the question of adaptation is borne out more tangibly in series films, where the excuse to see your favorite actors repeat their signature personae, or to deplore the miscasting of the wrong ones, is one of the pleasures of the star system. We are then asked to judge how Bogart's classic Marlowe stacks up against Robert Mitchum, let alone James Garner, Robert or George Montgomery, or Dick Powell. Actually, Chandler, himself educated in England, imagined a rather more suave and more sophisticated character (Cary Grant, again, in fact); and it is true that the very first Marlowe (under a name change) was played by George Sanders in *The Falcon Takes Over* (1942). In fact, Mitchum is a far more "perfect" Marlowe than Bogart, even though he spoils everything with his musings on baseball (the thought that the real Marlowe ever wasted a minute on Joe DiMaggio is ludicrous). On the other hand, too perfect a fit can be perilous in itself: how many millions of people, against all evidence, still believe that Basil Rathbone is the real Sherlock Holmes (and this, despite the neurotic and high-strung Holmes of the wonderful Jeremy Brett). Yet perhaps such casting traditions give later adaptors something to play off and react against, as with Elliot Gould's Marlowe in Altman's extraordinary *The Long Goodbye* (1973), in which even the ending is changed.

Much depends, I suppose, on the strength of your initial impressions of the printed page: the annoyance with unpleasant discoveries (the filmic hero has a moustache, the filmic heroine turns out to be a blonde) is what ultimately led both Gide and Virginia Woolf to advocate novels without description, but the practice scarcely prevents you from fantasizing an "original" of your own.

Yet here we have found our way back to "fidelity" against our best intentions; and therefore I propose the following law: the novel and its film adaptation must not be of equal quality. A great film can be made from a mediocre novel; most great novels only yield second-rate movie versions. I omit the logical possibility of films being novelized for obvious reasons, although it exists.[3] I also omit some other variants: the remake of a film, for example, which might then have two originals, one in each medium. Perhaps one ought to distinguish that from the various film versions of a classical novel like *Madame Bovary,* which are not exactly remakes of one another. And obviously the series (whether in literature, as in the Marlowe novels, or in film, as in *Star Wars,* even though for the most part film series will have some distant literary or graphic original) presents different problems.

Now how does one defend a proposition of this kind? You might want to argue that if the film version is definitive (whatever that might mean), the novel will fall into disuse: yet people still read Margaret Mitchell, I assume.

And on the other hand, you might want to claim that even when the film version is excellent, that does not stop producers from making more versions of the same classic novel, as with Stoker's *Dracula:* but that, I would argue, falls into the category of performance, as with successive versions of *Hamlet.* Meanwhile, if it is a question of a contemporary novel, such as *The English Patient,* we are more likely to think of the new film version as a remake.

But let's finally take on the flat-out contradiction of my law: what some people might call its "exception." What about the situation in which it is simply a fact that the two texts—novel and film—really are of equal quality and merit? I leave it to Colin MacCabe to make his case for *The Butcher Boy.* But in the instance I plan to examine next, my law then has a corollary: yes, it can happen that the two texts are of equal merit, but then in that case the film must be utterly different from, utterly unfaithful to, its original. The novel must give rise to a filmic adaptation that is not only governed by a wholly different aesthetic, but that breathes an utterly different spirit altogether. My example[4] will be the *Solaris* (1972) of Andrei Tarkovsky, where the skeptical, Voltairean, satiric, and agnostic Roman philosophique of Stanislaw Lem has been transformed into a mystical, well-nigh Proustian vision.

2.

The 1961 Lem novel, ostensibly "hard-science" science fiction in its time (the Polish writer was the author of several lengthy treatises on cybernetics), actually turned on two variants of the theme of the relationship to the other. The first was scientific in the sense in which it raised the issue, not only of alien life, but also of our very possibility of understanding such life, and indeed nature as such. The second was a remarkable and highly original version of the age-old theme of doubles, ghosts, and aliens, as well as an anticipation of all kinds of recent concepts of androids, cyborgs, replicants, and the like. These two thematic levels echo each other, to be sure, but have very different consequences for the plot, the first developing into metaphysical speculations, the second into what can only be characterized as a not unconventional love story.

Solaris is the name of a planet as well as the ocean that envelops it, about which various experiments—primarily measurements of the variation in its orbit—have suggested that it is in some way a sentient being. A whole new discipline of Solaristics then quickly developed, spawning some hundred years of inconclusive theories and speculations with the lone practical consequence that a scientific laboratory has been established in orbit around the enigmatic body. At the beginning of the novel, the lack of fresh breakthroughs along with a general deterioration of the station has prompted authorities to consider its abandonment; the astronaut Chris Kelvin is sent to assess the situation and make a report, which will no doubt be decisive. The novel begins with his landing on the space station.

It is quite otherwise with Tarkovsky's film version. The Russian director clearly found rich pretexts in the novel for the development of his own personal themes—memory, mortality, time, and nature; and his film can thus from that perspective be grasped as a form of what Dudley Andrew calls "borrowing"—a free and independent fantasia on motifs offered by an original text, to which its modifications have as little significant relationship as the first composer from whom a second borrows a musical subject for a set of variations. Tarkovsky is thus obliged to endow his protagonist with a past greatly exceeding the unhappy marriage that is the equivalent of the Lem situation. A whole new first section of the film (some fifty minutes long) gives us to see life on Earth in this presumably future period, and sensuously explores the father's house and grounds, in which we find Kelvin on the day before his departure. Here the sterility of the space station, and the unnatural landscape of the Solaris entity, is explicitly and thematically contrasted with a Utopian nature, whose vegetation may already in Tarkovsky's time have itself offered a pointed contrast to the ecological degradation well underway on the real earth itself. Only a seemingly endless trip on the complex autoroutes of this future world offers any material for a decision as to whether this future has indeed taken a dystopian rather than a Utopian turn (this elaborate movement sequence then perhaps replacing the space flight as such, which the film omits). Yet the omnipresence of Tarkovsky's privileged imagery of water in this first nature sequence makes an immediate link with the liquid being of Solaris itself. (Meanwhile, the Utopian is suggested by the wonderment of a little boy seeing a horse for the first time, reminding us of LeGuin's Shevek glimpsing animal life for the first time on Urras, itself at first sight suggesting paradise.) But Solaris's liquid has nothing of this transparent (Bachelardian) flow and is often closer to the Sartrean viscous than to the tonic qualities of earthly oceans; most often, however, it simply connotes changeability and infinite mutability, much like the variety of human moods and humors.

The inhabitants of the space station (initially three, but reduced by a suicide until Kelvin's arrival) turn out to be plagued by an unusual phenomenon, somewhat distinct from the more usual and even conventional literary one of haunting and of ghosts. They are indeed haunted, but by material incorporations and literal replications of beings from their own pasts (or from their own fantasies; the source remains unclear). These "guests," as the cosmonauts decide to call them, cannot be destroyed (without at once reappearing or even resurrecting), and they have—whether wanted or unwanted—the additional property of requiring the physical presence of their host at all times, a potentially most annoying characteristic to which we owe one of the most dramatic scenes in the novel and film alike: the one in which Kelvin's visitor, a frail and lovely creature, shut by accident into the bathroom by herself and not understanding that the door opens inward, tears open the heavy metal surface with her own ineffectual and bleeding hands. (It is appropriate at this point to recall the other climactic moments at which book and film coincide: little is lost of the novel's power when in the film Chris also discovers that Hari's dress has been reproduced seamlessly; the buttons serve no purpose, for the process of reproduction has been so literal that the garment can only be removed with scissors. Then too, the cruel moment in which the replicant Hari is dispatched by locking her into the space-shuttle capsule and firing her into outer space; will the simulacrum still exist up there in orbit as its duplicate reappears on the station?)

All these episodes, however, document Lem's originality in the imagination of these beings: less for their materiality (they are no mere subjective projections or hallucinations like ghosts) than for their putative consciousness. The standard science fiction question always had to do with that: from when do machines become conscious to the nature of the consciousness of aliens (like animals? like gods?). Philip K. Dick will invent what I call the android cogito, the moment in which the android reaches the shattering conclusion: I think, therefore I am not (human).[5] Here Lem short-circuits the dilemma by imagining a consciousness that can exist only turned toward its object (in some ghastly mechanical parody of the sickest forms of the human love passion, if not a caricature of patriarchy's view of women).

To be sure, the simulacrum has no past (in this, rather different from the invented pasts and doctored family and childhood photo albums in *Blade Runner* [Scott, 1982], except perhaps for the past of the character herself in real life, as remembered by the "host"—it is obviously a very important exception!). And now we should say that in both Lem and Tarkovsky, part of the drama of *Solaris* is the gradual "becoming conscious," that is to say, "becoming human," of one of these figures (Kelvin's dead wife Rheya, in the film called Hari, perhaps for reasons of Russian pronunciation). But what in Lem is a cybernetic learning process is in Tarkovsky the mixture of Soviet humanism and Russian mysticism that ultimately has to do with the soul itself.

Both novel and film turn on this dilemma, namely, how to get rid of these unwanted "visitors," and to a lesser degree, on the problem of where they came from in the first place and what they tell us about the entity that seems to have sent them. But Chris does not really want to get rid of Hari (Rheya), as he is still (again?) in love with her, and continues to love her avatars further, even as they develop away from the "original": for him it is truly a more-than-Proustian resurrection of a literally dead past, a victory over time itself and mortality, yet one severely limited by its conditions of possibility (the replicated lover can only continue to exist within the space station, in proximity to Solaris itself). In the long run, I think that for both Lem and Tarkovsky (but in very different ways), those limits are allegorical of the autonomy of the work of art itself and the differentiation of the imaginary. On this view, then, both works are ultimately autoreferential and assert the autonomy of the aesthetic, but Tarkovsky's does so in the name of the filmic image (various forms of black-and-white footage are vanquished by the glorious color stock), while Lem's foregrounds a qualified and relatively mathematical privilege of the imagination as such (we would have to read his Polish to grasp the status of language in his work in any reliable way; the English translation of this novel is disgracefully a transfer from the French one, yet verbal and comic deliria of the type of his *Futurological Congress* suggest a very real kinship with Philip K. Dick[6]).

This is the point at which to raise issues of causality: why do the simulacra appear? What can be the ocean's motive, after so many years of human research exploration (although we remember the episode of the dead astronaut's enormous child in the very early years of the exploration)? There must remain open two basic hypotheses, in order to preserve the otherness and incommunicability of Solaris: they are (1) as revenge for the new doses of radiation applied to it out of the scientists' desperation; or (2) its own curiosity and its psychic palpation of its own human guests, which is able to touch their most intense memories or fantasies. This must remain undecidable (in the historiographic rather than the Heisenbergian sense), but it would seem that Tarkovsky leans toward the first alternative, and Lem toward the second.

The matter of causality then offers an ambivalence that can serve to differentiate the two works, and we can articulate it by way of a distinction not always marked as such in some of the European languages, namely that between "conscience" and "consciousness." An emphasis on the former, then, with its overtones of guilt and responsibility, will shift the focus to the ethical and the metaphysical, or in other words to Tarkovsky's "humanist" themes. The weighting of the dilemma in the direction of consciousness as such—in Lem—moves us toward the science-fictional and toward science and scientific or materialistic explanations. In Tarkovsky's version, the projection of the simulacra is clearly a retaliation on the part of the ocean to repeated "attacks" in the form of radiation: the ocean has thus isolated and activated the sources of the most intense guilt in the cosmonauts' consciousness (in the case of Kelvin, he has been responsible for his wife's suicide).

In Lem, it is not so clear, and we are allowed to conjecture that the radiation doses have merely attracted the attention of the ocean to these human beings, otherwise as insignificant for it "as ants on an elephant." In this case, it seems possible that the ocean has merely activated the most intense memory traces retained by the humans, without any particular understanding of the good or bad connotations they may have. In fact, it even seems possible, as one of the characters suggests toward the end of the novel, that the ocean's intentions toward these alien creatures is a benevolent one and that it "wishes us well...perhaps it wants to please us but doesn't quite know how to set about the job. It spies out desires in our brains...."[7] At any rate, it should now be clearer how Lem's focus shifts us more centrally back to the problem of the ocean as such (and its intentions), while Tarkovsky's reading moves us, on the contrary, in the direction of the great metaphysical questions (what is human? what is memory and time? what is death?). (Lem himself was disgusted with this reorientation and after serious arguments in Moscow with the filmmaker, went back home and abandoned the project to its fate.)

But does this discussion really engage our topic of adaptation in any useful or interesting technical sense? I take it for granted that any student of script- or screen-writing will not need any commentary on the practicalities of the transfer from novel to film: concentration of plot, reduction of dialogue, omissions, substitutions, and so on. Rather, this doubt stands at the very heart of all current debates about "theory," namely the usefulness of interpretation as such, for it is essentially on the difference between Lem's and Tarkovsky's interpretations of their little fable that my comments have so far dwelled.

Indeed, one is tempted to endorse such doubts on occasion during the more long-winded philosophical debates Tarkovsky stages on the nature of the human and the meaning of human passions, desires, and sufferings. "Meaning" here simply becomes a pretext for the film as such, and we are tempted to indulge the director in whatever metaphysics he likes, as long as he offers us the bonus of pleasure of his unique filmic and visual style. That is, to be sure, the way the Russian Formalists saw the matter some sixty years before Tarkovsky: "meaning" was simply the "motivation of the device" of the work itself, the formal pretext for a practice of the art or craft as such. (Lem's skeptical-scientific thoughts, more modestly presented and more imminently novelistic, would of course equally count as pretexts.)

This remains a productive approach insofar as it ultimately moves us toward an account of what the Aristotelians used to call the "peculiar pleasures" of the different media in question. Nor are these the abstract, empty questions of some traditional aesthetics or system of the fine arts: in works like these, the "powers" of literature (or film) pass directly through the styles and "powers" of the artists themselves. You cannot appreciate Lem's genius, that is, his exercise of certain of the unique possibilities of literature by way of his own unique talents and obsessions, unless you begin to feel the sublimity of his imagination of possible and nonexistent creations. This is not an exercise of the imagination in general, but of a very peculiar form of imagination, in which, as in his book reviews of imaginary works, he begins to project a profusion of texts and forms that do not exist in our world. Such is, for example, the discipline of Solaristics, whose hundred-year-long history and well-nigh scholastic variety—its bitter debates and personal rivalries, its institutional status, its rigor and possibilities as an imaginary science—is given to us with a richness of detail—comic and tragic, passionate and crank-obsessional—that film could not begin to match (nor would it wish to).

The climax of such seeming digressions, which make up the most remarkable achievements of Lem's literary practice, comes upon us in the detailed enumeration of the ephemeral formations at play, in emergence or disintegration, on the ocean's surface (111–24). Indeed, if the ocean is a living and sentient being—like God, the only one of its kind—it may be wondered what it finds to think about, and what it can possibly do with its time. God, at least, had other possibilities, and according to some theological traditions, it is out of his infinite and eternal boredom (or, as with Schelling, his psychotic distress) that he was motivated to create the world and to people it with creatures. (This is the point at which to note Lem's explanation for the ocean's consciousness: if the latter is ultimately the result of challenges to the organism and the necessity for evolving responses, then for Solaris the dilemma is the instability of the planet's existence between the two suns that draw it into contradictory orbits; the ocean's "will" then emerges as its need to reconcile these claims by assuring its own unique stability between them.)

And as for the passage of time, it may be said that, as in Utopia, Solaris whiles away its immortality by aesthetic creation, by producing innumerable forms—"tree-mountains," "extensors," "fungoids," "mimoids," "symmetriads" and "asymmetriads," "vertebrids," and "agilus" (111)—which it then just as indifferently abandons. Lem imagines these extraordinary forms with the mental assistance of mathematical entities (which possess, to be sure, their own kind of semi-autonomy and non-referentiality): they never repeat and are all rigorously "singular" in the current sense of the word; and yet within them the strange process called, from earliest times, mimesis, is somehow at work, and the Solaris formations may be said to embody Lem's already-embodied reflexions on mimesis within themselves (he then extrapolates that "reflexion" to the new phenomenon of the "guests," the mimesis of humans on Solaris Station). Yet in another way these extraordinary creations may be said to be Solaris's thoughts, material thoughts and concepts as it were, utterly nominalistic and yet without languages, a colloidal *pensée sauvage* without taxonomy or utility. And of course they are also Lem's final thoughts on art as such.

Tarkovsky, although he gives us views of the infinitely mutable oceanic landscape, cannot reproduce these formations in film (and were this to be achieved by way of animation or latter-day special effects, the result would scarcely be so impressive, inasmuch as Lem's descriptions also embody our own, the human, attempts to grasp the phenomena in question). Instead, Tarkovsky has literalized the account of islands in Lem—those few rocky outcroppings that are in a way echoed by the ephemeral "islands" of the mimoids and symmetriads—and which he translates into "islands of memory."

For here we find Solaris's ultimate transcendental gift to Kelvin: not the illusion of the flesh-and-blood Hari, but rather the memory of the house itself (another mimesis, a reproduction of Kelvin's grandfather's house), and the return of the film to its beginnings. Now we can understand better why in order to develop this theme of memory Tarkovsky had to add a whole first section absent from Lem and probably utterly alien to him. In this section, we meet Kelvin's father and we also register a science fiction motif that played no part in the apparently more generic science fiction of Lem himself, namely the fact that, given the enormous distances and shifting temporal effects of space travel, Kelvin will inevitably return (if he ever does) to an Earth from which his father along with all of Kelvin's other living contemporaries will have disappeared. The pain of non-reconciliation with the father is then the first mark of Kelvin's guilt in the Tarkovsky reading of the fable.

Yet the idyllic dacha and its wondrous grounds are not only the pretext for the indulgence of Tarkovsky's camera; they also lay the groundwork for the return of this vision in the concluding "island of memory": Kelvin alights on this mimoid, and even peers through the window at the figure of his father, going about his business in a house from which the son is not eternally absent. Tarkovsky's more purely filmic "genius" lies not even there, however, although it is a vision of great beauty. The punctum lies in the fact that here, in this landscape beyond time, it rains within the house and not outside. The commentators tell us that rain is here a religious motif and a symbol of redemption: *je veux bien,* but abstain from interpreting; for it is a purely filmic matter—this rain, this quintessentially Tarkovskian moist or drenching, soggy, damp, or streaming inundation.

But all is not yet said about the relation of these two works to each other. I want to comment briefly on yet another Tarkovskian addition to Lem's novel before reaching any conclusion about the competition between the media involved in this particular case of adaptation. What Tarkovsky has moved to the opening of his film, in the form of a black-and-white documentary featuring the committee's discussion and Berton's brief film about the apparition over the ocean (it can be considered the first of the so-called "guests"), was in Lem buried in an obscure Solaristics pamphlet that Kelvin manages to locate on the station, where it is initially an episode (albeit a very serious one) in Lem's account of Solaristics and the mountainous research to which it has given rise. But all these innumerable books and pamphlets—whole content can scarcely be dealt with cinematographically—become in Tarkovsky's camera a very elegant library in which the three living inhabitants of the station, along with Hari/Rheya, who has an important discussion with them about the nature of being human and being conscious, meet.

The detail I want to dwell on has to do with the furnishings of this room, so different from the *Brazil*-type shoddy plastic of the rest of the space station; even the library seems to exceed the reference requirements of a purely scientific research facility, since we glimpse for a passing moment an illustration from Gustave Doré's edition of *Don Quixote*. In the same slow panning shot, meanwhile, there appears a large wall reproduction of Breughel's *Hunters*, which the camera explores for a considerable amount of time, in much detail—the snowy landscape, the hunters appearing above the village with their dogs, returning from the day's search, while typical Breughel peasants skate on the frozen ponds below in the distance. This is not a point-of-view shot, although we later observe Hari sitting despondently nearby; nor does the Breughel painting (or any such art-historical or literary reference) appear in Lem. What can possibly explain this seemingly gratuitous digression, which takes up an unusual amount of filmic time, even in a work as leisurely and as full of visual digressions as this one?

I believe that we have here the substitution of the religion of art, a kind of modernist aesthetic or affirmation of art's unique truth-claims, not only for traditional religion as such, but also for the fundamentally skeptical Enlightenment burden of the novel. The Breughel interlude is there, not for us, but for the ocean! It is the ocean, through Hari, who is the essential beholder of this to-us-familiar painting, the ocean who is to learn about art, about human aesthetics, about a faculty no alien could ever guess or imagine in advance about an alien life form! The ocean (like Hari herself) has been undergoing a learning process in which, with some evident confusion, it glimpses something about human passions and relationships. Now, by way of the mimetic powers of human cultural production, it is to experience not only human art as such but also its object, and the human life world of earthly nature as such, something it will clearly have never been in a position to grasp even in a situation of human scientific exploration. The seasons, the weariness of the hunt, the joyousness of human celebration on the ice, birds, trees—all this will have conveyed something to the sentient ocean for which its own lonely experience as the god of an empty world will have had no equivalent. Tarkovsky here seems to suggest yet an additional motive for the ocean's decision—its causes otherwise seemingly undecideable—to suspend the "guests" and to move into a new phase in its relationship to its human visitors (one which Tarkovsky begins to fill in, but which in Lem's conclud-ing sentence—"I persisted in the faith that the time of cruel miracles was not past"—is left open).

And yet...and yet...is it so certain the ocean knows nothing about art? What then are the mimoids and the symmetriads, if not spontaneous pro-ductions of a kind of unique art, proper to its own unique ideas and inspira-tions, toyed with as far as the most complex elaborations and then tossed aside, with the impatience human artists know well? Even mimesis has its equivalent here (as the name of the mimoid suggests), despite the fact that there is nothing here to imitate except the clouds that pass overhead.

But what is mimesis for the filmmaker exactly, and what finally con-stitutes the ideological role played for him—one which has no equivalent in Lem, unless it be a Galilean conception of mathematics—of that ulti-mate object of mimesis which is Nature itself? This is the point at which we approach the very different contradictions that lie at the heart of these two very different artists: these distinct contradictions are ultimately the object of our comparison here, and yet they greatly transcend the matter of adapta-tion, save in making it clearer why the two very different media—film and literature, the visual and the verbal—prove to be the vehicles of their expres-sion, if not their resolution.

Lem faces a dilemma, which is no doubt that of every literary artist in a more general way, namely to assure the seeming independence and auton-omy, the externality, of the object of his narratives: even dreams and the most subjective ruminations of the author or narrative must somehow seem to exist out there in order to be the content of the narrative. But in Lem's case, this universal aesthetic problem is sharpened into urgency and height-ened by a far more serious ideological dilemma, which turns on his ultimate message as a science fiction writer and theorist. Lem's entire work—which I have loosely characterized as skeptical—is traversed by a far more unshak-ably negative conviction, namely that if alien life exists elsewhere in the cos-mos, if there exists somewhere an intelligence without any relationship to the earth from which our very bodies and senses, indeed our language as such, has sprung, then we would never be able to understand it. There could be no "translation" from such an alien language—emerging from a wholly different physical and biological situation—to our own; no transmission of our "thoughts" to them and vice versa—inasmuch as thinking itself is a response to our own unique earthly situation. In short, there could never be such a thing as "First Contact," never anything like communication, perhaps not even any form of recognition in its ultimate philosophical sense. Indeed, the whole of Solaris constitutes a lesson designed to convey this message, which is the strongest conviction of Lem's own experience as a medical doc-tor and a pioneer in cybernetic theory.

The problem, however, arises from his practice as a novelist: for the novel must somehow construct this enigmatic object with which we cannot communicate, and it must be invented for just such a purpose by the human writer himself. However strange and inaccessible it may appear to the human characters within the novel, it remains an intentional artifact, expressly designed to repel all readerly approaches. The novelist must set out to create a non-I, an utterly non-natural phenomenon, with his own natural human means; he must literally imagine the unimaginable, and must therefore inevitably trick us and cheat (in advance of the actual real-life discovery of such a thing about which we cannot even speculate). No wonder his artistic problems have so much in common with those of the attempts of scholastic theologians to describe that indescribable and unimaginable thing they call God.

In appearance, Tarkovsky's problem is a little simpler: for him, what will count is the invention or reinvention of a Utopian nature, in a world in which nature is everywhere in the process of being destroyed and thereby reduced to the sterility of Solaris and its space station and its ocean (and in which all kinds of human suffering and characterological degradation have deformed in the human soul). Yet if this Nature is to be truly Utopian, it will have to be estranged for us beyond all Romantic mistiness—the freestanding trees, the lone horse in the meadow, the art-nouveau dacha—it will have to approach something of the science-fictional alienation of Solaris itself. My feeling is that no one who approaches this film—not even those unaware that it concerns some kind of extraterrestrial yet watery or oceanic being—will have been able to avoid the authentic strangeness of its opening shot: algae streaming like hair in the moving water of the transparent lake, thick water foliage flowing before us with a stubborn tenacity of its own, extended fronds tugging in the same direction as the current that pulls them along—a perplexing image no still photograph could ever capture, a familiar combination of objects before which we are caught up short in something it is inexact to call mystery or confusion either....Such is our first encounter with some properly Tarkovskian nature, more strangely natural than the thing itself and yet as unnatural as any work of art.

And then it comes to us: these are Tarkovsky's own mimoids and symmetriads, this flowing water with its algae is Tarkovsky's own properly filmic thought, just as the mimoids are Solaris's (via Lem's imagination and properly science-fictional thinking). Tarkovsky has not here "imitated" nature but has in some sense created it for the first time; he has used nature to think his own strange filmic image-thought, transforming nature itself into art. This is not a religion of nature but an art-religion, a religion of film itself, in which (as in Lem) "mimesis" comes to have a wholly different meaning from the traditional ones. Tarkovsky's ambitions are thereby even more overweening than Lem's own: for beyond the invention of what lies beyond our nature, Tarkovsky has here laid a claim, like God, to create our own earthly nature itself, ex nihilo.

I have elsewhere commented on what to me is Tarkovsky's central contradiction, and it does not lie here, in this promethean competition with God the creator. It has to do rather with the reproductive technology that assures the delivery of these wondrous images, which offer themselves as an unmediated experience of nature.

> Tarkovsky's screen is notoriously the space in which we once again apprehend or intuit the natural world, or better still its "elements," as though we could sense its emergent constitution out of fire, earth, water and air, which show through in the crucial moments. This, no doubt, rather than Nature or some concrete fascination with the object-world as such, is Tarkovsky's religion, whose camera tracks the moments in which the elements speak—from the persistent rain of *Ivan's Childhood* (1962) to the glorious fire which ends *The Sacrifice* (1986). That fire was in reality dual, and we should not receive it without somehow including the more gruesome pyre of the human sacrifice in *Nostalghia* (1983)—which was, if you like, a way of securing the body's participation in the image, of warding off the disembodied contemplative vision of a spectator who might admire the house in flames without paying the price, without existential sweat, seeing it as sheer apocalyptic aesthetics that omit the ultimate active grimness and despair of immolation. The image remains beautiful and false unless that Kantian disinterested viewer's body can be somehow tricked back inside of it, to lend it truth: an uncertain matter, which the "ban on graven images" was meant to solve, too simply and peremptorily, by removing the problem. If, however, film is given in advance and here to stay, then what arises for a Tarkovsky is the rather different, but no less delicate, problem of the relationship between asceticism and visual pleasure, between a life-denying fascination with sacrifice and the wide-screen libido of a created world that gorges the eyes rather than putting them out (or, like a Bresson, starving them). [...]
>
> Tarkovsky has meanwhile invented a substitute mystery, rarer and thus more immediately fascinating: it is the sponginess of wet soil into which the soaking shoe presses, and from which it is then withdrawn, with the faintest of sucking noises. It is the truth of mosses, Being itself as swamp, in which the faint human traces still persist for a time, the water seeping into their contours—no longer Robinson's clue, nor the mystery of the Other, but instead the late and catastrophic anticipation of the tendential extinction of the human species from a technologically exhausted planet. Yet that particular "disappearance of Man" would draw its occurrence from the exhaustion of a Nature which in Tarkovsky on the contrary seems to *revive*, thriving on human sacrifices and drawing its blood from the extinction of the human, as though it had rid itself of planetary

vermin and were now restored, at least on the screen and in the image, to some rich and archaic ur-natural flourishing. The deepest contradiction in Tarkovsky is then that offered by a valorization of nature without human technology achieved by the highest technology of the photographic apparatus itself. No reflexivity acknowledges this second hidden presence, thus threatening to transform Tarkovskian nature-mysticism into the sheerest ideology.[8]

This fundamental contradiction between filmic technology and an outside world ideologically conceived as Nature is not to be resolved by any religion of film-art, since here that art conceals its production process (unlike what happens, for example, in Godard, where the process itself is repeatedly and insistently foregrounded on all its levels). Here, it is the very opposition between the artificial and the natural which is ideological, but which, as so often with ideological contradictions, is also the productive source of all those complexities whereby the work attempts to conceal this ideology from itself: they are the film as such, just as Lem's impossible imaginings come to existence as a text in the very process of denying their own possibility.

But now we need to add a new wrinkle: Steven Soderbergh has claimed that his fine new version of *Solaris* (2002) has nothing to do with Tarkovsky, but goes back to Lem's original for its inspiration. It is thus to be classified as a new adaptation rather than a remake, even though the very effort required to be *different* from Tarkovsky (it is successful in this) certainly establishes an active relationship to the earlier film. So what do we have here? Without the scientific skepticism of Lem, without the mysticism of memory of Tarkovsky, without the science fiction genre framework of alien worlds (albeit with a true science fiction twist at the end, which will not be revealed here), what results is a little more than a love story. But it is also nothing less than a love story, a most intelligent and touching one, far more interesting and complex than anything in the two previous texts, owing for the most part to the expansion of the role of Rheya, here played by the English-born Natasha McElhone, of whom the producer (James Cameron) observes that they wanted an unfamiliar face, but that this actress had the presence and maturity of the great women figures of the European 1960s and 1970s, like Jeanne Moreau, Monica Vitti, or Anna Karina. Otherwise the cast and film are extraordinarily American, leading us not only to the conclusion that Soderbergh's is an Americanization of the earlier works but, very much in the spirit of Jennifer Jeffers's recent book,[9] that the whole operation is an American annexation and appropriation of the great European New Wave art film of the older period! Poor Lem, poor Poland: first colonized by the Soviets, then thirty years later by the Americans!

What is the end result of this whole process? First of all, the love relationship becomes one that demands an absolute isolation from the society all around it: Rheya hates the New York social scene to which her husband is professionally wedded, and by implication, the United States itself. To endure, this love passion must transpire outside the world. It is a very privatized, individualistic dilemma, quite unthinkable in the dense and profound sociability of Europe. Then too, the alien being at the heart of all this has slipped from being a radically different life form to being God himself, with the paradoxical result that Solaris becomes potentially far more menacing and the possibility of real evil is here materialized: what if he wants to take over the earth? (But the final handshake does return us, with a difference, to Lem's novel.) Meanwhile, Rheya's quite proper antisocial malaise is then attributed to mental illness and instability: now shake this cocktail up and you have an authentically American set of contradictions, a whole new text that does exactly what new adaptations ought to be doing.

Identity or Difference: such is now the philosophical form of our adaptation debate, nor is it resolved by Lévi-Strauss's ingenious proposal: "What constitutes a myth is not the individual versions but all the versions together. In studying myth, what one does is study as many versions of the myth as can be found, then abstract from those versions a general pattern or sequence."[10] As is well known, he includes in his study of Oedipus both Sophocles and Freud, both the oldest "originals" and the newest "adaptations." Yet not only does this approach require a vast corpus for its best effects, its object lies outside the individual texts (or beneath or behind them) in that "general pattern or sequence" they express, itself the symptom of some deeper contradiction, either formal or social (a contradiction of the type we have attributed to Lem and to Tarkovsky in the preceding section). In short, and paradoxically—given this emphasis on contradiction—Lévi-Strauss's method demands the presupposition of some essential identity underlying all the versions in question.

The universal repudiation of "fidelity" we have noted above certainly constitutes some initial commitment to Difference: but why stop with this weak and purely logical category? Difference is also opposition, antagonism, struggle, and it seems possible that the differences between novel and film versions also harbor some more-active tension between word and image, if not literature and film themselves.

So far, indeed, it has been the individual versions, the individual texts, the novel and the film, which have seemed to repel each other and to entertain their most fruitful relations in the form of rich and complex antagonisms rather than of this or that in unison. For this level of the individual text we may retain Adorno's appropriation of the Hegelian formula—"each consciousness wills the death of the other." And, indeed, Adorno argued with much persuasiveness that, at least in modernism (for I take his aesthetics to be one of the fullest expressions of the logic of artistic modernity), the individual works, and even the oeuvre of the individual modern artists, seek each other's death, in the sense in which they brook no other gods beside themselves. The participation in the "world" of one of the great modernist styles is a quasi-religious conversion to a jealous and exclusive absolute, for which tolerance of the contemporaries and their trivial productions is mere idolatry. To immerse oneself in Lawrence is thus to render any Proustian velleities neurotic indulgences; to hold Kafka dear is soberly to resist either of these temptations. To be sure, we do pass from one to the other in real life; but that is our problem and our weakness, and does not alter the imperative of the works themselves, these literary absolutes. They have their equivalent in the world of the filmic auteurs themselves: for whoever acknowledges Hitchcock will find the others little more than a hobby, excusable only on account of the master's mortality, which prevented us from having more than fifty-seven films at our disposal.

This philosophical emphasis on antagonism and incompatibility does seem to me the most productive course to follow, allowing for an insistence on the material structure and constraints of the medium fully as much as on the latter's Aristotelian "peculiar pleasures" or on ideology and world-view, on psychoanalytic analysis or class receptivity—all dimensions calculated to become most visible in the process of comparison.

But it seems to me we may also usefully generalize this process to a level in which the media themselves—novel and film—come into play; and here the most appropriate dialectic would seem to be that of Bakhtin, taken in a somewhat different form than the emphasis on dialogism and polyphony, whose lessons have been profitable to so many students of adaptation (and perhaps most fully elaborated in Stam's own work).

This is rather the Bakhtin of the emphasis on the novel as form, which he wishes to disengage from the study of the classical genres, such as epic or tragedy, which have completed their development and are comparable to "dead languages" in contrast to the more problematic approaches to the novel, which are "like studying languages that are not only alive, but still young."[11] But it is in his account of the consequences of these historical differences that Bakhtin is the most relevant to our current topic:

> Compared with them [the classical genres] the novel appears to be a creature
> from an alien species. It gets on poorly with other genres. It fights for its
> hegemony in literature; wherever it triumphs, the older genres go into decline. (4)

The novel "gets on poorly with other genres," Bakhtin insists. "There can be no talk of a harmony deriving from mutual limitation and complementariness" (5), and he evokes parody and novelization, absorption and reflexivity, and a flexible multiplication of new features and alleged "generic characteristics," that make it impossible to fit this form into any stable theoretical scheme. He writes of its "struggle with other genres and with itself (with other dominant and fashionable variants of the novel" (9).

It is this perpetual struggle of the new and developing medium (the novel) with older fixed forms that will now be renewed in infinitely more complex and interesting ways when yet a newer form or genre or medium appears, and that is clearly how we must see film. Everything Bakhtin has to say about the novel can be reiterated for film, save that its adversaries, those genres with which film "gets on poorly," are no longer the dead or classical languages of epic and tragedy, but rather the languages of the novel as such, still very much alive and themselves developing at least in part by way of their struggle with the younger medium as such.[12] So now truly we witness a Hegelian "struggle for recognition" between these two media, a titanic struggle whose innumerable episodes are registered here and elsewhere in the expanding casebooks of "adaptation studies."

But if the novel's engagements with the dead monuments of its predecessors seem handily encompassed by various versions of parody, its intersections with its living competitors demand a far more complex set of accounts, which are scarcely simplified by the new form's struggle against its own younger adversaries in television and the digital media. Even so complex a rehearsal of these duels as Godard's *Contempt* (see Rick Warner's analysis above) did not yet have to take television into account, or rise to the historical occasion thus described by James Naremore: "We now live in a media-saturated environment dense with cross-references and filled with borrowings from movies, books, and every other form of representation. Books can become movies, but movies themselves can also become novels, published screenplays, Broadway musicals, television shows, remakes, and so on."[13] I have myself elsewhere evoked the competition between all these media that is implicit whenever a film pauses on a television monitor or a computer screen, whenever a television program projects a movie clip, or indeed when any of the visual media pause on the spectacle of someone reading a book.[14]

Only allegory can, I think, do justice to this unparalleled historical situation, and I want to propose that the individual works, either as external adaptations or as internal echo chambers of the various media, be grasped as allegories of their never-ending and unresolvable struggles for primacy. The novel, even when written for adaptation by film, necessarily wishes the latter's eclipse and death, and seeks to demonstrate the debility of a medium that has to rely on a literary "original." But at one and the same time film believes that its triumphant incorporation of the literary and linguistic hypotext into itself, in a generic cannibalism or anthropophagy, sufficiently enacts its primacy in the visual age (itself blissfully unaware of its stealthily approaching digital rivals). Such is the deeper allegorical sense of the encounters recorded here.

Notes

1. Robert Stam, *Literature Through Film* (Oxford: Blackwell, 2005), 4.

2. Dudley Andrew, *Concepts in Film Theory* (Oxford: Oxford University Press, 1984), 98.

3. See for example my review, "SF Novel/SF Film," in *Science-Fiction Studies* 7, no. 22, part 3 (November 1980): 319–22.

4. I should have liked to add four more topics to what is already a long discussion: the star system, in Marcel Carné's *La Marie du Port* (1950, from a Simenon novel); the question of deterritorialization in Marcel l'Herbier's *L'Argent* (1928, a "modern" version of Zola's novel); genre theory in Altman's *Short Cuts* (1993, based on stories by Raymond Carver); and finally my old hobby, the movie versions of Raymond Chandler. It might also have been amusing to ask oneself whether the later filming of a long-dormant screenplay can be considered a kind of adaptation, as with Orson Welles's original screenplay for *The Big Brass Ring* or some future filming of Chandler's Unknown Thriller.

5. See my chapter "History and Salvation in Philip K. Dick," in *Archaeologies of the Future: The Desire Called Utopia and Other Science-Fictions* (London: Verso, 2005), 363–83.

6. See Lem's "Phillip K. Dick: A Visionary among the Charlatans," trans. Robert Abernathy, *Science-Fiction Studies* 2, no. 5, part 1 (March 1975): 54–67.

7. Stanislaw Lem, *Solaris*, trans. Joanna Kilmartin and Steve Cox (San Diego: Harcourt Brace, 1961), 183. All further page references are to this edition and included parenthetically in the text.

8. Fredric Jameson, *The Geopolitical Aesthetic* (Bloomington: Indiana University Press, 1992), 97–100.

9. Jennifer Jeffers, *Britain Colonized: Hollywood's Appropriation of British Literature* (London: Palgrave, 2006).

10. Claude Lévi-Strauss, *Anthropologie structurale* (Paris: Plon, 1958), 235–37.

11. Mikhail Bakhtin, *The Dialogic Imagination*, ed. Michael Holquist, trans. Caryl Emerson and Michael Holquist (Austin: University of Texas Press, 1981), 3. All further references are to this edition and are cited parenthetically in the text.

12. See for example Claude-Edmonde Magny's pathbreaking study, *L'Age du roman américain* (Paris: Éditions du Seuil, 1948).

13. James Naremore, "Introduction: Film and the Reign of Adaptation," in *Film Adaptation*, ed. Naremore (New Brunswick, N.J.: Rutgers University Press, 2000), 12–13.

14. But I always credit Miriam Hansen for this idea.

CONTRIBUTORS

Dudley Andrew is the R. Selden Rose Professor of Film and Comparative Literature at Yale University. His various publications include *Mists of Regret: Culture and Sensibility in Classic French Film* (1995) and, as co-author, *Popular Front Paris and the Poetics of Culture* (2005).

Tom Gunning is the Edwin A. and Betty L. Bergman Distinguished Service Professor in the Department of Art History and the Chair of the Committee on Cinema and Media at the University of Chicago. He is the author of *D. W. Griffith and the Origins of American Narrative Film* (1991), *The Films of Fritz Lang: Allegories of Vision and Modernity* (2000), and well over a hundred articles on early cinema, film history and theory, avant-garde film, film genre, and cinema and modernism.

Fredric Jameson is Distinguished Professor of Comparative Literature at Duke University. He is the author of many books, including *Postmodernism, Or, The Cultural Logic of Late Capitalism* (1991), *A Singular Modernity: Essay on the Ontology of the Present* (2002), *The Modernist Papers* (2007), *Archaeologies of the Future: The Desire Called Utopia and Other Science Fictions* (2005), *Valences of the Dialectic* (2009) and *The Hegel Variations: On the Phenomenology of Spirit* (2010).

Jonathan Loucks was born and raised in Southern California. He has studied at the University of California, Berkeley (B.A., 20th-Century Literature) and the University of Pittsburgh (M.F.A. Poetry). His rock criticism has appeared in *Kitchen Sink* and *Fabula* magazines, and his poems have appeared in *The New Yinzer* and *Pittsburgh Post-Gazette*. He currently teaches writing and popular culture at the University of Pittsburgh and Duquesne University.

Colin MacCabe is Distinguished Professor of English and Film at the University of Pittsburgh, and Professor of English and Humanities at Birkbeck College, University of London. He is the editor of *Critical Quarterly* and the author of several books, including *The Butcher Boy* (2007), *T. S. Eliot* (2006), *Godard: A Portrait of the Artist at Seventy* (2003), *The Eloquence of the Vulgar* (1998), and *James Joyce and the Revolution of the Word* (1978, 2nd ed. 2002). He is currently writing a book on Clint Eastwood and a history of English Literature from Shakespeare to the present.

Stephanie McKnight earned her Master's degree in English Literature with a Certificate in Film Studies from the University of Pittsburgh. She focuses on representations of gender and sexuality in Hollywood film and popular culture. Her master's thesis, "Reverence and Annihilation: Motherhood in the Reagan-era Maternal Melodrama," addresses the social conservatism and maternal essentialism espoused in Reagan-era popular film melodrama.

Laura Mulvey is Professor of Film and Media Studies at Birbeck College, University of London, and the author of *Death 24x a Second: Stillness and the Moving Image* (2006), *Fetishism and Curiosity* (1996), *Citizen Kane* (1992), and *Visual and Other Pleasures* (1989).

Kathleen Murray is a doctoral candidate at the University of Pittsburgh. She received her M.A. in Media Studies from New School University in 2003. Her research and teaching interests include play and performance, adaptation studies, early narrative cinema, feminism and film, televisual studies and genre. Currently working on her dissertation, "Overlooking the Evidence: Modalities of the Female Detective," she is exploring the intersections of gender, genre, and narrative structures through the history of cinema and television as it circles around the recurring figure of the investigating woman.

James Naremore is Emeritus Chancellor's Professor of Communication and Culture and English at Indiana University. He is the author of a number of books, including *On Kubrick* (2007), *More than Night: Film Noir in its Contexts* (1998, updated and expanded ed. 2008), and *Acting in the Cinema* (1993).

Alison Patterson is a doctoral candidate at the University of Pittsburgh. She received an M.A. in Cinema Studies from Tisch School of the Arts, New York University and anticipates her PhD in English from Pittsburgh in 2010 under the direction of Marcia Landy. Her dissertation engages with literary and visual studies' senses of the terms "decoration" and "description" to illuminate certain cinematographic tendencies in a subset of history films.

Shelagh Patterson is a doctoral candidate at the University of Pittsburgh, where she studies literary collaboration, feminism, and the black radical imagination. A Cave Canem Fellow, she holds an M.F.A. in Creative Writing, Poetry, and a B.A. in Comparative Literature from CUNY Hunter College.

Rick Warner is a doctoral candidate at the University of Pittsburgh. He is the author of articles on New Taiwan Cinema, relations between "old" and "new" media, the films of Chris Marker, and the video projects of Jean-Luc Godard. He is guest editor of the *Critical Quarterly* special issue "The Late Work of Jean-Luc Godard" (October 2009). His dissertation examines cinematic uses of the essay form.

Jarrell D. Wright is a doctoral candidate at the University of Pittsburgh, where his principal research interests are seventeenth-century devotional poetry and theories of play. He earned a B.A. in government with high honors from The College of William and Mary in 1989, and a J.D. from the same institution in 1992. His contribution to this volume reflects a long-time interest in the works of Stanley Kubrick and Stephen King, and particularly *The Shining*. He is a pit-bull enthusiast.

INDEX

Lightning Source UK Ltd.
Milton Keynes UK
UKOW02f0937200815

257234UK00001B/50/P